Some of the material in this Advance Review Copy may not appear in the June 2006 publication date. Therefore, material from this book should not be quoted without first obtaining permission from the Author.

How To Save Money & Organize Your Finances

Tales of an Urban Consumer

by

Me'Shae Brooks-Rolling

Bloomington, IN

Milton Keynes, UK

AuthorHouse™
1663 Liberty Drive, Suite 200
Bloomington, IN 47403
www.authorhouse.com
Phone: 1-800-839-8640

AuthorHouse™ UK Ltd.
500 Avebury Boulevard
Central Milton Keynes, MK9 2BE
www.authorhouse.co.uk
Phone: 08001974150

First published by AuthorHouse 3/28/2006

ISBN: 1-4259-1618-X (sc)

Library of Congress Control Number: 2006901160

Printed in the United States of America
Bloomington, Indiana

This book is printed on acid-free paper.

Cover design by Brian Gaidry

TESTIMONIALS

"Reading this book challenged us in several ways on how to be better stewards of our income. This book provides strategies to be better, wiser spenders. We have applied several strategies to our finances and we must say that it's tried and true and it works! Me'Shae's personal testimony of what God did for her and her husband is encouraging. That testimony has taught my husband and I several things:

1) Be content with what you have.
2) Delayed gratification is not a bad thing.
3) How to get out of debt and stay out of it!"

Monique & Anselm Scrubb
New York City Residents

~ ~ ~

"If you do not see, hear or taste a powerful, life-changing, and positive experience as a result of reading this well-written book… or if it does not make it into Oprah's Book of the Month Club, then we all need some serious counseling by Dr. Phil!"

Nelson Soto
Artist
New York City

This publication contains the opinions and ideas of its author. It is sold with the understanding that the author/publisher is not engaged in rendering legal, tax, investment, financial, accounting, or other professional advice or services. This publication should not be used as a substitute for competent advice. If the reader requires such advice or services, then a competent professional should be consulted. Relevant laws vary from state to state. The strategies outlined in this book may not be suitable for every individual, and are not guaranteed or warranted to produce any particular results.

The author has taken reasonable precautions in the preparation of this book and believes the facts presented herein are accurate as of the date it was written. No warranty is made, however, with respect to the accuracy or completeness of the information contained herein, and the author/copyright holder and publisher specifically disclaim any responsibility for any liability, loss or risk, personal or otherwise, which is incurred as a consequence, directly or indirectly, of the use and application of any of the contents of this book.

Quoted financial information, operational data, and charts are strictly hypothetical. This publication does not purport get-rich-quick schemes or methods. While all of the stories and anecdotes described in this book are based on true experiences, most of the names are pseudonyms, and the situations have been changed slightly to protect each individual's privacy.

While a great deal of care has been taken to provide accurate and current information, the author bears no responsibility and has no control over websites and phone numbers that may have changed since publication.

HERE IS WHAT A CROSS-SECTION OF CONSUMERS, CLERGY, PROFESSIONALS AND SMALL BUSINESS OWNERS ARE SAYING ABOUT ME'SHAE'S BOOK:

"*How To Save Money & Organize Your Finances: Tales of an Urban Consumer* is the supersized Consumer Report with a gospel backbone to make you stand up right."

James Best
Chief Executive Officer
First Class of Color

"If hindsight were $20/$20, we would all be where we should be financially. Me'Shae brought it so gently into understanding."

Vivian Y. Black
Owner/Stylist
S'Hair-eng Styling Salon

I love the 'Me'Shae' flair that makes the reading fun while practical…moreso than most books on personal finances. I found myself immediately applying the principles before I read the next idea; I am already seeing the savings accumulate. Applying the principles has not even been that painful!"

Rick Capozzi
President/Founder
CapozziGroup

"Ms. Rolling's humorous tales of life in the city will make you smile as you read. You will quickly say to yourself, 'been there, done that.' More importantly, you will be inspired to believe that you can actually make it financially in the big city!"

Joe and Maria Diaz
jmr productions, LLC
New York City

"This book reminds us that we always have more than we think we have. It teaches us—the average consumer—how to turn pennies into dollars."

Brendaly Elizabeth Drayton
Author, *A Labor of Love*

"A valuable means of understanding the steps of successfully transitioning from renting to homeownership...Brooks-Rolling packed a lot of commonsensical observations and advice into a concise win-win opportunity which, if it takes hold, may help convert the age of Renting and Big Spending...into the Era of Owning and Saving in the 21st century."

Drunia M. Duvivier
Property Manager
O'Rancy Management, LLC

"This book is funny and informative. I echo a couple of the author's tips: eat before you go grocery shopping to avoid buying unnecessary items and buy sale items from the circulars, thus taking advantage of the sale of the week. Works for me! Also, Me'Shae challenges us: do we really need ten credit cards?"

Tricia Fraser
Special Events Planner
T. Fraser Productions

"Chapter 16's 'Earning Your Keep in the City: The Entrepreneurial Mindset & Spirit' is inspirational to me. I especially appreciate Me'Shae's use of scripture to awaken the spirit of gratefulness and to show how important it is for one to seek knowledge. As an entrepreneur, I believe that the financial concepts that were covered in this chapter are insightful and if not properly executed, well, let's just put it as Me'Shae would, "Could lead to financial hardship or disaster."

Christina Johnson
Partner
Panache Expressions, Inc.

"Before setting an appointment to preview homes or sit down with a mortgage broker, every first-time home buyer needs to study this book, especially the chapter on credit scores. In fact, I plan on giving every one of my new clients a copy of Me'Shae's book so that they can take control of their credit and become capable and empowered home buyers."

Nancy Love
Associate Broker
The *Corcoran* Group
Real Estate

"Throughout our nation, from government to the common person, spending and debt seem to be a way of life. Amidst the pressure of our spend-and-debt culture, the principles found in this book are refreshing."

Harold F. McKenzie
Senior Pastor
Unity Church of Jesus Christ

"Me'Shae does an excellent job in Chapter 7 explaining the wide variety of ways to make payments on your bills. She offers advantages and cautions on each method, thereby offering you a quick education to make your bill paying options more optimal. Chapter 8 is packed full on great suggestions on ways to get out of debt and stay out of debt. A lot of books tell you to "do it," but few offer you the in depth details on how to get out of debt like Me'Shae does."

Tammy A. Miller
International Director
Toastmasters International

"...Me'Shae begins the reader on a journey of being well informed and asking questions with the right attitude—that we can all live free of debt, free of financial predators and free to prosper."

Felix Papadakis, JD.
Strategies for Every Lifestyle
New York City

"I've reviewed **many** books to get the resources that this book encompasses. Me'Shae's recommendations on setting up a home office (Chapter 17) are worth it. You will save time and office supply store visits, and become more organized to make money. I highly recommend this book! It will…convert employees into employers."

Corey R. Pettway
Founder/Vice President of Operations
New York Inkjet, LLC

"Urbanites who have only dreamed of tasting financial freedom hear whispers of hope for their timely escapes from the "rate race" via an urban rate race escapee who returned to rescue others."

Pamela K. Pettway
President/CEO
(and Wife & Mother)
New York Inkjet, LLC

"This book reads like a high beam spotlight through the fog of personal finance. It should be required reading for everyone: from those aspiring to become financially independent to those who wish to maintain their wealth and financial independence. A must-read for young and mature alike."

Richard T. Phillip
Financial Advisor
President, Creative Financial Strategies

"Ms. Rolling's tasteful humor and practical advice diffuse the anxiety and helplessness associated with the sensitive topics of identity theft, debt collection, and bankruptcy. Chapter 11 is essential to financial literacy."

Sandra Beauvoir Soto
Educator
New York City

"Consistent and Persistent! When it comes to moving, the best advice is to take the emotion out of the move. Me'Shae does that throughout as she details the many facets of the moving process. She has given the reader great resources in helping them to conquer the move process. If you are consistent and persistent in following the author's step-by-step plan, then you will have a positive experience with your next move."

Michael Sullivan
President
Sullivan's Moving & Storage

"My clients love it when I keep it simple and they can understand exactly what I want them to do. This book does just that. Me'Shae has the power to take a subject that scares most people and not only make it easy to understand, but also easy to implement."

Alfred C. Varano, Jr., CSA
Varano Financial Group

"Straightforward. Easy to read. Practical. Motivates you to act upon the information right away!"

Hope Wade
Auto Sales Consultant

This book is dedicated to stay-at-home Moms, the 'Domestic CEOs' who sacrifice financial gain, and yet contribute significantly to their households, families, and society-at-large through their labor of love.

ACKNOWLEDGMENTS

Earnest thanks to:

My devoted husband of 13 years, James, a brilliant scholar, teacher, author and visual artist in his own right who has always been wholly supportive of my endeavors and is also my chief editor.

Clarissa Williams, Ph.D., my best friend of 20 years (and counting) who was my accountability partner on this passion project;

My 'baby' sister, Scarlett, an up-and-coming scholar who contributed to the editing of my book and challenged me in a way that only she knows about;

My late father, Edward L. Brooks, from whom I inherited my entrepreneurial mindset and spirit;

My mother, Betty Jean Brooks, for sacrificing her own dreams in life and deciding to be a stay-at-home Mom in order to invest in getting her five children where we all are today;

My mother-in-law, Sylvia Rolling, for all of her unselfish acts of giving;

My sister, Holly, for our numerous phone conversations on personal finances;

Stephanie Brooks, Evelyn Lugo, and my sister-in-law, Angie—all financially astute women who I'm so proud of!

R.J. Arraial of Wells Fargo, who epitomizes what superb customer service should be;

Pastor Jim and Carol Cymbala of The Brooklyn Tabernacle, who've provided the greatest example in my life of what it means to sow earthly blessings back into the kingdom of God;

Very special thanks to:

Anthony J. Cavallo, Esq., CPA; Pastor Frank O'Neill, Associate Pastor of The Brooklyn Tabernacle; Mark E. Rolling, Tax Professional; Fiona Phillip, Fashion Designer; Myrna R. Fields, Paralegal Specialist with the Department of Justice, Office of the United States Trustee; Tomerial Brooks, L.S.W., and Tammy Miller, Owner of Hugz & Company Consulting and Author of *The Lighter Side of Breast Cancer Recovery* for their important contributions.

Special thanks to:

Kevin Davis, Financial Representative representing Northwestern Mutual Financial Network; and Daniel Ritter—thanks for the technology!

Sincere thanks to:

The following authors I have never met, but whose Financial Ministries have had a profound impact on James' and my own personal financial journey—Mary Hunt, the late Larry Burkett, and Austin Pryor.

Asa Aarons, author of *The NY Daily News* consumer reports column *"Ask Asa"* that I have been faithfully reading for years.

All of my family and friends who supported and prayed for me during this project—including Charles and Sherrie, Allison, Duane and Letitia, my church families, ministries, and fellowship groups—you all know who you are!

Casting Crowns, for the songs *Voice of Truth* and *American Dream* on their *Casting Crowns* album (2003), which served as a constant reminder and encouragement to me as to why I'm doing this.

God, my Father, who is full of wisdom and provides for all of my needs; Jesus, His Son who died on the cross for my sins; and the Holy Spirit, who guides me in everyday decisions—financial and otherwise.

~ ~ ~

TABLE OF CONTENTS

PREFACE
WHY I WROTE THIS BOOK

~ Educating urban consumers determined to turn their financial situation around. ~

LET'S FACE IT: NEW YORK CITY is consistently ranked among cities in the nation with the highest cost of living. The borough of Manhattan, all by itself, is dubbed the playground of the rich. If you can't pay, you can't stay.

While this may very well be true, I have found that if one makes a decent income, steers clear of credit card debt and keeps everyday expenses to a minimum, it is quite possible to have a decent standard of living in the city. By this, I mean one can fund the basic needs of food, shelter, transportation, utilities and clothing without financial hardship or distress, while still contributing to church and charity, with money to spare for saving, investing, vacationing, gift-buying, etc. As a consumer and an urbanite, I've been there.

I am cognizant however that New Yorkers, like inhabitants of all other cities great and small, have financial situations as diverse as their demographic composition: fixed-income households just getting by on social security or disability insurance; limited education and/or language barriers directly impacting the kinds of job opportunities one qualifies for; both single and married households *with children* supported by only one income; renters' subject to an owner's decision to sell the building they live in right from underneath their feet; low-income residents living in subsidized housing; development threatening rent-stabilized apartments; a financially devastated widow; alimony payments on too little salary; and the list goes on and on and on.

Being a transplant from the Midwest, over time I became frustrated reading financial books by authors who advocate well-meaning, sound, basic principles to keep expenses low, eliminate or stay out of credit card debt, and own your own home. Yet, according to the National Low Income Housing Coalition, the top five states with the highest rental rates are: Hawaii, California, Massachusetts, New Jersey, and New York.[1] The top trio of cities with the most expensive rents (according to Reis Client Services and M/PF YieldStar) are New York City, San Francisco, and Los Angeles, with the average monthly rent in NYC being $2,400 in the 4th quarter of 2005.[2] Dilapidated brownstones are currently closing at a million dollars...for the shell alone![3] Hence, even the most well-meaning advice can fall short.

In other parts of the country, the mortgage on a 2,000 square-foot home is less than the rent on the average "shoebox" in New York. *"Other parts of the country don't have the same job, career and business opportunities as New York does,"* one may argue. True, but there is benefit in a dollar bill stretching further and with more quality for the buck. Consider this: two of my sisters in Indiana have rented *whole houses* in middle-class neighborhoods for between $350-$400 per month.[4]

I have long felt that there needed to be a book written, from one urban consumer to another, explaining *exactly how* one saves money when living in a large metropolitan marketplace that sucks your pockets dry. If we are not careful, the very nature of cities' hi-octane, fast-paced living correlates with money flying out the door like a Mariano Rivera fastball! The very same money we would like to use to eliminate credit card debt, build savings, and/or make a down payment on a co-op or condo becomes but a phantom.

A colleague at a non-profit institution made the following comment during my tenure: *"If a person walks through the door with torn jeans and old sneakers, send him or her straight to me. Most likely, he or she is the one with the penthouse on Park Avenue and a house in the Hamptons who wishes to contribute to our organization."* And so I began observing that New Yorkers who have money engage in spending habits that the rest of us may be unaware of or haven't yet chosen to adopt. Let's not overlook working-class immigrants, many of whom own their own businesses. Whether upper-, middle- or low-income, many have learned the glorious art of living within their means. Here's the bottom line, folks: city dwellers can't afford to do otherwise.

This book is not about "getting rich quick," or for that matter, about getting rich at all. The money-saving habits described herein require a tremendous amount of sacrifice, perseverance, discipline, delayed gratification, and common sense...all of the words advertisers and credit card companies would rather you not hear about. (Now that I've gotten that off my chest, this book is sure to be a bestseller!)

New York City is the backdrop for this book, because that is my particular frame of reference. Yet, even if you do not live in the metropolitan New York City area, the concepts of spending less money and becoming financially organized on a fundamental level are still applicable to you.

This book is also filled with a plethora of national or New York-specific resources and tips (located at the end of most chapters) in order to help you equip yourself on the path toward financial literacy and stewardship. The purpose of these resource sections is to point you in the right direction and to help you search out the answers specific to your particular situation.

Periodically, a tip or suggestion is preceded by a phrase such as, "from consumer-to-consumer," or "from one urban consumer to another." Since all "how to" books contain obligatory definitions, I looked up the definition of a consumer, quite certain s/he is "one who utilizes goods." Imagine my surprise when *Webster* further defines "to consume" as "to spend wastefully; squander."[5] Although we are all consumers, we are also stewards, defined by *Webster* as a fiscal agent appointed by an estate-holder to actively manage domestic affairs. This includes the supervision, provision, and distribution of food and drink.[6] As a consumer and a steward, I'm traveling on the same road as you. In fact, my own personal financial odyssey is told in Chapter 20.

Because personal finances are normally such a serious, private matter, I wrote this book in a light-hearted fashion including "only-in-New York" tales and anecdotes that I hope any reader can identify with and chuckle at. I have also prefaced many chapters with Bible verses because these are time-tested principles that have worked for me personally. Might they apply to your life, as well? I encourage you to read on and decide for yourself.

I do not advocate financial gain at another's expense; nor is the intent of this book to stifle your fun in the big cities of the world. Rather, my goal is to help **stop the flow of money that is hemorrhaging from multiple financial wounds so that you can redirect it toward the people, goals, and activities in your life that are meaningful and important to you.** Trust me, had I known a decade ago what I know now, I would be a lot further ahead financially. (By the way—why wasn't I taught financial literacy and concepts of financial stewardship in my formative years of schooling or in college? Why wasn't it a requirement for graduation?) I can, on the other hand, recommend over a dozen ways for you to become financially organized—both in terms of adapting the proper mindset and implementing the appropriate actions. I can also teach you over 40 ways to live within your means in the Big Apple or in any other big city.

That is precisely why I wrote this book. From one consumer, to another.

CHAPTER 1
JUST HOW FED UP ARE YOU?

"I do not understand what I do. For what I want to do I do not do, but what I hate I do."
~ Romans 7:15 ~

AFTER I HAVE CONDUCTED A FINANCIAL LITERACY SEMINAR, people oftentimes come up to me and say, *"I am in a financial mess. I really need your help!"* I then give them my phone number so we can talk. It is a test to see if they will really call back. For those who do not call, I surmise that they are keenly aware of how dire their situation is and are compelled enough to verbalize the problem, but are not quite yet at the stage where they want to do something about it. For those who do call, it is a strong sign that they are fed up enough with their situation that they are ready to take action. S/he is ready to stare his or her finances in the face, regardless of how bleak or dismal the picture. After our initial meeting, if a client has followed up on my recommendations, I know he or she is really ready. He or she is usually...

- Tired of being late with rent payments
- Embarrassed from swiping their subway MetroCard and it consistently reads "insufficient fare"

- Discouraged about borrowing from other people to meet their *needs*
- Ashamed by eating out and not being able to afford a decent tip
- Perturbed at getting hit hard with parking fines and fees
- Weary of paying bills late due to disorganization and consequently being slapped with late fees
- Distraught at debt collectors harassing them and the repo man showing up on their doorstep.
- Sad at feeling they have no choice but to allow the basket to pass them by in church
- Annoyed at not being able to afford to travel outside of the five boroughs of New York City

There are a variety of circumstances that led us on the road to our current financial situation—some controllable, such as exercising loose spending habits or answering phony e-mail letter scams; some uncontrollable, such as a devastating death or illness; some innocent, such as simply not knowing our rights when dealing with that nasty, mean 'ole debt collector.

Likewise, there are a myriad of psychological, spiritual, behavioral, socio-economic, geneological, and even historical issues that affect how each of us handles our finances. Issues can range from negative influences growing up; to the development of poor money management habits; the need for validation and approval; comparing ourselves to other people and keeping up with the Jones's; individual personality traits; lack of basic financial literacy; the absence of family wealth accumulated, properly managed, and passed on from one generation to the next; or just plain bad choices made in life.

The only problem in keeping up with the Jones's is that more likely than not, the Jones's have enough available credit with which to buy their stuff. What is not outwardly apparent, however, is the truckload of debt (and interest on that debt) that they are carrying.

It is said that we spend much of our adulthood getting over our childhood. I'm no psychiatrist, but there comes a point when we must:

a) assess just how fed up we are with things as they are;
b) determine what the ideal circumstances might be; and
c) take the appropriate action required to overcome any obstacles toward reaching our new goal.

Your choice to read this book is a good sign that you wish to head in a positive direction financially. If you live with someone with whom your finances are intimately involved, that person must be on the same page as you are. Otherwise, any financial improvements you are trying to make will feel like you're going up against a brick wall. While you are doing all you can to save money, your loved one may be bleeding the ATM machine, draining the savings account, or racking up debt. Three key ingredients in making joint personal finances work seamlessly are: **communication** (discussing finances), **coordination** (planning a course of action, such as developing a budget for payday), and **administration** (executing the agreed-upon plan). Have a conversation with all those who are significant in your life about what you are attempting to do.

"Don't copy the behavior and customs of this world, but let God transform you into a new person by changing the way you think..."
~ Romans 12:2 (NLT) ~

CHAPTER 2
THE ABSOLUTE IMPORTANCE OF A PERSONALIZED BUDGET

"Be sure you know the condition of your flocks;
give careful attention to your herds;
for riches do not endure forever..."
~ Proverbs 27:23, 24a ~

HAVE YOU EVER WONDERED WHAT HAPPENED to your money on payday? Payday came and went, but the money somehow slipped through the cracks in-between. Expenses accrue, bills pour in, debts pile up, and there is little or no money left. Not to mention the long-term consequences of late or missed payments: Late fees. Credit blotches. Trying to play catch-up later on. *"You can't squeeze blood from a turnip,"* you shrug.

The purpose of a budget sheet is to track how much money is coming in, and how much money is going out. In its simplest form, a budget (see Appendix A) records your Income; Church Tithe and/or Charity Donations; Housing and Transportation expenditures; Groceries; Utilities; Student Loans; Credit Cards; Household expenses such as Laundry (since many city dwellings do not have in-house laundry facilities), etc.

Personalized Budget Sheet

The purpose of a Personalized Budget Sheet is to reflect expenses specific to your circumstances. In a Personalized Budget Sheet, you record income earned and add it to the previous balance in your checking account. This will present an accurate picture of how much money is available for bi-monthly or monthly expenses.

A personalized budget not only records payee categories, due dates, and minimum payments, but the method of payment, as well. For instance, check-by-phone; pay-in-person; money order; check-by-mail; debit card; online; and auto-payment (see Chapter 7 for the pros and cons of various bill paying options).

I recommend that once you establish your Personalized Budget Sheet, type it up or ask someone to type it for you, and make 26 copies representing 26 pay periods if you get paid bi-monthly, or 12 copies if you get paid monthly. Place the copies in a three-ring binder or folder. This way, every time payday rolls around, you will not have to recreate your budget sheet categories from scratch. All you will have to do is fill in the blanks.

Have your bi-weekly or monthly calendar next to you while you devise your budget to remind you which activities require money. It's a good exercise in trimming the fat, too. Going over the budget in our household is sometimes like Congressional backroom deal-making:

> Me'Shae: *"I'll throw in the King Kong movie if you allow me to purchase something for the house."*
> James: *"You buy ham and bacon in the next grocery trip, and you can have that new dress that you've had your eye on."*
> Together: *"Deal!"*

I strongly recommend including a personal spending allowance in your personalized budget. Why? Because regardless of how frugal you try to be, it will be nearly impossible *not* to spend money on miscellaneous items. Therefore, budget the pocket money you need for items not categorized in your budget. It will help you steer clear of the ATM machine until your next payday.

Financial experts generally recommend that you save a minimum of anywhere between 3-8 months of living expenses as an emergency fund, so be sure to include a savings category in your budget as well.

Envelope System

The purpose of an "Envelope System" is to:

a) help you stick to your personalized budget;
b) organize the cash you need on hand for expenses; and
c) keep you from bleeding the ATM machine until the next payday.

Take categories from the budget sheet that you are paying with cash and write the categories on envelopes. For instance, after you budget a designated amount of money for "Restaurants and Dining Out," place that cash amount in the envelope, along with any applicable coupons and hold onto it until you dine out. If you are on a monthly budget plan, pace yourself to spend half of the money between the 1st and the 15th of the month, and the other half during the 16th through the 31st of the month. You may feel that's too restrictive. *Au contraire,* my dear. It is actually liberating because you are meeting your needs with cash (see Chapter 8 on "The Case For Cold, Hard Cash").

If there is a surplus leftover in an envelope at the end of the month, you can do two things with the money:

a) Reallocate it towards another area that was shortchanged.
b) Keep the money in the envelope and add the balance on the next payday.

For example, let's say you normally budget $100/month on food, and $75/month on gas. During the last week of the month, you have $20 leftover in the food envelope, but need an extra $20 to fill up the car before the next payday. You can either subtract $20 from the food envelope and use it for gas without hitting up the ATM machine; or you can retain the $20 in the food envelope, debit or charge the gas, and budget $80 the next paycheck to bring the food envelope back up to $100.

I have heard extremely disciplined individuals go as far to say that once the envelope has been depleted, that's it. *Finito. No mas* until the next payday. Of course, the cash envelope system requires cooperation by all members of one's household.

You don't know how much you are truly spending
unless you see it in black and white,
and a budget sheet takes the guesswork
out of where your money is going.
~ MBR ~

CHAPTER 3
BEING DISORGANIZED COSTS YOU MONEY

"But everything should be done in a fitting and orderly way."
~ I Corinthians 14:40 ~

SCENARIO A: Jane goes to the hospital. Jane pays her co-payment. Jane is released. Bill collector sends Jane notice of non-payment. Jane has no leg to stand on. Bill collector harasses Jane. Hospital refuses to help Jane.

SCENARIO B: Mike goes to the hospital. Mike pays his co-payment. Mike asks hospital for receipt. Mike files away receipt. Bill collector sends Mike notice of non-payment. Mike sends bill collector copy of payment receipt. Bill collector backs off.

Here are a few tips on how to become financially organized enough to be like Mike.

Every Sunday after church, my husband and I hash out the details of our upcoming weekly schedule: Who is doing what and when. How we are going to navigate transportation—are we going to park 'n ride? Is the car coming into the city? We also discuss our schedule from a *financial* viewpoint. For instance, we determine which days I am able to cook dinner and which days we will have no choice but to eat out. Do we have enough cash in the envelope (see Chapter 2) or enough money in the checking account to debit the cost of meals? Does the car need a filler-up with gas this week? Do we need to refill the subway MetroCard?

All of these questions are designed to make sure that in addition to the daily administration of our lives, **the unavoidable financial aspects are incorporated as a fact of life, as well.** The goal is to not be deeper in debt at week's end due to the lack of financial organization. What is the alternative? Details falling through the cracks and coming back to haunt you later, that's all.

Following are a few step-by-step short-, intermediate-, and long-term organizing procedures that have helped me to keep my finances in order.

Short-Term Financial Organizing: Managing Daily and Weekly Expenses

1) Verify your balance before debiting purchases
2) Make your purchase(s)
3) Immediately write purpose on receipt (trust me, it's a challenge to try and remember later);
4) Immediately input debits and ATM withdrawals into financial software when you get home (for up-to-date balances)
5) Put the remainder of the receipts into a designated paper bin until you can organize them later;
6) Organize receipts accordingly into labeled envelopes: cash – debit – credit – personal – business
7) When the credit card bill arrives, attach credit card receipts to your statement
8) Input all receipt amounts into financial software application by month's end
9) File away important receipts you wish to keep for long-term reference (i.e., for tax or business purposes)

Now you have an accurate record and snapshot of your household's financial picture!

Paying and Organizing Your Bills

1) Open statement with letter opener (for the sake of neatness);
2) Make sure funds are available at the time you pay the bill;
3) Indicate payment method on the bill (We will explore various bill-paying options in Chapter 7: cash, in-person, debit, check, check-by-phone, credit card, online):
    a) If paying by cash, check or debit **in person,** staple printed receipt to statement copy;
    b) If paying by debit, credit card, or check **by phone,** write check # (if applicable), which credit card used, and confirmation # on statement copy;
    c) If **mailing a check,** endorse check, and write check #/ indicate the date sent on your statement copy;
    d) If **mailing a money order,** staple money order receipt to your statement copy. In both cases, seal and place stamp on envelope, and remember to include your return address in the upper left-hand corner of the envelope;
    e) If **paying online,** retain e-confirmation, print out, and staple to statement copy;

5) Regardless of the payment method, purchase a "paid" and "sent" stamp from a local office supply store...it's worth the six or seven bucks; and
6) File away all of the above.

Make sure your bills are paid before you go on vacation.
The credit card company's computer doesn't
care that you're sunbathing in Aruba!
~ MBR ~

Intermediate Financial Organizing: Maintaining Your Organizational System

1) New mail comes in;
2) Separate important from unimportant mail;
3) Discard unimportant papers in recyclable bin;
4) Shred sensitive documents;
5) File important papers for future reference;

6) Address mail that requires immediate action:
    a) act upon it, and then;
    b) file it; or
    c) throw it away.
7) Create files by:
    a) stacking each subject matter in a different pile;
    b) name the pile by placing a sticky note on it, and;
    c) create subdivisions if necessary. For instance, the hanging file will be labeled "Utilities," and the folders may include:
        i) Electricity bills
        ii) Gas bills
        iii) Water bills

I spend almost as much time separating and
shredding the junk mail inserts
included in envelopes as I do paying the actual bill!
~ MBR ~

Resources:
To request that your name be removed from mailing lists, phone lists, and e-mail lists, call the sources directly (as in the case of mail order catalogs), or contact:

Federal Trade Commission
Toll Free 1(888) 382-1222 or www.donotcall.gov

Direct Marketing Association
national telephone marketing lists, mail lists, and e-mail marketing lists: www.dmaconsumers.org
DMA's New York City #: (212) 768-7277

-or-

To remove your name from mailing lists:
Direct Marketing Association
Mail Preference Service
P.O. Box 643
Carmel, NY 10512

To remove your name from telemarketing lists:
Direct Marketing Association
Telephone Preference Service
P.O. Box 1559
Carmel, NY 10512

For credit card offers:

- **"One-stop" opt-out** number for the three major credit bureaus, 1(888) 5-OPTOUT (888-567-8688) or online at www.optoutprescreen.com
- **Equifax Opts**, Marketing Decision Systems, P.O. Box 740123, Atlanta, GA 30374-0123
- **Experian Opt Out**, Target Marketing Services Division, ATTN: Mail Preference Service, P.O. Box 919, Allen, TX 75013-0919
- **TransUnion Name Removal Option**,
  P.O. Box 505, Woodlyn, PA 19094

Long-Term Financial Organizing

For your long-term financial organization, purchase computerized programs such as Quicken®, Quickbooks®, or Microsoft® Money. These software programs are set up like a checkbook.

Here are the basics for Quicken, used by our household:

1) Type method of transaction (i.e., check #, withdrawal, deposit, or transfer);
2) Type the payment amount in the debit or credit column (i.e., input your income amount in the credit column and your telephone bill amount in the debit column);
3) Type in Payee information.

Some of the categories are already pre-set, and they can be edited to suit your fancy; some you have to create. For instance, my financial software program came pre-loaded with the word "Fuel" under the "Auto" category. I prefer to use the word "Gas" instead of "Fuel." If you wish to write U.S. Postal Service for the post office, or your favorite supermarket under "Groceries," you can do that, too. Whatever you want.

Why is Financial Software Useful?

The most useful function of financial software is that once you input the figures, the software automatically calculates the balances and statistics. Let's say you wish to determine how much your dry cleaning bill was in the third quarter of last year. Assuming you correctly input the date, dry cleaning business name, "dry cleaning" category every time, and the amounts, all you have to do is type 07/01/05 to 09/30/05 and *viola!* Not only can you see how much you spent on dry cleaning that particular quarter, but the software also allows you to view how much of your total household budget was spent on that category. It also devises pie charts and graphs. Pretty neat, huh?

I can use this software to make projections, as well. If I wish to estimate how much money to budget for groceries or dining out, I can do so by simply typing in a beginning and ending time period, and Quicken® helps provide a good estimation of how much I need to set aside for dining out in subsequent months.

When the credit card bill comes due, I encourage you to itemize the amount of interest you are paying in the financial software. If you see in black and white how much money you are paying in interest, then it will discourage you from adding to your credit card debt.

Another word about itemization, from consumer-to-consumer: be sure to ask for a line-by-line breakdown of your bills, as opposed to accepting the ambiguous *"Your fee, sir, is $1,895. Will that be cash, check or credit card?"* For instance, you need to be able to see line-item hospital charges so that it is clearly understood by you that *nasal membrane eau de toilette* means a box of tissue! My husband and I recently got our vehicle registered. Here is a breakdown of the fees: permit, eye exam, title, registration, license plates, processing fee, and inspection. It helps so much to know how your money is being spent.

Financial software also helps you to be able to compare prices down the road so you can keep track of, be aware of, and if necessary, question fee increases. *"Ma'am, I paid $139 last year for my membership. Can you kindly explain why the fee increased to $141?"* While the inquiry in and of itself is not inclined to reduce your charges, my experience is that people with organized records get more respect.

Furthermore, I utilize Quicken® in conjunction with Excel® at tax time. The key here is to exercise consistency when inputting your figures. Many banks and financial institutions also offer online banking to interface with the software.

I am a frugal individual. Nonetheless, I am amazed at the amount of money that it takes to provide for the basic necessities and to simply operate and sustain our household. I guarantee you: to fill in the blanks of your budget sheet is one thing. To see the cold, hard summations in black and white is quite another.

All of the above is highly recommended for everyone, but due to varying tolerances to the time commitment of organizing one's finances, those who are ready and willing to make the necessary changes can be subdivided into the following profiles:

Financial Organizing Character Traits
Profile #1: "In a New York minute, please"
"Cut to the chase, will ya? In a New York minute, tell me what I absolutely need to do. I'm busy." (sound of a door slamming)

Profile #2: "Gimme the basics, lady"
"I don't have a lot of time to spend on getting financially organized, but I recognize the importance thereof. Gimme the basics, but please—be reasonable with the amount of work involved."

Profile #3: "Honey child, I ain't playin'
"Honey, I want the whole enchilada. I will ***make*** *and* ***find*** *the time to set up a system. My finances are such a wreck, the tow truck should*

have come a long time ago! I am thoroughly convinced this will help me in the long-run. Child, I ain't playin'!"

Following is a chart designed to characterize the method and scope of financial organizing each of the profiles might be willing to undertake.

Financial Organizing Profiles...Which One Best Describes Your Level of Commitment?

Action	Frequency	Materials needed	Profile #1 *"In an New York minute, please"*	Profile #2 *"Gimme the basics, lady"*	Profile #3 *"Honey child, I ain't playin'"*
Balance Checkbook	every time a transaction is made	Checkbook, pen, calculator	✓	✓	
Collect receipts	daily	Your receipts			✓
Devise envelope system	one-time set-up	Empty, letter-sized envelopes		✓	✓
Establish a personalized budget	in conjunction with payday	All bills; pay stubs	✓	✓	✓
Pay bills	every time a bill is due	letter opener; "Paid" &/or "Sent" stamp	✓	✓	✓
Create a filing system	one-time set-up	File labels, File folders, Hanging files, File caddy, bin or cabinet	✓	✓	✓
Install and utilize a financial software system	on-going	Windows '98 or higher; Excel® spreadsheet; Quicken®, Quickbooks®, or Microsoft® Money; your financial data (your receipts, budget sheet, and pay stubs)			✓

On more than one occasion, I have found myself with short cash flow. Do the methods outlined above magically enable me to have more money? No. But they help me to track what's coming in, and *when*; what's going out, *when* and *how*; they help me to pace my bill payments, as well as project future spending habits. That's pretty powerful stuff.

For those of you who retort that you are too busy to become financially organized, I challenge you: What in your life is so demanding that it is keeping you from organizing your finances? **A helpful rule of thumb is to take a large task and break it down into smaller tasks over a period of time.** This provides you with a sense of accomplishment as your move toward your goal. Strive for simplicity in your quest to become financially organized. Yes, it does take *time* to become financially organized, but it's, like, totally worth it, dude.

As a Professional Organizer, I often get asked how long one should retain certain documents before discarding them. Due to the sensitive nature of certain documents, by "discard," I mean to shred (see Chapter 11 on Identity Theft). The following are general guidelines:

Tax returns and supporting documentation – Keep actual tax returns indefinitely, and any supporting documentation for not less than seven years, because that is how far back the IRS may conduct an audit of your tax returns.[7] Personally, I keep my supporting documentation indefinitely, as well. This includes big-ticket items purchased, particularly for business and tax-related purposes.

Rental & Mortgage payment receipts – Keep receipts indefinitely; for renters, it may bode well with a new landlord if presented along with utility statements, to show history of on-time payments.

> *Additional note:* Anytime you pay rent, *especially* with cash, immediately obtain a receipt from the landlord. Preferably, the landlord should provide a receipt bearing his or her pertinent information. Buy your own receipt booklet, if you must! This is your only proof that you pay your rent on time.

If you are a homeowner, retain those major purchases, maintenance, repair, and improvement receipts indefinitely.[8]

Medical statements – Keep statements indefinitely, so you do not look up one day and, lo and behold, the debt collection agency is contacting you about a bill you had already paid to the hospital! Can you believe that this has happened to my husband and me?

Retirement & Investment statements – Retain quarterly statements and annual summaries; permanently retain beneficiary designations.

Wage/salary records and pay stubs – Retain wage/salary records and pay stubs at least seven years; retain pay stubs at least three years. Your W-2 or 1099 records (if you are self-employed) serve as income verification when you receive it from your employer in January or February.[9]

Credit card statements – Retain statements between three and seven years.[10] However, you should retain the first statement to show when the account was opened, and the last statement, showing zero balance and when the account was closed so that it concurs with your credit reports.

Bank statements – Retain statements a minimum of seven years.[11]

Utility and phone bill statements – Unless needed for business deductions, these statements may be discarded after one year.[12]

ATM withdrawal receipts – Receipts may be discarded after you record the transaction in your passbook register or financial software, or upon showing up on your monthly bank statement.[13]

Items suitable for a safe-deposit box at the bank, or fire-proof, anti-theft safe at home (includes, but not limited to): Will; Healthcare Power of Attorney; Birth Certificate; Marriage Certificate; Death Certificate; Passport; Citizenship Papers; Military and other pertinent documents; Insurance policies (Home, Auto, Health, Disability); Property Title and Deeds (e.g., home and auto); Stock and Bond certificates—you get the idea.[14]

Resource:
To locate a Professional Organizer specializing in Financial Organization, contact The National Association of Professional Organizers (NAPO) at:
-national headquarters/outside of metro NYC –
1(847) 375-4746 – www.napo.net
-within metro NYC - (212) 439-1088 – www.napo-ny.net

Commercial resources:
Quicken® for personal and home use –
1(800) 811-8766 – www.Quicken.com

Quickbooks® for businesses/small businesses –
1(877) 683-3259 – www.Quickbooks.com

Microsoft® Money for business and personal use:
www.Microsoft.com/money

Tip: Before purchasing financial software, be sure to first check the compatibility with your PC or Apple Mac computer.

The single, most important thing to keep in mind with regard to both financial and professional organizing is to assign each record of information, each piece of paper, and every object its own "home".
~ MBR ~

CHAPTER 4
APPRECIATING THE VALUE OF A SIMPLE DOLLAR BILL

"Whoever can be trusted with very little can
also be trusted with much, and
whoever is dishonest with very little will
also be dishonest with much."
~ Luke 16:10 ~

IF YOU FOUND A DOLLAR BILL ON THE SIDEWALK, what could you buy with it? What about five dollars? Ten? Before we can examine specific ways to save money, we need to evaluate and determine what the value of a dollar bill means to you. *"Fuggedaboudit! It's only a dollar here, a couple of dollars there,"* you cringe. That's exactly what I thought back in 2001. You see, we were living in Crown Heights, Brooklyn at the time and I asked myself one day, *"Are clipping coupons, waiting for sales, taking advantage of bargains and discounts, and catching billing errors really worth my time, or am I just spinning my wheels like a rat on the subway tracks?"*

And so for one full year, I began tracking any goods and services purchased in which the following was involved: coupons, sales and discounts; maintaining organized records; comparison shopping; catching retailer mistakes; and get this—simply paying attention!

For instance, I had booked a hotel room for a business trip. The rate provided by the toll-free 800 reservations number was different from the rate provided by the hotel chain's local front office. By requesting the lower rate, I paid 10 dollars less per night correlating into two nights' savings worth 20 bucks.

After tracking expenditures for a full year and tallying the figures, I discovered that:

- I saved an average 6-7% on groceries; and
- I could have spent $13,594 during the year; instead, I spent $11,290. (Remember, this is not reflective of all items purchased, just those items where saving money was involved).

That's 17 cents *saved* on every dollar *spent.* These savings freed up $2,304 to apply towards credit card debt; or $2,304 to be applied towards an emergency fund or to invest; or $2,304 to contributes towards my church's building fund or to donate to a charitable cause. Shall I go on?

I repeated this experiment when we moved to New Jersey. In the first seven months alone, between mistakes on our bills, establishing memberships, upgrading or downgrading services, taking advantage of sales, discounts and frequency points, etc. we saved $2,600! Friends, $2,600 encompasses an extra mortgage or car payment; fills our car's gas tank for 26 months, provides groceries in our household for 13 months, buys a new furniture set...you get the picture.

Here is my own personal conclusion as a result of this experiment: **One dollar—just one dollar—can make a difference, especially in places where bottled water costs that much or more.** I am not talking about being stingy at the expense of other people, but rather identifying *which* entities to be cautious with: the video rental place, the credit card companies, the pricey coffee shops, etc. Credit card companies, retailers and advertisers are vigilant in finding ways to help us part with our money, and we have to be just as vigilant in finding ways to hold onto it!

My husband, James, and I went bicycling during a Labor Day get-away on Martha's Vineyard. The rental guy told us that the per diem rental cost was $15 each. James later overheard two people talking about their $4 hourly cost from the same bicycle shop. Because we had a clambake later on that afternoon and knew we could only go riding for a couple of hours, we inquired about the hourly rental fee upon returning the bikes. At $4 each for two hours, the total cost of our lovely bike ride would be $16 rather than the $30 for a full day rental we were originally charged. Without haggling or hesitation, the $14 was refunded to us! What is $14 to me personally? $14 goes toward getting a wash, press and curl at my Brooklyn hairdresser of over a decade. $14 will partially pay for dinner at a mid-priced restaurant with my husband. $14 to me is a pretty blouse that I recently bought someone for her birthday.

Smirk, purse your lips, and roll your neck all you want...it doesn't change the fact that the money my husband and I *didn't* spend was redirected towards that steak and lobster dinner we enjoyed during the next vacation. The next time you're on a weeklong vacation, you might try doing what we did by:

a) taking public transportation instead of a taxicab;
b) flying for free using your frequent flyer miles;
c) being unashamed to whip out tourist restaurant coupons; and
d) conducting car rental price comparisons in conjunction with your AAA car rental discount. In our case, this particular excursion should have cost us $1,382.42, but actually cost us $947.07, representing a total savings of $435.35. Okay, okay, you win some, and you lose some. Deduct the $25 for the excess baggage fee imposed by our airline carrier, and the savings percentage is reduced a wee bit, mate.

The purpose of this chapter is not to tell you what, where, or how to purchase because these choices are all highly subjective. Perhaps the idea of making your own coffee is not as appealing to you as a fresh brewed cup from the coffee shop. Perhaps getting your nails done for 30 bucks is a treat. Or perhaps you are a jet-setting businessperson who lives on the cell phone and you need the most sophisticated phone plan possible, regardless of the cost. The idea here is to get you thinking about ways to cut *everyday, thoughtless* spending, which is the *real* and very silent money-eater. Unchecked daily spending is like termites that unknowingly nibble away at your wallet.

Now conduct your own experiment. For the next seven days, collect every single receipt from your purchases (food, newspapers, transporation, clothes, school supplies, pet food, etc.). You will have to ask the cashier because merchants in New York City generally do not render receipts nowadays unless requested (and even still, the cashiers look at me like I have green flourescent goo smeared all over my forehead when I do ask for one). Tuck the receipts neatly in your wallet or an envelope. Now tally the figures. You will be amazed at how much money has passed through your fingers in one week alone.

Here is a snapshot of the expenses incurred one morning as I took care of business in downtown Brooklyn:

- $5 (with E-ZPass) from New Jersey to New York via the Holland Tunnel
- $10 parking in downtown Brooklyn, including a dollar tip
- $4 (after comparison shopping) for 2 packs of synthetic hair for my hairdresser
- I managed to escape food and beverage expenses by bringing my own coffee and promptly driving back to Jersey to eat lunch at home
- Total amount of money spent within a couple of hours: close to $20

It would have been more had I taken the New Jersey Transit and the New York City subway. In that case, transporation *alone* would have been around $20. By the time I stand on platforms waiting around for trains, I would have bought a newspaper or magazine to read, and would have been too hungry to wait until I got home to eat. Therefore, my trip into the city would have cost me around $30.

Now let's put some rum in the punch: calculate money **you** spend on any given day within a specified timeframe or in a single mile radius. Finally, tell yourself (not in public, of course): *"That extra $X that I paid for Y could go to Z instead."*

And so when you're not avoiding spit on the sidewalks, let's save some real money, shall we?

Resource:
See Appendix E to keep track of money **you** could be saving!

~ According to a friend of mine, she and her husband simply began collecting their spare change daily since the time their baby was born. By the time the child was age 2, they had collected $900 in his piggy bank! ~

CHAPTER 5
40 SPECIFIC WAYS TO SAVE MONEY IN THE CITY

"One man pretends to be rich, yet has nothing;
another pretends to be poor, yet has great wealth."
~ Proverbs 13:7 ~

OKAY YOU CITY SLICKERS, DO YOU REMEMBER THE BEVERLY HILLBILLIES? How they moved into a huge California crib after striking it rich with oil, aka "black gold"? No, they didn't go out and buy a fully loaded Hummer with a V-8 engine, custom detailing, Dolby surround-sound stereos embedded in the leather headrests, gold Spreewell rims on their wheels and $18,000 worth of other upgrades. They continued to drive their beat-up jalopy.

The Hillbillies may not have been too far off the profile of the millionaires described in authors Thomas Stanley and William Danko's book, *The Millionaire Next Door.* Drs. Stanley and Danko identified millionaires as households whose net worth (not annual salaries) is one million dollars or more.[15] In fact, they generally live on an income equivalent to less than seven percent of their wealth. Ninety-seven percent are homeowners.[16] An interesting comment typical of the men profiled in the book is that most of their wives are "planners and meticulous budgeters".[17]

Stanley and Danko also discovered through their studies that a major characteristic of millionaires is that they are frugal people. They even classify themselves as "tightwads."[18] They are not necessarily the ones driving around in a luxury sedan or living in the fanciest house on the block, because they typically shun displays of high social status. The affluent live well below their means and engage in low consumption habits.[19]

Have you ever imagined rich people watching how they spend money on goods and services by using coupons and taking advantage of sales, bargains and discounts? Fascinating. I can substantiate this, as one of my clients—a millionairess—once asked me as her Financial Organizer to compare the cost of her prescription medication with her neighborhood pharmacy, a Canadian pharmaceutical company, and AARP (American Association for Retired Persons, www.aarp.com). I thought, *"If she can do it, then surely I'd better 'get with the program' and start checking around, too!"*

Newsflash: rich people like to save money and enjoy freebies, too. If you do not believe me, see if any of Hollywood's celebrities turn down their free gift bag filled with designers' goodies at Oscar's next post-awards bash.

And so I present you with 40 specific ways to save money in the Big Apple or in any other big city—without your last name having to be Trump, or Rockefeller, or Gates or Bloomberg, without having to ask the boss for a raise, without having to take on a second job.

5.1 Your W-2 Form...Is it Accurate?

After years of being a pauper in graduate school, I was recruited as an Auditor for a federal government agency in the early 1990's and was happy just to have a job with an annual salary of five figures instead of three. I assumed that when I filled out the employment papers, everything was alright and therefore took my paycheck at face value. To my dismay, I discovered later on that the "new guy from Jersey in the back office" had no clue that Brooklyn was a part of New York City and therefore, wasn't withholding my city taxes.

I ended up owing New York back-taxes for the next tax season. Please do not let this happen to you. Check your W-2 for accuracy before you take home your check so that the right amount of taxes, benefits, withholdings, etc. is being deducted and subsequently, your net income, aka disposable income, aka take-home pay, is accurate.

Resources:
FREE Social Security Statement:
www.ssa.gov/mystatement
1 (800) 772-1213
TTY: 1(800) 325-0778

www.salary.com to compare your salary level by occupation and by region
(i.e., What do 4th public school teachers make in Phoenix, AZ in comparison to their counterparts in Queens, NY?)

5.2 Employer Automatic Pre-Tax Savings Plan

It is easier to save money if you don't see it in your hands. Consequently, you can better discipline yourself to live on less disposable income. I have a relative whose job *mandates* a savings plan. He was complaining about it to me, to which I replied, *"That's great!"* It may hurt now, but he will be grateful when he sees how large his savings account has swelled later on. If your employer doesn't institute an automatic savings plan, then set it up in reverse by having your financial institution automatically withdraw a set amount each payday. *"How much?"* you may ask.

In his book, *Smart Women Finish Rich,* financial expert David Bach recommends that a fixed percentage or set amount of money be automatically transferred into your account or through payroll deductions in regular intervals in order to systematically build up savings.[20]

Hmmm...let's see—even if you are earning the national minimum wage of $5.15 per hour, assuming that you were to hypothetically squirrel away an hour's pay daily, that's $25.75 weekly; $51.50 bi-weekly; $103 monthly; $309 quarterly; and $1,236 annually. This further translates to over $6,000 in five years; doubles to over $12,000 in ten years...and I didn't even compound the interest in this scenario!

5.3 Other Pre-Tax Benefits

The premise here is that you save money as a result of deducting certain benefits pre-tax as opposed to post-tax. Many institutions offer a Flexible Spending Account to suit this purpose that is predicated upon "using it or losing it".

HYPOTHETICAL EXAMPLE OF PRE-TAX BENEFITS:

Let's say you have an Annual Salary of
$35,000, which translates into $1,346 bi-weekly
gross, and $2,692 monthly gross.
Assuming a 30% tax bracket,
the bi-weekly net is $942 and the monthly net is $1,884.

You go out and purchase a $76 monthly unlimited-use subway MetroCard *after* payday.
$1,884 (total monthly net) minus $76 = $1,808

On the other hand, let's say you ask your employer to deduct the cost of same $76 MetroCard *prior* to taxes.
$2,692 monthly gross minus $76 = $2,616
Now let's take out the taxes: $784.80
$1,831.20 is the monthly net pay.

Not only do you take home $23.20 more per month
(the difference between $1,808 & $1,831.20)
But the $76 is negligible because you
are getting reimbursed for it.
You save close to $100 per month:
$99.20 ($23.20 savings + $76 reimbursement), or
$1,190 per year by deducting your MetroCard
pre-tax, and—all factors being equal—that
hypothetically translates into an annual
savings of $2,380 for a two-income household.

5.4 Tax-Deductibles

Be tax savvy. By this, I don't mean cheat Uncle Sam aka the Tax Man! First, determine the correct tax withholding for your situation. Speak with your Accountant for advice on these matters. Examine legitimate tax-deductible expenses you are currently not claiming. For instance, if you provide a contribution or in-kind donation to a IRC (Internal Revenue Code) Section 501 (c) 3 non-profit organization, ask for a receipt and report it on your income taxes. Online tax resources are available to assist you. The following is a list of some, but not all items that may be tax-deductible (once again, check with your Certified Public Accountant in this regard to address your specific situation):[21]

- Contributions to church, synagogue, etc.
- Charitable contributions (monetary & in-kind)
- In-kind donations (i.e., Salvation Army)
- Home/Co-op/Condo Mortgage Interest, Maintenance, Property Taxes
- Educational Expenses (i.e., tuition, books, etc.)
- Professional Development (i.e., job-related continuing education)
- Medical (7½% of Adjusted Gross Income, and then only that portion that exceeds the 7½% floor)
- Child/Dependent care expenses
- Auto mileage/expenses for business purposes
- Job search-related expenses (i.e., postage, transportation)
- Moving (non-reimbursed for job move)
- Office-in-home (rent, utilities or portion thereof when room in dwelling is used exclusively or regularly as place to conduct business; often based on square footage)

~ Remember to obtain your receipts for tax purposes ~

Resources:

For more tax tip resources, visit H&R Block's Advice page – Tax 101 – on the "Most Overlooked Deductions" by visiting:

www.hrblock.com/taxes/fast_facts/articles/overlooked_deductions.html

-or-
Jeff Schnepper, tax attorney and author featured on MSN's tax page at:
http://www.moneycentral.msn.com/corner/Taxes/P71102.asp

Software that calculates the fair market value (FMV) of charitable donations:
TurboTax ItsDeductible www.itsdeductible.com or
DeductionPro® by H&R Block www.hrblock.com

Federal – www.IRS.gov or www.irs.ustreas.gov

NY–New York State Department of Taxation and Finance:
www.tax.state.ny.us
(There are District offices in Brooklyn, Queens, Manhattan & Nassau County)

5.5 Mortgage Pre-Payments

If you have a mortage, make an effort to pre-pay portions of it. This is one of the premises of Marc Eisenson's book *The Banker's Secret.* Did you know that by making just one extra mortgage payment on the principal amount per year on a 30-year fixed mortgage can reduce the length of your mortgage?[22]

Be cautious, however, that there are variable factors that should be taken into account when accelerating your mortgage payments. See your mortgage lender or consultant for details regarding your individual situation.

Resources:
Bank Rate monitoring website, www.bankrate.com

Jack M. Guttentag aka The Mortgage Professor, www.mtgprofessor.com

5.6 Assess Needs vs. Wants vs. Desires

Let's define these terms because they often get mixed up, and this is where a lot of people get into trouble.

Needs are a matter of survival and may be identified as food, shelter, basic utilities, transportation and basic clothing, enough to protect you from exposure to the elements. Wants are a matter of expanding our comfort zone. Desires are a matter of added luxury.

Let's take shoes, for example. Shoes are a basic need. We need something between our feet and the ground. One pair of shoes can meet that basic most need, but shoes become a want when we purchase several types of shoes for various occasions: white soft soles if you work as a Nurse, winter boots for the snowy outdoors. Running shoes to go jogging. High heels wouldn't make comfortable running shoes, right? Shoes become ostentatious (I got that word from my smart husband) when we go out and buy *several* pairs of Liz Claibourne, Timberland, Nike or Air Jordan athletic shoes when just one pair will do. The same shoe brand in a variety of colors. To match different outfits. To coordinate with the furniture. To advertise or display the fact that we stylin', yo. That's when we turn shoes into a luxurious commodity.

If you want to save money in Gotham, any other metropolis, or in a rural town for that matter, then it is absolutely imperative to keep in mind that **needs are to be met first.** *Las necessitas numero uno.* For instance, rent should be paid before going out and buying bling-bling. I once observed the judge on a court TV show bring the gavel down on the Defendant because she borrowed rent money from her relative, the Plaintiff. The Defendant's *baby* was decked out in designer clothing while the Defendant toted a designer handbag to court. The judge ordered the woman to pay the amount borrowed *plus interest* to the Plaintiff because she was relying on the Plaintiff to meet her needs, while she went out and bought the desires of her heart.

Needs, wants, and desires also exist on a sliding scale relative to different regions and cultures in our world. Why do I say this?

Because there are people in developing countries to whom a pair of shoes from Payless are a luxury, considering they have no shoes to wear at all (read Chapter 12).

Needs. Wants. Desires. Try to keep your priorities straight.

"And this same God who takes care of me
will supply all your needs from his
glorious riches, which have been given to us in Christ Jesus."
~ Philippians 4:19 ~

5.7 Take Inventory & Avoid Impulsive Shopping

The feeling of buying something, going back home, and then realizing you already have it is unlike any other! Before you go out shopping, determine whether or not you already have the item in stock. If so, consolidate items that are alike. Make a list. This is particularly true with school and home office supplies (e.g., pens and pencils). Before going out and buying children brand new school supplies, see what is usable and leftover from the previous school year.

When New Yorkers aren't eating, they're shopping. Listen up, urbanites: you've gotta curb your enthusiasm for impulse spending. Don't just say to your friend *"Let's go to the mall"* for fun and recreation. Chances are, you will leave with stuff you really do not need—including a wad of debt! Instead, replace shopping with a fun, free, healthy activity such as a walk in Central Park, a free outdoor concert, or a stroll across the Brooklyn Bridge.

5.8 Develop A Shopping List

There are so many occasions to purchase gifts: Birthdays, Bar Mitzvahs, Bas Mitzvahs, Engagements, Weddings, Baby Showers, Anniversaries, Retirement parties. The holiday season is the time people especially get into trouble. Mind you, the way I approach gift-giving is predicated on the assumption that no one in my family (to my knowledge) gets offended by my yearly informal surveys. I ask close friends and family to list 2-3 things they need, want or desire for Christmas. I then make a chart of what I am going to buy for whom, where I am going to shop for it and how much I am willing to spend. This way, 1) I'm confident that I am getting the recipient a gift that won't end up in his or her closet collecting dust, 2) the gift is still a surprise and 3) the gift fits my budget so I can avert post-holiday debt.

My mother-in-law favors a particular brand of perfume. However, she is happiest when surrounded by her sons, daughter-in-laws and grandchildren. One Christmas I opted to forego the perfume and instead ordered a $20 calendar personalized with digital photos of family gatherings taken throughout the years. Brand-name perfume set: 60 bucks. Personalized digital calendar: priceless...to my mother-in-law.

I had a holiday club account through my credit union for years, the purpose of which is to regularly deposit money throughout the year to fund our holiday (or vacation) spending. The credit union sends us a check in the spring for summer vacation, and a check around Thanksgiving for the holidays. That's all fine and dandy, but gifts do not always have to be material in nature. How about offering a raincheck on that fall road trip to the Adirondacks? What about spending some valuable time with an elderly shut-in? Some people even request that a gift be designated to a charity in lieu of flowers upon the death of a loved one. The most important thing to remember here is that the gift most meaningful to the recipient doesn't necessarily have to break your bank account or cause you to go deeper into credit card debt.

5.9 Comparison-shopping

Comparison-shopping is a delicate balancing act between time, money, and quality. I recall countless examples in New York City in which I am looking for an item in one store, and with a little research, can find the same or similar item at a lower price—from bottled water on a hot summer day to electronic equipment. When I bought my husband a DVD player for his graduation present, little did I know that I also had to purchase an RF modulator device in order to switch back and forth between the VCR and DVD players. I priced the modulator at $39.99 at one major electronics store. The exact same make/model was literally a few feet away at a neighboring store for $29.99. I highly recommend comparison-shopping before major purchases such as furniture, electronic appliances, and even clothing. I am not suggesting, however, that this be accomplished at the expense of quality.

Back in college, I simply wanted to listen to music tapes. CDs were not on the market yet. My fiancé warned me to purchase a name-brand cassette player, but I felt I did not have the money to do so. I purchased the cheap model anyway, and it broke down within a couple of months. That is when I learned my lesson. You have to assess the time it takes to shop around (sometimes it's as simple as looking at the Sunday ads) vs. the cost of purchasing a product without sacrificing quality.

We selected our healthcare plan by way of comparison. What will the co-payment be? What are the deductibles? How much is going to be deducted from our paycheck? What do sources we trust have to say about the caliber of service—so are we, like, going to be put on hold by the healthcare provider for 500 minutes when we call with a simple question?

~ Sunday newspaper circulars are a good resource for comparison shoppers. ~

5.10 Time Your Purchases

Did you know that just planning ahead and timing your purchases can help save you money in the long-run, such as when you are planning your next vacation? Take the following budgetary considerations into account: mode of travel (via ground, air or water, which can be further categorized into vehicle, shuttle, tour trolley, car rental, train, bus, boat or airfare); lodging; food & dining; R&R activities and entertainment; and miscellaneous expenses such as souvenirs, tips and emergency monies.

When James and I vacationed at DisneyWorld on the eve of the millenium, we timed our trip by saving the cash over a period of time for all of the above categories, including those items placed on the credit card that had to be later paid once the credit card bill arrived. I did not wish to be reminded by American Express in January what a fabulous time I had with Mickey & Minnie in December. When the AmEx bill did show up on our doorstep in January, we paid it all off in one shot. "Bam!" as Emeril the Chef would say.

How about something as mundane as the components involved with updating your visionware: Eye exam for the lenses? Purchase of the frames? Separate eye exam for the contacts? The contact lenses? There is a big difference between calling ahead to gather price quotes, and standing at the counter dazed, as the clerk announces, *"That'll be $279.99, sir."* My sister-in-law, Angie (a feline lover) points out, don't underestimate the cost of having a pet: veterinarian; pet food; pet toys; litter; carpet cleaner; dog walker or pet boarder, if you are away on vacation. It really pays to shop around, compare costs, collect coupons, and take advantage of sales and discounts based on your personal needs and preferences. Anticipate costs by planning ahead and timing your purchases accordingly.

I spend a considerable amount of time planning ahead,
and the rest executing plans, encountering very few
wrinkles during the implementation process.
~ MBR ~

5.11 Have a Pay-Off Plan in Place

I will make a case for using cash in Chapter 8, but if you *must* purchase via credit card, determine the following in advance: what it is you wish to buy; how much you are willing to spend after conducting pricing research; and which credit card you intend to use. But most importantly, develop a plan to pay off the debt *before* you even make the purchase! Some card companies offer a low interest rate; others, cash back or frequency points; factor in which card will give you the most back for charging the purchase. Or it may boil down to which card has a sufficient available line of credit for your purchase or the most useful record-keeping statement. There are some tax-related purchases my husband and I intentionally place on American Express, because AmEx sends us the year-end summary, which is beneficial to us at tax time.

The point is, avoid the potentially embarrassing situation of standing in line and chanting *"eeny-meeny-miny-moe,"* with your credit cards, and crossing your fingers that the cash register doesn't flash a big red rejection sign when paying for your purchases.

5.12 Generic Brands

Let's face it: paper clips are paper clips. Canned corn is canned corn. But if there are generic brands that are not comparable in quality to brand names according to your sophisticated estimation and palate, then so be it, Madame. My husband also cautions of the trauma of his mother cooking a generic brand of boxed frozen spinach so low-rent, he discovered half of a juicy green caterpillar on his dinner plate. Yum. Yum. Strangely, spinach is still his favorite vegetable...as long as it is a name brand. Choose even your generic brands with care.

5.13 Hotel, Airline & Car Rental Resources

Just a few short years ago, I would call the individual hotel chains to inquire about their rates, and the major airline carriers to ask them what their flights and fares were. Nowadays, you can go online to compare the costs of one airline and flight availability to another, including connecting flights...right down to the boarding pass and seat assignments! There are several online resources, in addition to the individual airline carriers, with searches linked to combined airline, hotel and car rental deals. Here are but a few (fees may apply):

www.bestfares.com
www.cheaptickets.com
www.expedia.com
www.fly4less.com
www.hotels.com
www.orbitz.com

www.priceline.com
www.sidestep.com (search engine for travelers)
www.travelocity.com

While online deals may be found, the downside of going online is restrictions that may accompany the lower price quote. For example, is that airline ticket you are purchasing online restricted or unrestricted; should an emergency arise where you cannot take the trip, can a refund be obtained or the ticket applied towards a future trip? You have to ask the airline carrier. Tip: you may be able to snag a free round-trip domestic airline ticket for a future flight if you give up your seat on an overbooked flight.

When booking hotels online, you may very well obtain a lower rate, but you will have to pay for the hotel upfront or be subject to a cancellation fee, and/or only a partial refund should you have to cancel. On the other hand, if you book directly with the hotel, there is a chance you could pay a slightly higher rate, but the cancellation policy could be much more flexible.

Consider the following. A hotel online rate: \$87/night plus tax. vs. \$119/night plus tax. If I book online, the \$87+ rate will be assessed to my credit card regardless of emergency occurrences where I may have to cancel. At the \$119+ rate, I can cancel up until 6 p.m. on the check-in date with no payment penalties at most major hotel chains.

Now let's look at car rental resources. I am simply amazed that a recent Internet search I conducted for a week-long car rental among the top national car rental chains yielded a difference of \$323.20 between the highest and lowest base price quoted, and when I identified myself as a AAA member, the discount margin widened by over 50%. Same car make/model. Same time frame. Same airport code. Same insurance terms. Same payment method. Different prices. (Don't these guys check out their fellow competitors' prices?) It took me a half-hour, tops, to comparison shop on the Internet.

Now before you ask, *"What did the car look like? You get what you pay for, ya know."* That's what I halfway expected—a modest-looking car, but our aim wasn't "to be stylin' in Florida". However, we were assigned an economy late model Ford Taurus 4-door sedan. Nice color, too.

Also, be sure to look for car rental companies that offer unlimited mileage unless you are certain that you are not going to exceed the mileage allowed in conjunction with the rate. Unless your circumstances dictate it, assign one driver, as opposed to two, since an additional driver incurs an additional charge. Avoid incurring an additional hourly fee by returning the vehicle around the same time you pick the car up. For example, James and I rented a car from Friday at 2 p.m. to Monday at 2 p.m. If we were to return the car on Monday at 3 p.m., we would have had to pay for an additional hour. Be sure to fill up the tank with gas before returning the vehicle. If applying for your car rental online and you happen to have any coupons to apply toward your purchase, be sure to enter that all-important coupon code online. Things are so automated nowadays, that I as a consumer became quite frustrated when the behind-the-counter staff of one of the major car rental suppliers indicated "the system" would not allow them to enter a coupon for our rental over-the-counter—it had to have been done over the Internet at the time of our reservation. This represented significant savings lost on our week-long rental.

Car rental discounts in conjunction with airline and hotel frequency points, professional associations, AAA, etc. are widely available. Now repeat after me: *"There is no reason for me to pay full price for my car rental. There is no reason for me to pay full price for my car rental. There is no reason for..."*

Resources:
Alamo.com, 1(800) GO ALAMO / 462-5266
Avis.com, 1(800)230-4898
Budget.com, 1(800) 527-0700
Dollar.com, 1(800) 800-4000

Enterprise.com, 1(800) 261-7331
Hertz.com, 1(800) 654-3131
NationalCar.com, 1(800) CAR-RENT / 227-7368
Thrifty.com, 1(800)847-4389
CarRentals.com (between airports)

Major tip:
Compare the base price, fees and taxes cost between your local or neighborhood car rental and the nearest airport car rental

~ New Century Travel Service provides daily express bus service between Chinatown in New York & Washington, D.C. for only $35 round trip; and between Chinatown in New York & Philadelphia for only $20 round trip. ~

5.14 Post Office Mailings

My husband and I attended a convention in Florida and needed to send boxes back to Manhattan. The hotel's courier office was more than willing to send the boxes to NYC the fastest way possible (translation: mo' money). But how fast did it really need to get there? We thought about it and decided the contents of the box were not such that we needed them ASAP. Also, prioritize which mailings require return receipt, signature confirmation, etc. Sometimes the time sensitivity or importance of a package indeed warrants using FedEx or UPS. With the ever-rising costs of postage, save the 39 cents if you can pay a bill check-by-phone without incurring a surcharge for doing so.

Next time you're at the Post Office, before starting to growl, give the person in front of you more of a grace period than half of a nano second to move to the next available window as the light turns green. Promise?
~ MBR ~

Resource: when locating a zip code, tracking confirmation receipt or fulfilling other postal needs, access the U.S. Postal

Service's website. Here is the contact info for the Post Office and other major carriers:

U.S. Postal Service - www.USPS.com -
1(800) ASK-USPS / 275-8777
DHL Express - www.DHL.com - 1(800) CALL-DHL / 225-5345
Federal Express - www.FedEx.com -
1(800) GO-FEDEX / 463-3339
United Parcel Service - www.UPS.com -
1(800) PICK-UPS / 742-5877

5.15 Receipts, Reimbursements, Rebates, Returns, Refunds, Recyclables, & Referrals

Check Your Receipts
Human error does occur, but you do not want it to be at your expense. Whenever you make a purchase or dine out, double check the bill for accuracy before paying.

I know, I know. I know all too well what it is like to be at the supermarket, attempting to strategically place the shopping cart between you and the person behind you to give yourself breathing room, all the while hoping the cashier doesn't sling your eggs around or mash your bread, and praying that a passerby isn't lifting your fabric softener at the end of the conveyer belt while you're paying for your goods as you hunch over your debit card keypad screen so an identity thief doesn't steal your Personal Identification Number. But do the best you can. And check your receipt before you vacate the premises.

Reimbursements
Send in those job-related and healthcare receipts for reimbursement. In a previous job of mine, I was reimbursed dinner and transportation expenses for overtime spent beyond 9 to 5. That amounted to about 8 bucks extra in each paycheck. If you multiply that by 26 pay periods, that's $208 annually.

Manufacturer Rebates

When you purchase a piece of equipment that comes with a money-back offer guarantee, fill out the form and send away for the rebate. I regularly receive rebates from office supplies that I purchase. I recently redeemed ten bucks I received on a piece of capital equipment and recycled it back into my business for miscellaneous supplies.

Returns

If you purchase an item that you need to return for any reason, pay careful attention to the return policy (i.e., store credit, exchange or refund). Avoid hassles by returning the merchandise within the specified time period printed on the receipt or posted near the cash register. I recently bought a pair of black denim jeans and because I hadn't bought any new articles of clothing in a very long time, I forgot which size I wore. I bought both a size 8 and 10, went home and tried them both on because there were no dressing rooms on store premises, and took one pair back (a lady doesn't tell which size) with no hassle. It is also a good idea to scope out which stores have open return policies so you don't feel hemmed in (pun intended). Some stores are now keeping track of customers who repeatedly return merchandise and may reserve the right to deny refunds to repeat returners, so try and be as close to sure as possible that you're purchasing merchandise you wish to keep.

Refunds

Why should you have to pay now because the system hasn't reconciled its records yet? We have a bundled telephone-Internet-cable package from Company A. Company A (telephone and internet) subcontracts with Company B for the cable. Company B installed cable equipment and then took it away due to incompatibility issues. The bill from Company A was higher than usual due to Company B's add-on equipment charges. However, the credit for the returned equipment had not yet shown up in Company A's records. Company A set up a three-way call between Company B and myself, where I politely explained that it would be difficult to advance the full amount. Company B saw the return on its computer screen, and conceded that it had not yet been communicated to Company A. The latter assured me that it was all right to send in the full amount less the refund. One may justifiably argue, *"Why not just wait for the adjustment on the next bill? You'll owe less the next time around."* Valid point, but we happened to be on a tight budget that month and needed the extra money to go towards other bills.

C'mon, you know how it is, especially with large refunds—if **you** owe money, the bill is in the mail pronto and was due yesterday. Your name has already been forwarded to a bill collection agency (or so the letter threatens). If another entity owes **you** money, it takes an Executive Board of 15 people requiring a notorized affidavit in the presence of Supreme Court Justices before **your** refund can be issued.

Also, have you ever noticed that when you go to the store and buy soda or bottled water (which, by the way, is a multi-billion dollar business in the United States according to *Time* magazine[23]), you are charged a nickel to drink out of the container? Well, you are. If you can, return the thing and get your nickel back.

Recyclables

Speaking of recyclables, I once returned my ink cartridges, and the office supply store clerk promptly handed me a free ream of paper (their monthly special), valued at $4.39. I was also given the alternative of $2.50 off the purchase of my next ink cartridge. Apparently, re-manufactured ink cartridges are big business and also help to lower the cost for consumers. (Check your local post office, as I have discovered that some offer the service of collecting your old ink cartridges and forwarding them to re-manufacturers.) Gee whiz…I was just trying to do my little bit to help the environment. Who knew?

Referrals

Some establishments such as banks and storage facilities offer cash rewards as an incentive for you to refer a friend (i.e., refer a friend and get $10 off). Are there any such companies or vendors you currently do business with that provide money for referrals without as many catches as there are people in New York? Conversely, make sure it is a place you yourself have an account with or can refer in good faith. In other words, don't refer them to a bad place and then run off with the 10 bucks! Geesh.

Should you receive an unexpected windfall
(i.e., monetary gift, inheritance), try to treat the money as
"special," and don't blow it on frivolity.
~ MBR ~

5.16 Prepare Your Own Coffee, Tea & Lunch

My favorite tea is Lipton. I usually don't get into flavored teas. So for the sake of simplicity, let's use plain 'ole Lipton as an example. A box of 100 tea bags at the supermarket costs me $3.29. If I go to a street vendor, he will charge me a *minimum* of 85 cents to dip a tea bag into a paper cup of hot water. Not to mention if I were to sip my coffee at a café. I won't even go there. For the same 100 tea bags, I would pay $85 to the vendor versus somewhere between 3 to 4 cents per tea bag by buying it myself. If someone handed me the difference of $81.31 right now, would I be able to use that cash? Did a man house a tiger and an alligator in his Harlem apartment? Then I rest my case.

According to industry tracker Technomic, coffee is a low-overhead, high profit commodity for restaurateur.[24] Take it from one urban consumer to another—go buy yourself a coffeemaker, kettle and thermal mug. Brew your coffee or boil your water while you are getting ready for work. Take the thermal mug with you in your car, train or bus; and the next morning rush hour as you watch those long lines of people paying for their beverages, think of the money you are saving. Plus, you get it flavored exactly the way you like. And if it is free at your place of work—well then!

David Bach, author of *The Automatic Millionaire* specifically refers to this coffee craze as the "Latté Factor™." He challenges us to calculate how much money we spend on coffee, and to redirect that same money towards savings. Multiply the amount spent on coffee out by a month, quarter, year, two years. "What is *your* latté?," Bach probes.[25] Is it clothes? Sweets? Video games? Whatever it is, is it worth depleting savings for?

~ When I buy my favorite White Chocolate Mocha at Starbuck's, it's a rare treat and not a ritual ~

"Yo quiero un café con leche y azucar de quatro, por favor?" (Non Spanish-speaking me, attempting to order my coffee in Spanish from my favorite street vendor near Grand Central Station because New York is about interesting experiences, and not just money)

My mother made lunches from the time I was in Kindergarten through Middle School. By the time I went to High School, I didn't *want* school cafeteria food. Although I admit, I had to get rid of the metal lunchbox with a picture of a watermelon on it by the time I got to Junior High. The practice of making my own lunch followed me well into my professional years. While my colleagues were buying deli sandwiches for $7-8 bucks a pop, I brought dinner leftovers, canned soup or made my own sandwiches. If you do not have time to make lunch, at least bring your own cold beverages to work with you. On a hot, summer day, bring bottled water with you from your apartment so you will not be tempted to stop by a store and buy it.

Don't get too overconfident about having a full-time salaried position. When you are fortunate enough have a stable job, that is *especially* the time to be saving your money. Yes, you may have a steady income, but transportation and expenses associated with simply having a job are no doubt already eating into your discretionary income. God forbid, should you ever lose your job someday, you will at least rest assured knowing you were financially prudent while you were working 9 to 5.

5.17 Utility Usage

Turn off the lights when you're done," we were told as kids. In many high-rise Manhattan office buildings, lights and restroom water faucets are motion-sensored to automatically turn off. If the big guys can save money on utility usage, then so can you and I. Utility companies such as ConEd and KeySpan offer level paying plans. Level payment plans are when your average heating and electrical usage is leveled-out over time to equalize the payments, as opposed to generating hi vs. low bills.

Resources:
Edison Energy Institute – www.eei.org/wiseuse
Consumer Energy Center – www.consumerenergycenter.org

5.18 Telephone, Cell Phone, Internet, & Cable TV Service Providers

1) Analyze your usage by reviewing past bills—don't rely entirely on how much usage you *think* you talk on the phone. Chances are, your usage is more than you think.

2) Identify a plan that best encompasses your usage pattern and fits your budget. TV viewers, for instance, are offered a plethora of choices nowadays: basic cable, satellite TV, pay-per-view movies-on-demand; or TiVo.

3) Review the financial anatomy and accuracy of your bills for the breakdown of sub-categorized charges (i.e., roaming, off-peak, airtime, national long distance, etc.)

There is no cookie-cutter approach, because each of us utilizes these services differently. I prefer to make and receive calls through my home (office) phone because our home phone has an *unlimited* national, regional and local package, and my husband and I have a *limited* amount of monthly cell phone minutes that we share for incoming and outgoing calls. Included in the plan is unlimited mobile-to-mobile (me to him and him to me...how cute is that?). We don't make international calls. I am extremely satisfied with both our landline and cell phone bills (each bill is *under* $70 per month including taxes, fees and surcharges).

Yet, I know people who opt to talk only on their cell because it is more cost-effective *for them.* Some use long-distance or international calling pre-fix numbers or pre-paid calling cards. Or as New Yorkers would say, *'coiling cods.'* One of my family members only pays for a fixed amount of minutes for dial-up Internet usage. Many feel that new retirement home they built in the Poconos will be finished before that dial-up Internet Service Provider logs on. Hi-speed DSL may be too expensive for others. Some bundle Internet usage with their cable and/or telephone. (In which case, be sure to ask your service provider upfront whether or not a 911 operator will be able to locate the exact location of your call in case of an emergency since the call is originating from the Internet). I attended a conference where a consultant demonstrated VoIP (Voice over Internet Protocol). His Manhattan number shows up on his client's caller I.D., even though he may very well be calling out of state! Have you ever heard of pre-paid virtual vanity toll-free 800 numbers? Hey, whatever floats your boat.

The point is, only you can decide which service package and provider best suits your needs. Also, make sure you are not paying multiple companies for access to the Internet. I hate to say this, but half of the people I know do not even answer from the e-mail addresses they do have in effect.

Depending on the caliber of service—and no, not all cell phone plans are equal in this regard—do not pay more than you have to by exceeding the prescribed base rate. Periodically check with your cell phone company for the latest deals. I have called my carrier about other matters and ended up getting extra minutes for the same or less cost. What's the catch? You may have to agree to a contract extension. Be cognizant that early termination fees are applicable should you decide to discontinue a cell phone contract.

Conversely, if you are paying for more than your usage, think about that, too. For instance, if you are not home much of the time and you subscribe to the premium cable package with all of the bells and whistles, consider downgrading. The big cable companies won't like me for this, but why pay for something you are too busy to watch?

Bundling: Convenience vs. Cost

Company A, which is already our telephone-Internet-cable service provider, cheerfully reminded me that my cell phone plan is not with them, to which I replied, *"Is that a fact?"* Seriously, I challenged: My husband and I are currently paying around $60 a month to Company B for two phones, and when the contract expires, we're even thinking about leaving Company B and going to pre-paid cell phone minutes based on our very low usage. So tell me—can you beat $60 a month? Their reply? We offer the convenience of placing it all on one bill for you. They totally skirted the cost issue. (I happen to know that their plan is at least $70 per month for shared minutes). So this is where you as a consumer have to decide which is best for you: the convenience of having everything on one bill, or possibly paying more. In fairness to Company A, we're already receiving across-the-board discounts as a result of having a bundled package.

In conclusion, from consumer-to-consumer, research the market's offerings, assess your needs, and analyze what your budget can support.

~ Netiquette ~
Observe your party's preferred method of
communication. Is it the telephone? Then don't send them a
bunch of e-mails and expect them to reply promptly.
Is it the Internet? Then don't call incessantly on their cell phone.
Respect your party's right-to-privacy by
creating a list of undisclosed recipients.
Avoid e-spats.
Also, is posting your RSVP to the entire listserv truly necessary?
Hey, I'm just asking.

Resource:

www.SaveOnPhone.com for a comparison on various phone and wireless plans

5.19 Features You Did Not Subscribe To

Check your bills for errors to make sure you are not being charged for something you did not subscribe to. Address errors as soon as you receive your bill so that the credit assessed to your statement is reflected on the very next billing cycle. One of the major airline carriers erroneously charged us for mailing our tickets. Everything from booking the flight to printing out the boarding tickets was processed electronically online, so our credit card company had no problem crediting us the surcharges. One call. Problem corrected.

Even after repeated phone calls, our cellular provider insisted on charging us for text messaging. I finally got through to them that if I wanted to vote for Ruben Studdard or Clay Aiken, I would call the toll-free number directly, but we are not interested in this feature, which for our household is a frivolous charge. Same way with our phone company...they were charging us a nominal fee for a second line. There's only one teensy weensy little problem: we don't have a second line!

5.20 Consider Making Advanced Payments

If there are services you subscribe to that you are reasonably sure to retain over a long period of time, inquire about discount rates available for making advance payments if you are financially able to do so. We try to do this with our insurance policy premium payments in order to avoid the quarterly processing fee.

5.21 Coupons, Sales, Discounts & Clearances

I could go on and on about this one. To begin with, although you risk the desired item not being available (which may very well be the case in New York), you may choose to wait it out for the lower price. Merchandise eventually goes on sale, especially during off-season and major holidays. You may even find what you're looking for on the clearance rack for more than 50% off. I once found an elegant, perfectly color- coordinated bathroom set (soap dispenser, toothbrush holder, and soap dish) on the clearance shelf for a total of $23 when I could have easily paid double the price.

Do not purchase items, particularly food, *just because* you have a coupon. That can be a waste of money. Buy it because you really need it *and* you happen to have a coupon. Just today, my lunch cost $1.25 because I responded to a survey regarding service at a burger joint. The system gave me a code after I completed the survey, I took the coded card to the restaurant; and I enjoyed a big, fat, juicy bacon mushroom cheeseburger for free, paid for the fries, and drank water (to wash down all the grease). Coupons may be found in the yellow pages and are available online, as well. I bought a box of mashed potato buds for $5 at the supermarket. I later bought 2 boxes for half that price ($2.50) by printing my coupon online. In that vein...

5.22 On-line Deals

Utilize the Internet to find deals &/or items you'd normally purchase offline. I hardly ever pay retail for (used) books I order online through Amazon.com, BN.com (Barnes & Noble), or ChristianBook.com; not to mention that you can throw in membership and coupon codes when placing your order.

Rather than calling directory assistance and getting charged not only for the call, but also their dialing the number for you (get a life!), access www.411.com. Or try calling 1-800-FREE-411. You are already paying for access to the information superhighway if you have Internet service.

The same can be applied with the TV Guide included with cable TV packages. Unless you *want* or *desire* that magazine readily available at your fingertips on your coffee table, access the Internet or check the back page of your daily local newspaper to see when your favorite shows are airing. We shaved 4 bucks a month off of our basic cable bill by doing this. Could you use an extra 48 bucks in *your* pocket at year's end to apply towards the kids' Christmas gifts?

5.23 Merchant Partnering

Utilize deals offered through merchant cross-partnering, particularly teacher discounts, student discounts, union discounts and professional association discounts. For instance, as a member of my special events association, I get 30% off all Kinko's orders. If you are a member of AAA, you can get a discount at Lenscrafters and Payless Shoe Source. If you are a Student Advantage Member, you can get 15% off an Amtrak train ticket. My husband once got $20 off a pair of $100 Nike sneakers because he was a member of Student Advantage.

5.24 Dollar Stores, 99-Cent Stores, Discount Outlets & Consignment Shops

Growing up, I remember my mother shopping at the Goodwill, the Salvation Army and at the dollar store. In New York, 99-cent stores are more prevelant. With my father working to support a wife and five children, K-Mart and Target were a "step up" for us. My brother's joke was that by the time we got our clothes out of the lay-away, they were too small to fit (LoL)! My mother always taught us it's not what you have, but how well you take care of and maintain what you have. Do I hear an "Amen," somebody? Mom bought hand-me-downs. After she sewed, cleaned and pressed the second-hand clothing, no one—not even the kids who made fun of you from the back of the bus—knew the difference between the pair of $5 jeans bought at the Goodwill vs. the $50 pair from the fancy retail store.

Conversely, when donating goods in-kind, be sure to obtain a receipt for goods rendered so that you can assess the fair market value during tax time. Sometimes we've given stuff away, and sometimes consignment shops have paid us for the items (i.e., furniture).

I do understand that quality may be an issue, so simply identify what merchandise you are willing to purchase from the dollar store, 99-cent store, or other discount outlet. I have found rock-bottom prices on the following overstocked or irregular close-outs at outlet stores: candy, attractive-looking stationery and paper supplies, party supplies, kitchen and bathroom accessories, socks, name-brand cereal, batteries (yes, Duracell and Energizer), and the list goes on!

~ *"One man's junk is another man's treasure." (Author Unknown)* ~

~ *Visit a thrift shop on the Upper East Side of Manhattan one day.* ~

5.25 Frequency Points, Rewards & Cash-back Bonuses

If it's free and has a frequency reward for usage, take it. Make sure you have all of those supermarket, drug store, office supply store, bookstore, airline, hotel and car rental frequency cards and numbers. Even Amtrak sponsors such a program. Some major retailers such as Barnes & Noble, Best Buy, and GNC charge a nominal fee in order to be assigned a frequency rewards I.D. number and/or to receive special discounts.

Be extremely organized with your points. The more our lives become automated, I feel like pulling out my hair in terms of keeping track of all of the account numbers, user I.D.s, and passwords.

When making purchases, **remember to have the cashier to scan the key card or provide your I.D. number when placing orders over the phone or Internet. If your card isn't being scanned, then you are not accumulating the points!** It is often difficult if not impossible to have the points retroactively credited after the transaction has been completed.

My only real criticism about frequency points programs is that you have to ask yourself if the redemption terms are too restrictive and if the redemption points are equitable to the purchase. For instance, if a $100 leather designer purse takes 10,000 points to redeem, then conceivably you accumulated $10,000 in charges in a 1:1 ratio. If you had the cash, would you have spent $10,000 on that purse? Unless you're a spoiled socialite, probably not. So why trade those kinds of points (unless you really, really want the bag)? I could not believe my eyes when one of the major credit card companies was offering a bag of popcorn and soda at the movie theatre for a redemption of 2,000 points. I know movie snacks are expensive, but is it really worth 2,000 points? On the other hand, 25,000 points is usually the minimum requirement for a round-trip domestic coach airline ticket. I've redeemed frequent flyer miles with the click of a mouse. Pretty neat, huh? But the key here is the accumulation of points. There is one caveat you should keep in mind. I recently attempted to redeem frequent flyer points (albeit at the last minute, **and** during

Christmastime). Not one, but several airline reps told me I couldn't redeem points because the carriers had already allocated a certain number of seats to passengers using their frequent flyer miles.

Before writing this book, I was an uncompromising believer in paying cash for consumables such as groceries, gasoline, and pharmaceuticals. *"Why pay in August for groceries charged in July?"* Plus, it feels good pulling out the pre-budgeted cash envelope at the gas pump. However, purchases on these very kinds of items often yield double or more points or cash-back bonuses by major credit and charge cards. Our household experimented with the idea of accumulating rewards for these everyday items. The $250 my husband spent on groceries at Thanksgiving could have translated into 500 double rewards points, or $12 (5%) worth of cash rebates on down the line. We would have had to shell out the grocery money anyway at some point or another. If we tie cash-back rebates to our credit card, and make certain there are no late payments, paying the bill is just later as opposed to sooner. It's totally up to you to decide for yourself.

From one consumer to another, I still must heavily caution: a) Avoid racking up credit card debt for the sake of points/rewards *alone*—examine how much interest you are paying. b) Be committed to paying off the credit card balance in full. c) Ask the following questions before enrolling in a points or cash-back rewards program: how many points per dollar spent will I accumulate? Do the points ever expire? What is the cash-back rebate percentage? A simple phone call told me that 1.5% rebate is tied to Card A, and 5% cash back is tied to Card B. Which card do you think we're enticed to use? (Although we intend to pay the card in full every month—just in case we can't—Card B has a lower, fixed interest rate than Card A's higher, variable interest rate.) Is the cash-back automatically posted as a credit to the account, or can I call and request a check? (We prefer the cash rebate checks so that we can deposit them into an interest-bearing account. Other consumers may prefer that a credit be posted to their account.) Is there a waiting period before the points can be redeemed or the cash rebate check cut?

Assessing which credit card to use is one thing (see Chapter 8); closely examining the types of rewards offered relative to your spending tastes and habits requires different analysis.

Resource: www.Points.com is a free online service that consolidates points accrued from participating airlines, hotels, retailers, etc. Track, trade, earn, or buy points points around for goods, services and gift certificates.

5.26 Points Redemption, Gift Cards & Certificates

Racking up the points is one thing; *redeeming* the points is another. Redeem those points parked on your credit cards and frequency programs. Let's not forget those free hams and turkeys at the supermarket during the holidays. I can vouch for the $30 coupon sent to me by Staples for being a frequent rewards participant (www.staplesrewardscenter.com for business use, personal use or for teachers). I bought a $34.99 black ink cartridge for our home office printer. After-coupon cost: $4.99 plus tax. In another instance, I didn't have enough points accumulated on one of my airline frequency accounts to qualify for a free plane ticket (heard they were going bankrupt, anyway). Instead, I redeemed a portion of the points to subscribe for 12 issues to a business-oriented magazine. Newsstand price: $4.99 per issue. I saved 60 bucks. Sorry, I can't resist one other story: five Mothers Day cards should have cost me 15 bucks. Armed with ten dollars' worth of Hallmark Gold Crown® coupons, however, the cost ended up being $3.95 plus tax (www.hallmark.com). What should have cost me $110 in the above examples cost me around $9. **The $101 saved was redirected towards other purchases in our household.**

Whether or not you send free cards from the Internet is a matter of taste: how do you think the recipient will feel about the gesture? I regularly send friends and family free e-cards with music and sound effects from DaySpring at www.dayspring.com. To send out an invitation to an event you are planning (and to manage the RSVPs), check out www.evite.com.

Gift cards are more conspicuously displayed at stores than they used to be. You can now purchase a movie gift card at the office supply store, or a department store gift card at the grocery store. If you receive a gift card or certificate, carefully read the terms and conditions, as well as note the expiration date. Do not hold onto the gift card for too long; redeem sooner as opposed to later so you will not encounter any difficulty from the retailer honoring the gift card.

~ Do not underestimate the long-term buying power of points that generate coupons. ~

5.27 ATM Fees & ATM Machines

Consider banking with an institution that doesn't charge you to withdraw or draft a check on your own money. Make sure the designated bank is conveniently located near your residence or place of employment so that you are not forced to use a different bank that will assess an ATM surcharge to your account. If a nearby bank is not possible, then go make a small purchase, perhaps at a nearby grocery store, use your ATM debit card, and select "cash back" as a way to obtain cash fee-free.

Beware of ATM machines not directly located on bank premises where you can seek and obtain assistance if need be. Merchants subleasing ATM machines on their property claim that they are limited in terms of assisting you if a problem arises. They cannot refund money lost because the machine is "not really theirs". Yet, they are profiting a cut from the surcharge.

Make sure the ATM machine is bona fide, and use the mirror to watch over your shoulder anytime you input your personal identification number to protect sensitive card information from the eyes of prying thieves. Take your ATM receipts with you. To err on the side of caution, do not leave them scattered on the floor of the bank foyer. Even in the supermarket, place the grocery cart between you and the person behind you when swiping your card and entering your PIN. Take no prisoners when it comes to protecting your credit and debit bank cards (see Chapter 11 on Identify Theft, etc.).

5.28 Avoiding Late Fees

We will discuss late fees on credit cards later, but let's use my favorite example: videos. If you return a DVD or video after its due date, it can cost up to 5 bucks. Now that may not seem a lot to you, but look at it from the merchant's point of view: if 100,000 people across the county return a video late at 5 bucks each, that is half a million dollars! Pure profit. They did not have to pay advertising dollars. No additional overhead. A cool half a mil earned from customers returning videos late. Do not allow money you work hard for go straight into company's war chest because you cannot return a video on time. Think of it this way: The President & CEO of the video rental company is living in nice digs in a posh neighborhood (Hamptons, perhaps)? His or her kids are attending a private boarding school, and he or she is driving a Mercedes, no—Cadillac Escalade (for the kids as they get dropped off at the door of their private school)—all because you can't seem to turn the video in on time.

5.29 Going To The Movies

If you *must* see Tom H., or Brad or Denzel or Nicole or Halle or Julia or Will, you don't have to see them at 10 bucks a pop. Be selective, discriminating, and check listings for matinee times, which cost less. Or you might wait until the movie comes out on video/DVD, cable, or pay-per-view. True, performing artists and their associates in the film and motion picture industry have a right to fair compensation and royalties for their talent and expertise so the viewing public can be entertained, yada yada. I am not suggesting, however, that you buy pirated video and audio goods; doing so hurts someone else. What I am saying is that while we are on our couch munching potato chips and watching them, celebrities, filmmakers, movie companies, distributors, etc. are still making money off of stuff they did over twenty years ago! *Drum roll.*

AMC Theatres has a frequency club. Visit MovieWatcher.com for details. You accumulate 2 points per movie, and these points may be applied towards a minimum reward of a free small popcorn, up to a maximum reward of a free movie ticket, small popcorn, and small drink at the concession stand. (With the cost of hotdogs, soda and popcorn, you'll need it!) Downside: must see 50 movies in order to qualify for the one free movie. Just thought I'd let you know. Also, which theatre is your favorite movie playing at? Sometimes the movie I wish to see is at Loews Cineplex, and not at AMC. Yet, I'd accumulate the rewards at AMC. But I guess that won't matter soon, as Loews and AMC plan to merge as of this writing.[26] Ahh, don't you just love our free enterprise system?

Resource: Movie Phone (212) 777-FILM / 3456

5.30 Resources Available At Your Local Library

Unless you wish to make a book a part of your permanent library collection, checking out books, videos, CDs, and DVDs from your local library is the cheaper alternative to buying. Read your favorite newspapers and magazines at the library, as well. Don't forget your tax-paying dollars are supporting the library, so take advantage.

5.31 Subscriptions & Memberships

If you do not read the magazines you subscribe to or go to the gym you are a member of, then cancel the membership, regardless of how much of a discount you are being offered. If you are not taking advantage of it—regardless of how well-intentioned—then the money is still *diñero out the door-o.*

On the other hand, if you *are* reading those magazines, then do subscribe to it (or visit the library) versus paying the newsstand price. Example: pay a cover price of $3.95 yielding $47.40 annually versus $20 for a year's subscription. That's more than 50% off of the newsstand price. Then be a good neighbor and recycle its use by passing it on to friends and establishments such as barber and beauty shops, doctor's office or better yet, nursing homes. Be sure to black out your name and address on the label. (See section 5.26 on redeeming points, gift cards & certificates on a way to get your fave magazine for absolutely free!)

Resource: www.bestdealsmagazines.com

5.32 Early-Bird Specials

If there is an early bird special and you know with a degree of certainty that you plan on attending an association meeting, conference, trade show, convention, etc., then make sure you read the cancellation policy carefully. I regularly save anywhere between 5 and 10 bucks just by sending my payment in early for an association meeting. (Hey, these associations can be expensive to join and to attend!) Early bird specials also apply to shopping, such as when a department store opens its doors early for loyal shoppers to take advantage of drastic discounts. During the holiday season, many merchandisers offer customers a discount if they place their order shortly after Thanksgiving in order to avoid the last-minute holiday rush. According to one major office supply store, if I order 100 personalized Christmas cards before December 10th, it will cost me $128.24. After the 10th, it will cost an extra $42.74. And of course, taxes will be added on top of that, making it close to a difference of 50 bucks.

~ *Mark your calendar to remind yourself of early bird deadline dates, sale dates, or coupon expiration dates.* ~

5.33 Personal Maintenance

I remember the priest at the Catholic elementary school I attended asking me if my Mom pressed my hair by placing my head on the ironing board to make it so straight and shiny. That's not quite the way it worked, but my hair styles have metamorphised over the years from wash and press, to perms, to braids, back to perms and then back to braids. But in the end, the health of my—or anyone else's hair—is much more important than style alone. My husband has learned to cut his own hair, thereby saving $12-$15 bucks a month. Some women feel it necessary to pay someone else to do their nails, so nails is a hard one. However, if you choose to spend money to paint your *dog's* nails...well, it's a free country, but we don't have to get silly, do we?

5.34 Shopping For Clothes

Who says you have to dress expensively to look nice? NYC is the fashion capital of the world, so this is a real hard one. Without impeding on your preference of a favorite store or name brand manufacturer, I'll take a stab at it (no pun intended, New York).

The fashion industry, designers and marketing and advertising would have you believe that if you do not have a certain item with so-and-so's label made with a particular fabric, daa-ling, then you are *so* last season. This highbrow, chi-chi-pooh-pah attitude aside, nothing beats every New Yorker's must-have: basic black and white in our wardrobe.

1) Assess what clothing items are a need vs. a want vs. a desire.

2) Avoid fads and opt to buy with an eye for the future—will you still look good in it 10 years from now? Remember, fashion recycles itself, so if do buy fashionable articles and they stay in the closet long enough, chances are they will be back in style.

3) Carefully assess what color schemes and clothing types look good on you. Just because it looks good on Tyra Banks or "O" may not necessarily mean that it looks good on you. I have learned that dressing nicely is sometimes simply a matter of putting the right colors together to compliment our skin tone and fit our body contour. As a woman, I admiringly compliment other women on their hairdo or outfit. I remember one lady who wore a simple, casual baby blue sweatsuit with just the right accessories. She confessed, *"Honey, this entire outfit cost me less than $50, including the accessories."*

4) Accessorize each season as opposed to going out and buying a whole new wardrobe. Slowly build up your classics.

5) Would you at all consider wearing unisex clothing? Allow me to put this in context before you look askance. When James and I revisted our alma mater, I had an inclination to purchase university paraphernalia, the affordability of which was out of question when

I was a student. I wanted to buy us both a pair of sweatpants and a T-shirt. Of course, this cost more than the regular, average jersey and tee due to the branded logo. Ultimately, I bought a large T-shirt and one pair of medium sweatpants—small enough to fit my 5'4" height, and large enough to fit James' tall frame. Hey, this is not a fashion show—just something to lounge around the house in. I paid $21.99 and $24.99 respectively, totaling 50 bucks with tax vs. $100 to purchase two separate outfits for both of us.

6) Don't be ashamed to buy from the Salvation Army, Goodwill or consignment shop. Have you ever been to the consignment shops on Manhattan's Upper East or Upper West side? The selections can be incredible! If you do not live in the city, visit the thrift shops located somewhere near the upper crusty neighborhoods.

7) Once you do make a purchase, keep it clean and well-maintained so that it lasts for years to come.

Personally speaking, I bought most of my wardrobe during my professional working years, when I had the budget to pay for it. Twelve years later, I still wear the same clothes, and they look like new because I bought them with an eye toward the future. Some don't fit, so I donated these articles of clothing to charities promoting women in the workforce. But both my husband and I are blessed to have the basics in our wardrobe: khakis, jeans, polos, shirts, blouses, skirts, suits. If we do purchase a new piece of clothing, it is a want or a desire that we make every effort to pay for with cash.

The important thing to know about the clothing industry is that it is cyclical. The industry revolves around the four distinct seasons of Spring, Summer, Fall, and Winter. Styles are designed and manufactured one year in advance, and promoted at least one season in advance. For example, Fall collections are designed the previous Fall; you see ads promoting Summer fashions in the preceding Winter season. Whatever clothing consumers do not buy is considered surplus inventory, and gets shipped out to odds and ends stores at factory/discount outlets once the season is over. Local outlets also receive clothing from main retail stores.[27] Bottom line: a friend of mine has gotten a $100-$200 dress that she would have bought in-season at a department store for $18-$20 out-of-season on the clearance rack at the outlet.

The best time to shop for deep discounts on summer merchandise is in June (as retailers are clearing inventory to make way for Fall merchandise) and immediately following July 4th; and the week after New Year's up until February for winter items.[28]

~ New York State periodically sponsors a sales tax-free week on clothing and footware purchases that cost less than $110 per item. ~

~ Macy's is one of the department store in New York City that has a hosiery club: purchase 12 pairs of stockings, get the 13th pair free. ~

Donate your slightly worn coats to:
New York Cares Coat Drive – www.nycares.org, (212) 228-5000 (Who can forget the image of the Statue of Liberty freezing in the wintertime?)

5.35 Dry Cleaning & Laundry

As I have said before, sometimes other factors are more important than money. After my husband and I moved to Spanish Harlem, we continued to travel to our dry cleaners of choice on Flatbush Avenue in Brooklyn because for over ten years, the owner/manager came to know us. There comes a point, in a city with millions of people, where you cherish personal affiliations. As a matter of fact, when we moved, the dry cleaner got teary-eyed because he thought he was losing us to one of those "uptown cats".

Here's an urban tale for you. I used to go to a certain laundromat due to its proximity to our apartment. It was across the street. Can't beat that. Then one hot summer day, a big, fat roach walked in with his sunglasses on like he was a preferred customer. I shrieked, everyone ducked, and the other patrons glared at me as if to say, *"You got a problem, lady?"* Needless to say, I changed my laundromat venue as fast as an O.J. trial.

Ya'll think I'm making this up, don't you? (This entire tale is true except for the sunglasses part.)

5.36 Pharmacy Needs

Comparison-shopping is particularly important with prescription medications. Shop your prescriptions around. From what I hear, some people are getting theirs as far away as Canada. I didn't go that far...I priced mine at local neighborhood pharmacies Rite Aid, Duane Reade and Walgreen's. The price for the very same prescription differed slightly at each place! I then asked myself which location is the most convenient. Certainly, I am not going to travel from one borough to another just to save a few pennies a month (had you fooled, didn't I?). I settled on a mid-town location that, incidentally, offered the lowest price quotation. It also offered an efficient telephone refill service, thereby saving me time. And the savings differential from the highest-priced quote? Five bucks a month, or $60/year.

5.37 Asking All Of The Right Questions

Don't just ask questions; ask all of the *right* questions before agreeing to anything, especially major purchases! Upon entering a corporate, hi-rise Manhattan office building to attend a meeting of one of my professional/business organizations that I am a member of, security snaps a grainy black and white photo that makes me look like I am being booked for Rikers Island. Security then prints out a visitor's badge, and screens me by asking who I am there to see in order to verify that I truly have business in the building. If I mention a specific name, I am taking a chance that individual may or may not be at his or her desk. As security calls my party, I may end up getting stuck in the lobby. However, if I state that *"I am here to attend the Network of Enterprising Women's affiliate chapter of the National Association of Female Executives,"* then s/he doesn't even bother to pick-up the phone and sends me on up. Don't take this the wrong way; I am not trying to dodge security protocol, but I know what answers to provide in order to expedite the nature of my business. Likewise, when it comes to being astute with your finances, it is not enough to ask questions. You have to be able to ask all of the *right* questions:

- What is the interest rate on this batch of unsolicited convenience checks you have sent to me?
- What will the interest rate or the monthly cost jack up to after the introductory offer period?
- How much will you deduct from my checking account when I request a new batch of checks or pre-printed deposit slips?
- Do I need to lock-in the lower interest rate now as I'm making this deposit on an automobile?
- If I pay this merchandise off early, will I be assessed an early termination fee?
- What are the terms of your return policy?
- What exactly does the extended warranty cover?
- I have dial-up, so if I switch to your lower-cost phone service, will my callers receive a busy signal or voice mail when I'm online?
- How much will it cost me to have your organization to consolidate my debt? What, precisely, are your fees for assisting me in doing so?
- Is the fare you are quoting me over the phone the same as if I booked online?
- What is your base rate? And please identify all of the applicable fees and charges I can expect to see in addition to the base rate.
- Am I going to be assessed a fee if I don't maintain a minimum balance? If so, how much?
- Is the cost you're quoting me for labor only, or are the materials included as well?
- Are you the Buyer's broker, Seller's broker, or a Dual agent?
- You are offering me a free 3-day/2-night hotel stay and complimentary dinner for two...what's the catch? What

are you requiring that I do or attend in order to be eligible for this offer?

- If I convert to satellite cable, will I lose my ability to videotape a program on one TV station while I'm simultaneously watching a TV program on another station?

For everything the sales rep on the other end of the phone says or the postcard in the mail advertises in order to convince you to make a purchase, what are they *not* communicating? You have to ask yourself, "*How* are they making their profit for servicing me?"

A local bank offered us a higher interest rate on our savings account if we deposited a certain amount of new monies by a certain date. We obtained the sum of money, but they revoked the offer because our funds were electronically transferred through a family member's account within the same bank, as opposed being rendered in the form of a paper check. Because the required amount was deposited from one account to another at same bank, there should not have been any difference between paper and electronic transfer. It did not matter to them. We missed out on the higher-yielding interest rate simply because we didn't ask, "*How* is the deposit to be transferred in order for us to be eligible for your special offer?" I called and complained to their marketing department but still, who woulda thunk?

~ Don't be afraid to ask...you're a force to be reckoned with! ~

5.38 Salespeople, Telemarketers & Freebies

Do not let salespeople or telemarketers talk you into anything you don't need or can't afford...is the freebie *really* worth all of the hassle? When James and I moved into our new home, telemarketers calling to sell us everything from newspapers to a home delivery meat service absolutely besieged us. First of all, there is no banner on your forehead announcing that just because you are a new homeowner or renter, you suddenly require every service that comes along. Once again, ascertain whether what is being offered is a need, a want or a desire. Then look at your budget to determine whether or not you can afford or spare the cost.

When you appear consumer-literate, solicitation can go both ways. I have found that when I indulge the telemarketers a little bit and start talking in budgetary language, they actually want me as a customer *even more.* I suppose that is what happens when one even remotely appears to be an astute consumer, because astute consumers are usually financially responsible people. Translation: "If I can convince this 'hard sell," then my company should have no problem getting paid when the invoice is sent out."

On the other hand, I once had a telemarketer hang up on *me* because I told her I'd have to first discuss her company's offering further with my husband, and that we also had to weigh all of the freebies for signing on the dotted line with the distasteful prospect of carrying new debt. The telemarketer tersely told me to have a good day and hung up on *me*...how's that for a switcheroo? Good thing I didn't verbalize what was really on my mind: "What will I have to do to earn the freebie—stand upside down on a balancing beam at the *Cirque du Soleil* while pinching my nose with my eyes closed?" So what is the deeper meaning of this exchange...if you want to get rid of telemarketers, talk intelligently?

Think of it this way: If you sign up for something you can't afford to pay down the line, the merchant or vendor will be the first ones to send debt collectors after you like bloodhounds on a rabbit trail! (See Chapter 11 on Debt Collectors, et. al.)

Let's look at the time factor involved with getting freebies. Will you actually *read* every issue of *The Daily Trumpet* that is delivered on your doorstep? If not, why pay for a subscription? Free introductory issues mean nothing if you don't have time to read them. Also, if mistakes occur in the order, now it's taking up your time to place a call to correct the situation. Is your valuable time worth whatever promotional discount they are offering? My husband warned me about accepting any free promo offers until I finally relented and let someone talk me into a free daily newspaper for a week or two and 99 cents per week thereafter. I was told I could cancel the invoice at any time. No questions asked. I relented to the sales pitch, rationalizing that James may wish to read it on the train on his way to work. Even though the promo freebie week wasn't up, they had already sent me a post-dated invoice! Thank goodness no problems occurred when I cancelled (even at $4 per month, that $48 annual amount needs to remain in our household). Still it took more out of my time than I wanted to call repeatedly and make sure the agreement was nullified. Remember, the clock starts ticking on promotional offers the moment you agree to receive the materials. The odds are that people won't be organized enough to cancel the offer within the preview period. Telemarketers are betting on this.

And as for the home delivery meat service, since I am a home-based consultant who breaks at a certain time many weekdays to fix dinner for my husband, we decided against it because there is a wholesale and seafood market not too far from our residence. I concede, however, that it might have been a different story had I worked in the city.

I am not saying that all promos are bad or illegitimate; it's just that you have to think critically before subscribing to any of them. Last tip: Should you decide to go forward with so-and-so's home delivery vacuum steam system, have a pen and notepad handy to write down the date, time, item, cost and promo dates so that if any problems arise, it might be an indication of servicing later on down the road. (See Appendix C for a sample tracking form for organizing information on orders)

"An educated consumer is our best customer"
~ a slogan from Syms Clothing ~

~ a.m. New York and Metro NY are two FREE New York newspapers handed out on the streets weekday mornings. ~

Fact: Under the Federal Telephone Consumer Protection Act, telemarketers are prohibited from making unsolicited sales calls before 8 a.m. and after 9 p.m.[29]

Resources:
The Federal Communications Commission National Do Not Call Registry (including mobile phone users)

www.fcc.gov/cgb
1(888) CALL-FCC / 225-5322
1(888) TELL-FCC / 835-5322
- or -
www.donotcall.gov - 1(888) 382-1222

Do Not Call Registry in order to limit the amount of information in circulation about you, your spending habits, your credit, etc. for research and marketing purposes: The Direct Marketing Association – www.the-dma.org

Visit the New York State Office of Attorney General's website to read press releases regarding consumer advocacy cases right here in New York City, such as top consumer complaints; and cases involving landlord/tenant issues, predatory lending, funeral home monopoly, beer bottle redemption scheme, used bed scam, a station transferring rogue waste, etc. Who needs reality TV?

New York State Attorney General's Office – www.oag.state.ny.us
Consumer Helpline within NYS: 1(800) 771-7755
Executive Office – (212) 416-8000

New York State Consumer Protection Board –
www.consumer.state.ny.us
1 (800) 697-1220 (within NYS)

5.39 Warding Off Administrative Glitches

During my very first visit to New York City to visit my then-boyfriend, James, I arrived via a Greyhound bus from Syracuse. As I waited for him to pick me up, I crouched in the corner of the Port Authority's 42nd Street & 8th Avenue entrance like a scared, lost kitty cat. My mind may have said to strangers, *"please don't approach, bother, maim or mug me,"* but my body language broadcast exactly the opposite message. Now all of these years later, I strut through the Port Authority like I *own* the place. *What?* Well, New York'll do that to ya. By the same token, warding off administrative errors is not for the faint of heart. When booking appointments, sending in payments, or faxing verification information, from one consumer-to-another, consider implementing the following:

Get the name of the customer service representative, executive/administrative assistant or receptionist assisting you. Politely inform the party that you are jotting down detailed notes on the conversation. Note the date, time, and further action regarding the issue at hand. If there is a timeline involved, mark the follow-up task on your calendar of things to do and treat it accordingly.

For instance, if you have enjoyed free introductory, no-obligation Internet service for three months and you decide not to subscribe to that particular product or service, make sure you call prior to the deadline date and obtain a cancellation number so you will not be billed. Many companies make a sure bet that people are not *organized enough* to mark their calendar for cancellations, but rest assured, *their* computer is "fixed" to send you out an invoice at the appropriate time.

When faxing, 1) put the total number of pages being transmitted on the cover sheet, 2) call to make sure your fax is received in someone's hands and 3) note whom you spoke with so that you can reference the conversation should problems occur later. I admit that I often get annoyed when asked, *"Whom did you speak with?"* Like I'm supposed to remember Barbara's name from the 1-800-number on October 10th. The onus is apparently on the consumer. But I *have* discovered that when I indeed refer to my conversation with Barbara on October 10th, I receive more efficient service to my call.

When ordering merchandise over the Internet, print out and save the confirmation. Via phone, get all of the details. I once stopped ordering merchandise from catalogs cold turkey because there often seemed to be some sort of a problem.

This all boils down to being **proactive** on your part and making the recipient accountable. If you make the people you deal with on the phone accountable for the information involved, you are more likely to yield better results.

Always be polite (that still gets you somewhere in this town), but no-nonsense. Whenever I receive bad service, I tend to be vocal. The way I rationalize it: *"How will the owner or manager know if he or she has lost my business if I don't tell him or her?"*

On the flip side, offer to compliment a Customer Service Representative to his or her Supervisor. I realized that I can be quick to complain about shoddy service, but what about when I receive good service? This is what I inadvertently found: when I am willing to convey glowing compliments to the Customer Service Rep's Supervisor—provided of course he or she processes my request satisfactorily—not only do they process my request courteously and accurately, but guess what? I am patched through to their Supervisor much quicker than when I am voicing a complaint! Remember, you can catch more flies with honey than you can with vinegar. Now why in the world anyone but a frog would want to catch flies, I don't know, but that's the way it is.

The alternative to not addressing administrative glitches when they occur is to allow incidences to blow up in your face. The last thing you need is to show up at your doctor's office for an appointment you took time off of work to attend and booked three months in advance—only to find that the front office didn't receive your primary care physician's referral. Or to realize late in the game that your intended recipient did not receive page two of an important fax. Such errors are probably more costly in time than in money, and as we discussed earlier in this chapter, your time is just as valuable.

Technological Access and Capabilities

On a final administrative note, either invest in a computer/fax machine/scanner so that you can properly process paperwork, or make sure you have access to capital equipment.

You cannot, for instance, fax over your information verification to the mortgage company so they can finish processing your loan application if you do not have fax capabilities; you cannot provide your only copy of an important statement to another party if you do not duplicate it and retain a copy for your own files.

You can buy a basic fax machine for under $100. Hint: fax machines also make copies. Some online companies offer fax service delivered directly to your e-mailbox for a small monthly fee, so you don't even have to buy the stand-alone machine. If necessary, go to your local UPS Store, or FedEx Kinkos, or local neighborhood copy center to acquire access to these services.

When faxing a document, call and leave a voice mail or an e-mail with the following script:

"Good day, Marlene, this is [your name]. I have just faxed [#] pages to you at [fax number]. If you have indeed received the fax, no need to call me back. If I do not hear from you, I will safely assume that you have received the document. If, however, you have not received the fax, please contact me, and I will be more than happy to re-send the fax to you."

I cannot begin to describe how this single act has prevented administrative glitches from occurring. I am not taking up any more of the recipient's time by having them to contact me; and yet, the onus is on him/her if action is not executed, because I made it crystal clear to contact me if there is a problem. It is crucial to include the number where you sent the fax. I once had an incident where the fax number location for something I had sent out was on the other side of the building from where the recipient's cubicle was located. My call helped the recipient to know exactly where to pick-up the fax.

The digital divide is ever widening between the rich and poor. Do not be left out in the cold due to the absence of technological capabilities.

*~ Extra tip specific to New York City:
When booking appointments, always get cross
streets in addition to the address. ~*

5.40 Paying Attention (With So Much Stimuli In The City)

As a native Hoosier, the constant hustle and bustle of the urban scene is something I never got quite totally acclimated to. If I did learn to go with the flow, it was out of necessity because I can easily become discombobulated. You know, survival of the fittest...yada, yada. With so much environmental stimuli in the city—cashiers punching in numbers, registers chirping and people huffing and puffing behind you in line while you can actually *hear* their eyeballs rolling with impatience—remember to stay focused on what you purchased, how you're paying for it, and make sure you are charged the advertised price. On more than one occasion, I had to bring the actual sign bearing the advertised price of an item to the cash register because the sticker price was incongruent with what the register rung up. If necessary, ask for receipts (yes, nowadays you have to ask because receipts are not always automatically given to you). If you are a student or a self-employed business consultant, some of your expenses may very well be tax-deductible, so it is especially important to collect a receipt. Slide to the side, check your receipt for accuracy, count your change, and make sure all of your change or credit card is safely in your purse or wallet before walking away.

*~ Walgreens promises that your purchase is free
if the cashier fails to issue a receipt. ~*

Consumer Resources:

Consumer Reports – www.consumerreports.org

J. D. Power and Associates conducts research based on millions of consumer responses to products and services, and ranks the results—industries pay attention!

www.jdpower.com

NYC Dept. of Consumer Affairs (DCA)
www.nyc.gov/consumers or (212) NEW-YORK / 639-9675
(Outside of the five boroughs)

Call 3-1-1 for FREE guides:

- Consumer Advertising Guide
- Debt Collection Guide
- Auto Leasing, Rental & Repair Guide
- Generic Drug Guide
- Administrative Hearing Guide
- Funeral Planning Guide
- Tax Preparation Services

FREE Reports on the New York State Attorney General's website www.oag.state.ny.us:

- Automobiles (Lemon Law & Related Topics)
- Charitable Giving/Organizations
- Consumer Tips
- Civil Rights/Special Needs
- Courts
- Crime & Safety
- Environmental
- Health
- Housing
- Internet
- Investor Protection
- Labor
- Senior Citizens
- Telecommunications
- Publications Available in Spanish & Other Languages
- Various Other Reports

CHAPTER 6
BIG-TIME CITY EXPENSES: GRUB & TRANSPORTATION

"In the house of the wise are stores of choice food and oil..."
~ Proverbs 21:20a ~

BIG-TIME CITY EXPENSE #1: GRUB

THE COST OF EATING IS UNEQUIVOCALLY the next largest monthly expense behind housing and transportation; in our household, it even exceeds transportation. This fact is substantiated by Consumer Expenditure surveys compiled by the U.S. Department of Labor-Bureau of Labor Statistics.[30] Another hard, cold fact: We gotta eat. But it *is* possible to chow down in a cost-efficient manner. For starters, eat only when you're hungry and not just for the sake of eating. When dining out, let it be a treat and not a necessity.

Grocery and Convenience Stores

Before going grocery shopping, take inventory of what you already have and make a list. To take it a step further, use the blank list in Appendix B and post it on your refrigerator to check off your grocery items. Pre-determine if you are going to go to the grocery store, drug store, 99-cent store, a large chain franchise, or wholesale club for the items.

Of course, you may buy something not on your list, but the purpose of the list is to keep you on track. Arm yourself with coupons before you go. However, be aware of a downside of coupons; they are often for manufacturer brand-name items, whose products usually cost more in the first place. Simply assess: Do you like the brand name or generic product? Then compare the cost of brand name with the coupon to the store or generic name without a coupon. Which are you willing and able to pay?

If the purchase price is not clearly visible, then you have the right as a consumer to know the price before purchasing the product. On more than one occasion, I have had to ask a cashier to ring up two similar items so I can compare the cost. I use it as an opportunity to voice my complaint that it is not my intent to put him or her through extra work, but I would not have to do so if the store marked the prices clearly; and I'm not about to purchase an item blindly. Price check scanners are extremely useful in this regard.

Resources:
www.TheGroceryGame.com (nominal fee)
www.TheCouponMom.com (Free)
www.CouponClippers.com (S&H fee)

Wholesale Clubs

Whether or not you shop at wholesale clubs such as BJ's, Costco, or Sam's Club is a function of access, affordability and storage space. I am partial to buying in bulk because all you have to do is do the math. Paper towels are a non-perishable item you will use no matter what. Compare the following: 8 individual rolls of paper towels at \$1.39 each totaling \$11.12 vs. \$5.50 per pack of eight. I once spotted my favorite frozen dinner at the supermarket at \$8.99 for one serving. The same meal could be had at the wholesale club at \$12.99 for two servings/box. Eating solo? Spend the 9 bucks. Buying for two or want seconds? Save \$6 by shopping wholesale. A 60-oz. container of mayonnaise at $3.99 will last me for months as opposed to a small jar at $2.99, which will last as fast as it takes the #2 train to go by. And for crying out loud, *puh-leeez* don't buy a dinky box of detergent at your neighborhood laundromat when you can purchase a big 'ole 200 fl. oz. (1.56 gal.) jug at the supermarket. However, with wholesale clubs, be prepared to pay more upfront *now* for savings *later*.

There is an annual fee to join these clubs—generally $35-$40 per year for basic membership, which often includes a household member. A challenge particular to city dwellers is the issue of storage space and even transportation. When my husband and I lived in Manhattan, going to a wholesale club in Brooklyn was a trek that involved planning and coordination. My mother-in-law drove me, and my husband was annoyed at coming home and seeing paper towels lined alongside our living room wall. Additionally, it may be more prudent for single persons and smaller families to purchase non-perishables in bulk—which are going to be consumed no matter what—as opposed to purchasing perishables. You don't want 18 eggs spoiling in your refrigerator. New York has enough unidentifiable odors already. Nor should that extra package of bread begin to mold because you are not eating it fast enough, unless you want to feed that second package to the pigeons. Before it begins to mold, of course.

Restaurants & Fast Food

I am thoroughly convinced that I was severely deprived as a child by not having eaten brown rice and beans and roti growing up. That is one of the wonderful things about NYC—its varied ethnic cuisines. However, eating out and sampling those wonderful restaurants out there can get expensive. Still, in spite of trying to save a buck or two, sometimes we have a taste for Italian food, or price doesn't matter as much because we want to go someplace on a special occasion or with a lively (or subdued) atmosphere. There are times when we want Texas-sized portions at Rhode Island-sized prices without the New York attitude.

Recognizing that different criteria are important at different times, here are factors to take into account when selecting a restaurant:

- Ambiance
- Specialty cuisine
- Service
- Cleanliness
- Price
- Recommendation

The cleanliness of a restaurant's restroom
is a good indicator of the cleanliness of the restaurant's kitchen.
~ MBR ~

According to a study of 1,000 New Yorkers conducted by The Bank of New York, restaurants and take-out are a poison to the pocketbook, as half of those sampled said they spend too much money on food.[31] During each of the three moves James and I have recently made, we had a joke in our household: McDonald's had become our personal chef. Please don't allow this to happen to you on a daily basis. Consider a recent scenario we encountered at a NYC restaurant. As soon as we sat down, our waiter was trained to ask the following questions:

Waiter: Would you like drinks from the bar? (We were shown a menu that included virgin pina coladas & strawberry daiquiris starting at 8 bucks per glass). I ordered water. Hey, it's healthier, anyway. We both ordered a chicken entrée.

Waiter: White meat or dark meat? (White meat selections cost a buck extra).

We both ordered dark meat.

Waiter: BBQ or honey roasted? (Either selection was another buck extra). The trick here was to say "neither", since the chicken is already deliciously baked and a great barbeque sauce is provided for free on each table. My husband caught the trick. I missed the trick and was served a treat: honey roasted dark meat, which had basically been dipped in a vat of honey. Yum-yum. Sugar high.

Waiter: Would you like to upgrade to a super-sized drink? (Regular size had shrunk by 1/3 since the last time we ate at this restaurant, and yet the super-size was another buck extra). We ordered regular-sized drinks.

Waiter: May I get you an appetizer while you wait?

We had just ordered a half chicken—each. We declined.

So, ladies and gentlemen, had we said yes to all of the extras above, our bill would have been jacked up by **at least 15 bucks** *in addition to the tax and tip.*

Stock up your fridge with as many beverages as you like, and when dining out, curb your appetite for beverages that jack up your check by ordering water. A non-refillable glass of soda, for instance, can cost 3 bucks. Double-check your bill before paying for your meal to make sure that you were not accidentally charged for food you were not served (e.g., additional beverage, appetizer). It happens. And now, many eateries have the audacity to keep your change. How presumptuous! Can you imagine if an establishment kept 4 *pennies* per 100 customers for a whole week? That's $16 monthly in that restaurant's coffers! Let's bring it on home: $192 a year! I am not against a business owner making his/her profit (they have to be or they'd be out of business). Yet, it is important to bear in mind that **while it is a businessperson's responsibility to watch his or her bottom line, you and I have to be just as diligent as consumers in watching and protecting our own bottom line.**

Food prepared by our own hands, in our own kitchen is more cost efficient and can be fun to make. These days, I e-mail my husband "Today's Menu" so he will not be tempted to buy dinner. Because I am an offspring of parents from North Carolina and Alabama, I was practically raised on cornbread, pig's feet, black-eyed peas, hamhocks, and chitlins. Honey, back in the day, *Fear Factor* had nothin' on us! Once my edumacated husband explained to me the true anatomical origin of chitterlings, however, I immediately revised our menu to reflect the following:

Fresh salad with ingredients from the Farmers Market
Grilled Salmon or Lamb Chops
Jasmine Rice or Boiled Potato
Side Vegetable Dish such as Garlic Spinach
White Peach Grape Juice
Apple Crisp a la mode (OK, OK, so the dessert is actually from a bakery, but I sprinkle a little flour on my face so he'll think I've been slaving over the hot stove.)

This same meal will easily cost $40-$50 bucks for two at a nice sit-down restaurant, and there's no coaxing involved to get him home from work!

For you drivers out there, take snacks in the car with you in a sandwich baggie for yourself and the kids so as to curtail situations where you are forced to eat out while on the road. Better yet, on those road trips, bring the cooler along, stocked with ice, bottled water, juices, soda, fruit, homemade sandwiches, and snacks. Plunk it down in the hotel room, so that you won't have to pay 85 cents for a miniscule bag containing 3-4 potato chips.

The biggest thing to keep in mind here is that eating in an urban environment is definitely a constant conflict between time and money. Less time to cook translates into having to eat out and spend more money. More time spent shopping for, preparing and cooking meals equals less time eating out and consequently, less money spent.

Downsize The Supersize
My dear friends, do not underestimate the amount of money that "fries" out the window when you consistently buy a $6-7 meal deal here, a 99 cent cheeseburger there, and supersize to a biggie wiggie soda for 59 cents more. This all adds up!

Food tastes even better when you're hungry.
~ MBR ~

Tipping

I read somewhere that the word "tip" is an acronym for "to insure promptness". Tipping is generally optional, not mandatory. Remember, however, that service and hospitality providers such as waiters and waitresses generally earn minimum wages and rely on tips to survive, so be absolutely sure to tip for good service. The standard is 15%, and 18% for parties of 4 or more. If you receive poor service, however, tipping under 15% gets the message across. There are *so many* people to tip in New Yawk:

- Doorman
- Handyman
- Super
- Nanny
- Housekeeper
- Cook
- Butler
- Gardener
- Taxicab and Car Service Drivers
- Valet Parking Attendant
- Hotel Bell Hop
- Hairdresser
- Nail Salon
- Mailman
- Delivery personnel, etc., etc. etc.

Extra tips:

~ Pick-up dinner portions at lunch special prices. ~

~ Ask for a doggie-bag of your uneaten meal at the restaurant— it could be tomorrow's lunch! ~

Resources:

Zagat Survey, www.zagat.com - 1(800) 333-3421 or (212) 977-6000 in NYC

Time Out New York Annual Eating & Drinking Guide
www.eatdrink.timeoutny.com - (646) 432-3000

BIG-TIME CITY EXPENSE #2: TRANSPORTATION

NYC has the most extensive public transportation system in the country. busses, express busses, trains, ferries, taxicabs, liveries, car services, rail, shuttles, limo services, and even helicopter transport.

But costs associated with getting to and fro can quickly add up considerably. Unless you are visiting NYC, this is that part where you can "get off the bus" and proceed to Chapter 7.

MTA MetroCard

When I began writing this book, MTA was threatening another fare hike. As this book is going to press, it's a done deal. If you as a frequent rider can ante up the $76 now, you can enjoy a full month to ride the subway without having to feed money into a machine on a per-ride basis with MTA's monthly unlimited MetroCard. Compare the following: the 30-day monthly unlimited MetroCard at a flat rate of $76 is more economical than a month's worth of 7-day weekly unlimited cards at a total of $88 ($24/week x 4 weeks). In this scenario, you save $12 per month, or $144 per year. A reduced fare MetroCard is available to people age 65 and over, as well as for persons with disabilities who qualify.

If you have family members whose work schedules don't coincide, how about trading off the unlimited MetroCard? Due to ministry commitments, there are times when I have to be at church in Brooklyn sooner than my husband. I borrow his New Jersey Transit pass, as well as his unlimited MetroCard until he drives the car into the city so we can link up later. Savings: $16.90. *Cha-ching.*

Did You Know...

If your 30-day unlimited MetroCard gets lost or stolen, all you have to do is call (212) METROCARD (638-7622) with your credit card, debit card or ATM account number, and the unused number of days from the date you notify MTA of the loss will be credited back to your account at a pro-rated amount of $2.53 per diem. Stipulations: The card must be purchased from a vending machine, not from a transit clerk. Only two claims per calendar year accepted. The first claim will be processed free of charge. The second claim is subject to a $5 administrative handling fee.

Contact Info:
Metropolitan Transportation Authority
www.mta.info, (212) 878-7000

New York City Transit (NYCT)
www.mta.nyc.ny.us/nyct, (718) 330-1234

MTA NYCT Fareline: (718) 243-4999

Commuter Bus/Rail

As of July 1, 2005, New Jersey Transit increased its fares, as well. If you are a suburban commuter, allow yourself enough time to purchase bus or rail tickets in advance to avoid a surcharge. My husband forgot his monthly New Jersey Transit pass *and* MetroCard one morning. What should have been a $12.90 round trip ride cost him $26.90: a $5 surcharge both ways plus the round trip MTA MetroCard. Yee-ouch.

Contact Info:
MetroNorth
www.mta.nyc.ny.us/mnr
(212) 532-4900 – within NYC / 1(800) 638-7646 – outside NYC

Long Island Railroad (LIRR)
www.mta.nyc.ny.us/lirr
(718) 217-5477 – within NYC / (516) 822-5477 – outside NYC

New Jersey Transit (NJT bus and rail)
www.njtransit.com – 1(800) 772-2222

PATH
Port Authority of New York and New Jersey
www.panynj.gov - (212) 435-7000

Amtrak
www.amtrak.com -1(800) 872-7245

Greyhound
www.greyhound.com - **1(800) Go-Greyhound (231-2222)**
(Also provides companion fare discount)

While you are at it, check out MetroNorth and LIRR's one-day get-aways on their respective websites. It's nice to get out of the city sometimes.

Vehicle Maintenance and Gas
Regularly servicing your vehicle adds to its longetivity. We have a manufacturer's scheduled maintenance guide that let's us know what should be done to the car at the appropriate mileage interval. I have observed that New Yorkers' cars are usually very clean and clutter-free (to avoid tempting theives, I suppose?). This yields an inadvertent advantage: the lighter weight of the vehicle increases fuel economy. Keep your car maintained with a regular tune-up, and check the oil, air and tire pressure. The last thing you need after a Nor'easter is for the car to break down in the dead middle of winter on the expressway.

When we first got our car, we noticed several gas stations advertising different prices for regular unleaded. We asked friends who were more experienced drivers, *"Er, please forgive us for wasting your time with this silly little question, but...is it the same gas?"*

Identify which gas station nearest you consistently offers the lowest prices per gallon. Why pay $20.50 for ten gallons of gas, when you can pay $18.60? Treat yourself to 1/3 cup of a café latte with that $1.90. Just kidding—go buy a couple of doughnuts.

During the summer of 2005, gas prices reached astronomical levels, peaking to as high as 3 bucks per gallon nationwide. One way we offset this was by paying a pre-set amount, say 20 bucks worth of gas until the price decreased. The risk, of course, is determining how far a pre-set gas amount will get you in terms of your travel needs. Alternatives that commuters around the country employed during this difficult time included taking mass transit, car-pooling, biking, and good old-fashioned walking.

Organize your errands geographically to
save yourself some travel time.
~ MBR ~

Resources:
These sites will provide you with updated price rankings on regional and national gas prices. For example, click on your region and zip code:

www.gasbuddy.com, which will redirect you to your state or city:
www.NewYorkStateGasPrices.com
www.ChicagoGasPrices.com
www.LosAngelesGasPrices.com
www.GeorgiaGasPrices.com
www.TwinCitiesGasPrices.com
-and-
www.gaspricewatch.com

E-ZPass

If you frequently drive to NYC, it's worth it to get the E-ZPass. The cost declines by $1 during rush hour ($6 cash per car vs. $5 E-ZPass during rush hour). Plus, you move through the George Washington Bridge, Lincoln and Holland Tunnels quicker with E-ZPass. From consumer-to-consumer: understand, however, that should you opt to have your trips auto-charged to your credit card as opposed to mailing in check or money order, be sure to read the fine print and understand the financial ramifications associated with the ease of zippin' on through the toll because the E-ZPass is tied to your credit card. For example, according to our own personal E-ZPass statement based on our usage, E-ZPass changed our replenishment amount: *"On evaluation of toll usage, your replenishment has been changed from $25 to $40."* End quote. No consent from us required at the point of the decision. (To give them the benefit of the doubt, it's possible we signed something without reading the fine print when we set up the account, but an alert sure would have been appreciated.)

See Appendix D to maintain your own travel log in order to compare your records with E-ZPass' and to identify the nature of your trips.
Contact: www.EZPass.com - 1 (888) 288-6865

Getting to the Airport
There are several ways to get to the airport, but let's take a moment for an "only in New York" tale. Let me say first, that not all liveries in Brooklyn are bad. Now that the disclaimer is squarely in place, let's get on with the story. I once hailed a livery in Crown Heights, Brooklyn to drop my sister off at Laguardia Airport. The livery stopped, picked us up, stopped by to get gas, turned around and asked us for the money for the gas, and by the time we did all of that, my sister missed her flight. I'm speechless to this day and have no words, let alone suggestions. Next section.

Van Shuttle

Pro: Economical; costs less than the price of a yellow taxi taking you to the airport.

Con: Shared ride, so the shuttle may pick you up three hours prior to your flight departure and you'd have to hope that your fellow passengers are waiting for the shuttle in their vestibule with their luggage so you do not have to sit in the van waiting on them.

Resource: www.supershuttle.com
(servicing shared-ride airport transportation in 18 major U.S. cities)
1(800) Blue-Van (258-3826) / (212) Blue-Van (258-3826) for Manhattan service

Yellow TaxiCab

Let's take a look at the prohibitive costs for the average New Yorker first:

- between Manhattan and JFK Airport – $45 flat fee plus tolls
- between Manhattan and Laguardia Airport – meter plus tolls
- from Manhattan to Newark Liberty Airport – meter plus $10 flat fee
- from Newark Liberty Airport to Manhattan – meter only

Pro: Unless you share a ride with a stranger who is traveling to the same vicinity as you are at those ambiguous prices, you'll have the privilege of being the cabbie's only passenger. Awww, how special... don't forget to tip.

Con: The tip.

Contact the New York City Taxi and Limousine Commission at:
www.nyc.gov, call 311 in NYC, or
(212) NEW-YORK / 639-9675 (outside of NYC)

Inform the taxicab driver of the route to your destination so you don't get taken for a ride (in your pocketbook).
~ MBR ~

Alternative Modes of Transportation to the Airport

New York City's local subway, buses and shuttle services also provide travelers with convenient connections to airline terminals, rental car facilities, hotels, and airport parking lots. Consider...

•M60 Bus to Laguardia Airport. Same cost as a single-ride mass transit fare (depending on the type of MetroCard you normally purchase). Otherwise, $2 one-way.

•AirTrain JFK is the light rail shuttle service between the MTA Long Island Rail Road (LIRR) train via the Jamaica station and John F. Kennedy International Airport. $5 one-way. Take the A (Howard Beach), E, or J/Z trains (via Jamaica Station) to the JFK AirTrain connection. The A, E, J/Z trains cost the same as a single-ride mass transit fare (depending on the type of MetroCard you normally purchase). Otherwise, the cost is $2 one-way.

•There is also an AirTrain service available if you don't feel like paying in the neighborhood of $50 or more to have a car service take you to Newark Liberty, depending on where you live in Jersey. Connect to the Newark Liberty International Airport Train Station via NJTransit or Amtrak trains, and then transfer to AirTrain to make the connection to your terminal. The cost is $5 one way (discounted fare with your NJT monthly pass, if you have one). Children under five years old ride for free.

Contact info:
www.panynj.gov/airtrain
www.panynj.gov/airtrainnewark
www.newarkairport.com
1(888) EWR-INFO (397-4636)

- Olympia Trail provides airport express bus service with frequent daily departures between Penn Station, Grand Central, Port Authority and downtown Manhattan and Newark Liberty Airport (www.coachusa.com/olympia). As of this writing, the cost is $22 round-trip; $13 one-way, with discount fares available for children, students, persons living with disabilities, and senior citizens. You will have to pick-up mass transit or a taxi to finish the journey home.

- New York Airport Service provides airport express bus service with frequent daily departures between Penn Station, Grand Central, Port Authority, midtown hotels; and JFK and Laguardia Airports (www.newyorkairportservice.com). As of this writing, the cost ranges between $12-$15 one-way, and $21-$33 round-trip depending on your destination, with discount fares available for students and senior citizens. You will have to pick-up mass transit or a taxi to finish the journey home.

Car Service/Livery

If you reside in an area of New York City where yellow taxicabs do not frequent, then you need a reliable car service you can call from time to time. Collect business cards from neighboring services and compare the cost to your destination. All it takes is a couple of phone calls.

After grocery shopping, I relied on liveries to take me to Crown Heights because, quite frankly, yellow taxicabs didn't travel in that neck of the woods. Liveries are just trying to make an honest living. I once got a driver, though, who was on his cell phone the whole time, trying to direct someone by the name of Pookie Dookie off of the Jackie Robinson Parkway. If the driver actually gets out of the van to help you with the groceries, give him a tip.

Shared Ride

I recently attended a seminar at the Meadowlands Convention Center in New Jersey. The cost of the taxicab from the train station to the convention center: $12. I inquired of three other safe-looking women standing nearby if they were going to the same destination (gotta have those antennas up). They were. The cost of the shared taxi ride: $3 each one-way. Yet, we were still a little regretful as we passed by the public express bus to the convention center, which I later found out was $1.10 one-way. Still not bad. My estimated savings in transportation costs between the train station and convention center that day: around 18 bucks, because the round-trip taxicab ride would have cost me $24. If you are a parent, you can literally tuck that money away towards your child's summer camp.

CHAPTER 7
BILL-PAYING OPTIONS: WHAT'S IN YOUR BEST INTEREST?

"Give everyone what you owe him: If you owe taxes, pay taxes; if revenue, then revenue..."
~ Romans 13:7a ~

CAREFULLY WEIGH THE PLETHORA OF BILL-PAYING OPTIONS that were not available to us even a short decade ago. Back in the day, our bill arrived in the mail, we wrote a check, and mailed the bill. The way we pay our bills has been totally revolutionized. From a consumer viewpoint, sometimes I get the feeling that companies are trying to lure me from paying the traditional way—with a check—or maybe it's just my imagination. (But I have to wonder how encouraging me to pay by phone and then imposing a fee for doing so provides me with an incentive?) Here are the pros and cons associated with bill-paying options that we have in the 21st century:

Pay-By-Phone
Description: Payment is debited/deducted from your account (or charged to your credit card) when you pick up the phone and pay the bill.

Advantage: Check clears within 24-48 hours; you have control over when the bill gets paid, which is slightly different from auto-payment (see page 90).

Disadvantage/caution: Make sure you are not charged a fee for this service.

In some cases, there is a charge if I process my payments through an automated system; in other cases, no charge is involved. For example, as of this writing, Con Edison does not assess a fee for you to pay your electricity bill by phone. I can also pay my American Express bill in this manner (although AmEx does have an annual membership fee). With regard to my business credit card: if the operator takes my payment info, then there is a $15 fee. Inquire of entities you regularly render payments as to whether or not a fee is involved for taking payments over the phone, whether by an auto-attendant or a live customer service representative.

Pay-In-Person

Advantage: No worries about the payment getting lost or delayed in the mail.

Disadvantage/caution: If you are using an intermediary such as a check-cashing place, remember to ask yourself: *"Self, will the payment post to my account through the intermediary on time?"* When paying at a department store, for instance, check to make sure the payment will post to your account immediately.

Money Order

Advantage: As good as cash.

Disadvantage/caution: Costs approximately 95 cents, depending on where you buy it (Post Office, vs. supermarket or convenience store vs. Western Union, etc.).

Check By Mail
Advantage: As good as cash...provided the funds are liquid.

Disadvantages/caution: Must mail 7-10 days in advance in order for it to be received on time. Identify where the payment is going: southeast to Delaware, or west to Los Angeles? Remember to endorse the check. Avoid the risk of bouncing the check by "floating" it. Floating is when you submit the check knowing money is not yet in your bank account to cover it, but will be there by the time the payee cashes it. Those days are over. As of this writing, banks have instituted Check Clearing for the 21st Century Act to expedite clearance, whether the funds are in your account or not (therefore, possibly incurring a bounced check fee). More about this relatively recent legislation in Chapter 8. Also consider whether or not your bank charges you extra for writing your own checks. Remember to include the cost of periodically reordering checks into your budget.

Debit Card
Advantage: As good as cash, especially with a MasterCard or Visa logo.

Disadvantage/caution: Less fraud protection than with credit card; plus, if there is a dispute with a payee/vendor regarding services or merchandise, you can contest the charge and appeal to your credit card company to issue a refund. Asking the bank to put the money back into your account will be more difficult.[32] For these reasons, if at all possible, try to avoid paying bills online with your debit card. Also beware of scamming (see Chapter 11 on Identity Theft et. al.).

Online
Description: According to *USA Today,* the three most common ways consumers pay their bills online are: paying the vendor directly through its website; through a bank's online services; or through an intermediary such as AOL, MSN or Yahoo.[33]

Advantage: Payment is considered to be on time, but bear in mind that it may still take between 24-48 hours for the payment to post to your account.

Disadvantage/caution: Investigate whether or not there is a charge. If so, ascertain whether or not this factor is important to you. Privacy issues; risk of hacking or identity theft. Make absolutely certain you are on a secure site. Never, ever give out sensitive, personal information unless you initiated contact with the website yourself (see "Identity Theft" in Chapter 11). What is considered sensitive? Your Social Security Number, Date of Birth, Mother's Maiden Name, and PINs. An entity that I conduct business with once asked me to e-mail my social security number. Are you kidding? No way!

Autopayment

Description: This is different from you picking up the phone and paying by phone. You set-up your account to be paid automatically by providing your credit card or debit/checking account number in advance. The bill(s) is/are paid at a pre-set interval.

Advantage: You do not have to worry about the bill being paid on time. The system automatically debits or charges your account on time. This method is advantageous if the account being debited consistently has available funds.

Disadvantage/caution: Make sure funds are available. Even though the vendor/payee is making it convenient for you, still be aware of what is coming out and when (including fees, if applicable). Carefully think about whether you want to give a company that level of access to your account. Remember to notify the company auto-charging your account if you have decided you are no longer using the same credit or debit card that you originally authorized the payments to be made from.

Here's an example for you. We took advantage of the *convenience* of allowing E-ZPass to charge our credit card automatically for tolls usage in our neck of the woods. Nobody wants to get to a tunnel or bridge, be short of cash, and not be able to get through, right? However, one day as I was inputting the credit card expenses into Quicken®, I thought *"We're paying E-ZPass an awful lot of money for the amount of car trips we're making into New York"*. I compared the charges against our travel log (see Appendix D), called customer service, and discovered that due to the amount of trips we made into the city at one point during a particular month, the system defaulted to auto-charge us $40 instead of $25. What the system didn't know was that over time, we had adjusted the frequency and mode of our modus operandi so that the car didn't come into the city as much. We were now using rail service a lot more. Too late. We had to wait 90 days before the system would allow us to re-set the auto-charge at $25. In the meantime, we had $40 assessed to our account. Talk about hardball. Plus, if we are unable for any reason to pay off the credit card balance in full, interest is added on top of that $40. But technically, that's not E-ZPass' (or any other entity auto-charging your credit card) concern or problem. Think, New York, think.

Also, inquire about how difficult or easy acquiring a refund will be. I was in a situation where I no longer needed to use a particular pre-paid calling card anymore. We'll call them Calling Card Company #1, cast them in the dark shadows and distort their voice to sound like Darth Vader. When the balance got low, Calling Card Company #1 auto-charged my credit card. It seemed convenient at the time, but I had a credit balance that I wanted the refund for since I was not going to use it *and* I wanted to prevent the card from being auto-charged. Want more scoop? I found a dirt-cheap card provided by a reputable and reliable company (Calling Card Company #2) with hundreds more available minutes, but that's none of Calling Card Company #1's business. Anyway, it was like pulling teeth to obtain my refund from Calling Card Company #1 and even then, I had to appeal to the **credit card company** to credit me because the Calling Card #1's customer service branch simply did not address my request. Interesting...they were not hard to find when they asked for my credit card number in order to replenish my account automatically. Buyer beware.

Dates Are Very, Very Important

Pay close attention to when monthly banking fees, credit card late fees, etc., if applicable, might be assessed against your account.

From one consumer to another, here's a personal example: James and I were going to switch banks from fee-crazy Bank A to no-fee Bank B. Our balance was most certainly going to fall way below the amount needed in order to maintain our "no-fee checking" arrangement. There was only one outstanding check that needed to clear before I could write a balance-transfer check from Bank A to Bank B. However, we had no control over when the payee would present that last check for payment.

What we did know, however, was that Bank A was going to assess a fee of $30 on the 4th business day of the month due to our balance falling below the minimum requirement. That day just so happened to fall around a holiday weekend, and I was told by the customer service rep (you have to pick up the phone and call to find out these things!) that the fee may very well be deducted on the 2nd business day of the month instead of the 4th. Bank personnel apparently had holiday parades they needed to attend…

Anyway, since we did not have overdraft protection, we gritted our teeth and went ahead and made sure a balance totaling the amount of the very last check written *plus* $30 was left in Bank A. Why didn't we just leave the amount of the last check in the account and call it a day? We didn't want the possibility of the bank's fee to swoop in first and cause that last check to bounce. Got it?

"So you're telling me, Me'Shae, to write dates pertaining to my finances in my calendar alongside my dental appointment?" You betcha! If I were walking in the city, and found $30 on the sidewalk—the same fee amount the bank would have charged us in the scenario above—I'd pick it up...wouldn't you? If we would pick-up $30 in the street, we should keep $30 in the bank. Get it?

Tip

~Before you establish an account with a new entity, inquire about the mechanics of the account set-up.~

CHAPTER 8
THE CASE FOR COLD, HARD CASH: AVOIDING, MANAGING AND ELIMINATING CREDIT CARD DEBT

"Do not co-sign another person's note or put
up a guarantee for someone else's loan.
If you can't pay, even your bed will be snatched from under you."
~Proverbs 22:26-27 (NLT) ~

LET'S CUT TO THE CHASE ON THIS ONE, shall we? Some schools of thought strictly advocate "zero tolerance" for credit card debt. If you can't pay cash, you can't afford to purchase it, period, they surmise. *"But what about when I have to buy things such as airline tickets?"* you ask. To that question, they respond that debit cards have Visa and MasterCard logos nowadays. Such debit cards make the use of credit cards unnecessary, or so the argument goes.

Then there is the more liberal approach that it is OK to have one or two credit cards. From an urban consumer standpoint, my verdict is somewhere in-between. In theory, I agree wholeheartedly with the total abstinence of credit card usage, and I most certainly advocate living on an all-cash basis. I just do not know how realistic it is when one's income is insufficient to meet expenses, particularly in cities with outrageous costs of living. Furthermore, we all need a credit history so that potential lenders have criteria on which to base credit and lending decisions.

As you will read in Chapter 20, "Our Tale," at one point in our financial journey, both James and I enjoyed good incomes and kept daily living expenses to a minimum, thereby creating surplus savings for emergency situations. This is an ideal situation to be in. On the other hand, we have also experienced the stress and challenge of having cash resources totally exhausted due to our expenses. For example, what are you going to do when the tires go flat on your car? Wait until the next payday rolls around? Of course, we used the credit available to us. It was convenient, and we were cash-strapped.

"But I am one of those few Americans who *does* pay their monthly bill on time," you rationalize. This is what I have to say to you: you are still parceling out portions of your future paycheck to pay back a loan. Consider the following sequence of events:

- You purchase goods or services on your credit card.
- The credit card company pays the merchant for the goods or services you purchased.
- The credit card company bills you.
- You have somewhere in the neighborhood of 25-30 days to repay the credit card company without having to pay a finance charge. (Translation: penalty)
- You may very well pay within that timeframe, but a portion of your future paycheck is already "spoken for". Translation: The plastic already has dibs on your next paycheck.
- Ultimately, it is a loan because you are borrowing on credit to pay for it, and you must view it as such. When you buy a dress with credit card, just say to yourself, *"I am taking out a loan to buy this dress, and if I do not pay off the dress in full, I will be paying interest on top of the original price tag, even if I got it on sale."*

There is a distinction between credit card networks and issuers. Networks are credit card companies such as American Express, Visa, MasterCard, and Discover. Issuers are a consortium of banks/ lending institutions that issue cards through MasterCard and Visa. [34] Nevertheless, for the purposes of this chapter, I will refer to the term "credit card companies" for simplicity.

According to CardWeb, a credit card industry tracker, American households with at least one credit card carried an average debt load of $8,940 in 2002.[35] By the end of 2005, that figure rose to $9,312.[36] According to Federal Reserve statistics, the total amount of revolving and non-revolving consumer credit continues to rise steadily.[37] More specifically, *Time* magazine reports that this figure aggregately climbed to $801.5 billion in September 2005.[38] This is an amount approaching one trillion dollars of consumer debt! Is some of your debt included in these statistics? This staggering figure certainly makes a case for zero tolerance of credit card debt.

Have you ever *called* your credit card company to ask a question or to resolve a matter? Here is a hypothetical account. It begins by my phone call to a toll-free number:

- *"Hi, I'm Julie, your Virtual Customer Service Representative, and welcome to Pay-thru-your-nose Credit Card Service."*
- *"For English, press 1."*
- *"Para espanol, oprima el número dos."*
  (I press "1").
- *"Please enter your credit card number, followed by the pound sign."*
  (I enter 16 digits).
- *"For balance, available credit, or payment information, press or say 1."*
- *"To make a payment, press or say 2."*
- *"For our mailing address to make sure your payment reaches us on time so we won't be forced into a situation where we will have to smear your name with the credit bureau, press or say 3."*

- *"To enter your bank routing number so we can access your account and seize the money we lent to you, press or say 4."*
- *"To FedEx your payment, press or say 5."*
- *"OK, we're almost done."* (Is this some sort of a lame attempt to make the computer sound like my homey?)

Tip: Simply press "zero" several times to bypass the voice automation and to get through to a real Homo sapien.

- *"Your call is very important to us. Your approximate wait time is less than 72 minutes. Please hold for the next Live Trained Customer Care Quality Services Professional Technician."*

~ Elevator Music ~

(If my call is so important, then why am I on hold for the same amount of minutes as I have available on my pre-paid calling card?)

- *"Your call is being transferred. This call is being monitored for quality assurance and training purposes."*

- *"Hello, this is Nick Kiamfromaforeigncountry. May I have the last four digits of your account number, please?"* (Didn't Julie, the Virtual Representative prompt me for all 16 digits at the very beginning of this phone call? Oh, well...now this is where it *really* gets interesting…)

- *"May I have your name, please?"*
  Me'Shae Rolling.
- *Please verify your address, Mrs. Rolling.*
- *And your phone number?*
- *Your date of birth?*
- *The zip code of the hospital you were born at?*
- *Mother's maiden name?*
- *Last four digits of your husband's social security number, please?*

- *Cousin's mama's sister's nephew's daughter's maiden name?*
- *When is the last time you ate a chicken Caesar salad, Mrs. Rolling?*
- *Got indigestion?*
- *Mrs. Rolling, what is your blood type?*
- *Please bear with me as I finish pulling up the screen. Our system is slow today.*
  (Never mind that it's only 8 a.m.)
- *To verify your identity, may I have a DNA sample, please?*
  (I suppose with the rate of modern technology, we'll be able to transmit blood samples through the landline, digitally—or via satellite—as the case may be)
- *OK, Mrs. Rolling, how may I help you?*

By the time I get through all of that, I forgot what I called about in the first place!

It is both responsible and unfortunate to have to interject here that high incidences of white collar crime and identity theft must be the reason for the polygraph before I can get my questions answered (see dumpster diving, scamming, phishing, and surfing in Chapter 11).

Enough of the soap opera. Let's examine some of the advantages of cash:

Cash places you in a better negotiating position. I have heard more than one story of consumers going into a furniture store, eyeing a $1,300 dining room set, and laying out 8 "Benjamins" on the counter, saying, "I'll take *that* dining room set for $800. Take it or leave it," and walking away with a set for $500 less than if they had they charged it to their credit card. I have a relative who bought her car with cold, hard cash—no financing—and paid significantly less than the sticker price.

Cash is immediate. It's paid for. It's a done deal. No bills in the mail. No interest on top of the base price. No inability to pay for it later. No harrassment by debt collectors.

Urbanites, let's brainstorm for a minute: are there any items in your cramped apartment—clothes, furniture, appliances, trinkets, doodads—that you are paying more on than you should due to compounding interest?

If I have not convinced you yet, here is my final plea: waiting to budget the cash for purchases forces you to re-think your needs vs. your wants vs. your desires (re-visit section 5.6). Try and use cash or debit card for consumables such as groceries and gas. From a consumer standpoint, it doesn't make a hill of beans worth of sense to buy groceries and gas in July, put it on a credit card, get billed in August, and pay in early September for that food and gas consumed in July! This is a toughie, because credit card companies offer more reward points and cash-back bonuses at the supermarket and at the gas pump (revisit section 5.25 on Frequency Points & Rewards, and Cash-back bonuses/rebates).

You know what? The process of getting out from under debt builds discipline. Once you have the experience of living on an all-cash basis, it's like taking in a deep breath of fresh, Catskill mountain air. A load gets lifted off of your hard-working shoulders. Whenever you go into a mall or a boutique or elsewhere, you are able to say, *"Just because I have cash in my wallet doesn't mean that I have to buy it if I don't really need it."* We can climb the mountaintop, echo and proclaim the words of the Rev. Dr. Martin Luther King, Jr.: *"Free at last, free at last! Thank God Almighty, I am free at last!"*

Resource: www.Bankrate.com for nationwide bank interest rates

In this chapter, we will learn simple ways to avoid debt altogether. If you already have it, let's manage it properly, and if you have way too much of it, let's work on eliminating it.

Psychologically, consumers are more likely to buy merchandise priced at $19.95 vs. $20. Why? Because they see the $19 first, never mind that it's only a nickel away from $20. And whassup with the music playing—whether Beethoven in the chic boutique, bubblegum pop in the discount store, or urban hip hop in the jean shop—while you're browsing the store to "get you in the right mood" to shop? Did you know that companies instruct stock workers to strategically place their merchandise on the shelves at eyeball level so that you will see it in front of your face and consequently, buy it? Next time you go into a supermarket, casually glance at the logo on the shirt of the person stocking the shelves to ascertain whether s/he is a supermarket employee, or works for the company whose item s/he is stocking the shelf with. Personnel at the cash register are trained to ask you if you want "something else" for just $2 more. The answer is no! When placing a mail order over the phone, I am presumptuously asked *"...and what is your **second** item, Mrs. Rolling?"* (Pssst...this is all called Sales & Marketing 101).

Retailing 101: Even if merchandise is marked 50% off, the retailer, wholesaler/distributor and manufacurer are all still going to make their profit. Money has already exchanged hands between the time the merchandise is manufactured, and the time you purchase it at the cash register.

Fact: Consumers generally purchase more goods when paying with a credit card than when they pay with cash.

Fact: A certain major department store earns more off of the interest payments from its store brand credit card than it does from the sale of the actual merchandise!

Don't Even Go There: Avoiding Credit Card Debt

If you do not need a new credit card, just say "no". I receive calls all of the time from credit card companies querying: *"We have a fabulous credit card we'd like to offer you. Mrs. Rolling, I'd like to confirm that your address is..."* Did I miss something between their offer and confirmation of my address? That's where I stop them dead in their tracks, as I scratch my forehead and realize:

a) I am not afforded the opportunity to decline the offer;
b) If they send the me the card, then it means the credit card issuer has already made a credit inquiry and, with my implicit permission, will run a credit check on me, which I may not want at this particular time for whatever reason;
c) There is no voluntary disclosure in the sales representative's script about what the interest rate is...I have to ask!
d) It doesn't matter that they'll put a picture of a little kitty cat on the credit card. If I want a pwetty wittle kitty cat, I'll get one from the humane society! If I don't need the credit card, then I won't get it. Period.

Credit cards are treated like some sort of status symbol. Salespeople are trained to ask if you wish to apply for the store's credit card on the spot: *"Like, would you like to apply for our store's credit card on-the-spot er, uh (peering at my merchandise receipt) Ms. Rolling?"* I once gleefully indulged a young lady and replied *"Like, what's the interest rate?"* To which she replied, *"Like, I don't know."* To which I replied, *"Like, almost 30%!"* I once experienced passive-aggressive behavior when a saleswoman at a wholesale club offered to escort me to the service desk to apply for a credit card. For a moment there, I felt like a visiting Ambassador to the United Nations. Likewise, don't let the drug dealers—sorry, I mean credit card companies—approach you with their trench coat half open while you're all alone on the dark alley of your telephone, with no one else around, to talk you into getting hooked on some dope...I mean debt. Just like we were all taught in our high school D.A.R.E program, *"Just say no!"*

Now some of you may be exclaiming, *"Are you nuts? You're so fortunate to have companies tripping all over their feet to extend credit to you! My credit is so shot, I donated the bullet proof vest to help raise proceeds for the Patrolmen's Benevolent Association."*

All I'm saying, is...am I likely to take advantage of a good deal if I really need it? Of course. Generally speaking, however, all I see **personally** when these offers are presented to me is the possibility of more debt and further entanglement.

Do not let the credit card companies prey on your desperation or bulldog you into acquiring something you don't need. Remember, making money is the nature of their legitimate business. Furthermore, make sure the company is indeed legitimate. One of my family members received a solicitious call about a credit card offer out of the blue, and accepted because he felt he needed it. He gave them his checking account routing number as a collateral deposit in order to establish a secure line of credit. The deposit cleared, but he received no card. My relative gave me the number so I could check the company out on his behalf, but I could not reach them. When I was finally able to do so, they had a mouthful of excuses and additional steps in order to obtain the card. Thankfully, my relative's checking account balance was already very low before this bogus company withdrew the deposit. I immediately advised him to place a fraud alert on his account with the bank and close the account altogether. By the way, he never did receive that card.

Credit cards are also treated like some sort of rite of passage or a badge of honor. In a study conducted by student loan agency Nellie Mae, 31% of college students carry between $3,000 and $7,000 in credit card debt.[39] As of this writing, legislation is being introduced to stop credit card companies from preying on college students, who are perceived as "fresh meat" because: *"They may get a job after graduation, so let's get them into debt now with the lure of quick cash, and they'll be indebted to us from now to eternity." (Sound of evil laughter).* More about teaching and protecting our young people in Chapter 19.

If you share a credit card account with someone else, pay close attention to how the account is initially set up. There is a huge difference between a joint account holder and an authorized user. A joint account holder means a credit card is in two cardholders' names, both have buying privileges, and may make balance transfers (which is considered to be a purchase), and both are responsible for the debt should one or the other default.[40]

In the case of an authorized user, the card is in the name of the primary account holder. The primary account holder may authorize other parties to use the credit card. However, only the primary account holder may do the following in order to safeguard against any unauthorized changes: Request a lower interest rate, ask for a credit line increase, or close the account.[41]

Should the primary account holder default, the creditor can only go after the primary account holder; the authorized user cannot be held liable (although I am curious what state laws say about this since we are married; state laws vary, you know), *but* positive or negative payment information will reflect on the authorized user's credit report.[42]

Further, unless the authorized user requests that his or her name be removed from the account **before** damage is done by the primary account holder, it will show up negatively on the authorized user's credit report.[43]

If you are an authorized user, you will have to ask your own card issuer whether or not you are allowed to make address changes; as I received two different answers from two different companies.[44] As of this writing, some credit card companies no longer allow joint credit card accounts due to high incidences of divorce.[45]

All of this explains why–although my husband and I have cards in both of our names–we have limited access to each other's accounts. In some cases, we are not the joint account holder but rather, authorized users only on each other's accounts. Personally speaking, when James is listed as the primary account holder, I have to go through extra lengths to request that credit bureaus to note a zero balance under my name, too, after we close a line of credit.

Resource: You have a right to prohibit information contained in your file from being used in connection with any credit transaction that is not initiated by you by calling the credit bureaus' centralized toll free number:
1(888) 5-OPT-OUT or 1(888) 567-8688 or by visiting:
www.optoutprescreen.com

Now That You're Stuck With It, Managing Credit Card Debt
Spanish lesson: I think it is interesting that a Spanish slang for "Credit Card" is *crédito de plástico.* How apropos. Just think: a 3½" x 2" piece of plastic ought to be pretty easy to keep a handle on. Why do we allow something so little to weigh so heavily on our lives? Credit card use is sometimes unavoidable, however. If you **must** pull out the *crédito de plástico,* then follow the guidelines below to use the credit card only as a last resort, to keep debt to a bare minimum, and to use the card responsibly.

• **Consider establishing a secure line of credit.** A secured line of credit is where the credit limit is equal to an amount of money you place on deposit with the card issuer. Your money is used as collateral.[46]

Let's say you send $500 to the card issuer to open a credit card. Your line of credit is $500. If you go purchase an item for $50, your available line of credit becomes $450. This is common for people with no credit history or a history of poor credit.

Robert McKinley and Marc Robinson, authors of *Managing Credit - What You Need To Know To Boost Your Buying Power* define an unsecured line of credit in that "a lender can't immediately take your property if you don't pay your bill."[47] No money was put up as collateral as in the case of a secured line of credit.

• **Why pay an annual fee?** Many revolving credit cards—that is, where you borrow, repay and borrow again against the principal amount repaid—do not charge an annual fee. [48]

• **Fixed interest rate or variable interest rate?** Compare which credit card offers charge less interest: a fixed low-rate card or a card with a high(er) variable interest rate? Each individual's circumstances and credit history differ vastly in this regard. Understand that depending on the terms outlined in your cardholder agreement or disclosure statement, your interest rate can increase due to late payments.

• **Make sure that in this competitive market, credit cards are providing *you* with some sort of incentives.** If you are carrying balances, obtain cards with the lowest possible interest rate first, followed by cash-back bonus awards or frequency points. These are called specialty cards in that they offer special advantages to the consumer. Specialty cards are often offered through affiliations, partnerships, major brand retailers, or service providers who offer rewards or some other earned benefit for your card usage. In my consumer-oriented opinion, out of all of the frills being offered to you, the best-case scenario is having a low interest rate. A contractor came to do work on our home one day. He noted we were charging his services on the same specialty credit card that he uses, and commented on the amount of frequency points he accumulates to fly with. But he can do that due to the volume of business he does. As a fellow consumer, I do not believe in racking up high interest rate credit card debt for the sole purpose of obtaining cash-back rebates or frequency points.

• **Stop and think before you shop.** Before you even step out the door, pick up the phone, or click the mouse with the intent to use your credit card, you must first mentally prioritize which purchases might go on the credit card. For instance, we charged my husband's books and tuition on American Express because 1) it compelled us to pay off the balance at the end of every month and 2) the AmEx Gold card provided us with a year-end itemized usage summary that we glean for tax purposes. Some Internet service providers obviously require a credit or debit card. The point is, you must decide what is best for *you.* **What** is being charged, **which** card is it being charged to, **why** that particular card, and **when** am I going to charge this? What is mean by this is. . .

• **Time your purchases.** If your next paycheck cannot support paying off the balance in full, then consider waiting to make a purchase until the day after the billing cycle ends so that the charge goes on the next bill and does not stress your incoming paycheck. *Sweet.*

• **Do not exceed your credit limit.** Your credit limit is the maximum line of credit you are allowed to borrow against. What are the penalties for doing so? You have to call and find out, since it may vary from individual to individual and from card to card. Generally speaking, this is what I found out as a consumer if you exceed your credit limit:

a) You risk a fee being assessed against your account.
b) You can trigger a higher interest rate.
c) It may negatively impact your credit score.
d) You may be removed from promotional offers.[49]

• **Pay bills on time.** Do not be late with a payment lest you: incur late fees and risk triggering an even higher interest rate; or worse, blemish your credit report if you are 30 days or more overdue with a payment. One of our credit cards goes as far as to include the date *and time* the payment must be received in order not to be considered late. I think it to be a very fair disclosure for a credit card company to make. Presuming there is money sitting in your checking account and you do not necessarily have to wait until payday for additional funds, have you considered paying bills upon their arrival? While I totally understand the notion of utilizing "free money" to pay for merchandise and services, I admire the way one fellow consumer put it: *"I don't deal with that grace-period stuff."*

Some credit card companies now assess a higher interest rate if you are late with an unrelated bill, such as cable or telephone, even though your utility bill has absolutely nothing to do with your being on time with the credit card company's bill. What? How? Huh? The story behind this is that entities such as telephone companies furnish the credit bureaus with your bill payment information, which affects your credit score, which has an effect on loan qualification, interest rates available to you, deposit requirements, etc.[50] Establish a good payment history with your telephone company, cell phone company, and utility providers by paying them on time!

• **If you already have a history of paying your bill on time, simply pick up the phone and ask for an interest rate reduction.** Do not be afraid; the worse they can do is say *"no."* By the way, are your interest rates clearly visible on your credit card statement, or is it placed obscurely so you cannot see it and therefore, pay no attention to it? You know—out of sight, out of mind. This tactic is synonymous to a mall not having clocks so you can lose track of time as you shop your 'lil heart away.

• **Pay off your balance in full each month.** This is not as difficult as it seems once you begin managing your purchases so that you only charge as much as you can pay in a given month. Plus, did I mention that you avoid paying interest on previous billing cycles' purchases by doing so?

• **Even if you pay your credit card bill in full every month...don't become an insect entangled in the credit card company's web.** If you pay your credit card bill in full and on time every month, watch your due dates closely. James and I had paid all of our bills prior to going on vacation once. Little did we know that one of our bills—which arrived while we were away—was now due on the 1st of the month, almost as soon as the wheels of the plane made contact with the blacktop on the runway. The normal due date was the 5th or 6th of the month which was perfect for us, as payday is on the 30th/31st of each month, and allows us time to drop a check in the mail. The credit card company indicated to me that because we pay *in full, on time each month,* the billing cycle had been rolled back from 25 days to 20 days. Get a load of that. I then calmly informed them as I brushed beach sand off of my toes that we'd pay off the small balance, cut up the card, and never use their services again. I had just had a week of de-stressing, you see. We have routines with regard to our paydates, and we know when we can cut a check (because they're sure not going to get direct access to our checking account). The customer service rep promptly replied that it was not a problem "rolling it back" to 25 days. Incidentally, they sent us this notice during the holiday season. I presume they assumed I was out racking up debt at Wal-Mart, shopping for a roasted hen, chopping down a pine tree for the living room, and running myself too haggard to notice. Here's something else to think about: imagine if this type of change triggered a late fee of $15 for 1 million consumers. That's $15 million in the credit card company's coffers. *Merry Christmas, Charlie Brown.*

• **If you cannot pay off your balance in full each month, at least pay the minimum balance. If you can pay more than the minimum balance, do so!** Avoid making just the minimum payment—remember that the bank makes oodles of money off of you by the interest rate it charges on your credit card balance. One of our credit cards indicates, "$15 reduced payment" in the minimum payment box. I need a magnifying glass to find the normal minimum monthly payment of $32. On our statement, the $15 reduced payment amount is easier to see than the $32. This placement is not by accident, ladies and gentlemen. Fifteen dollars may be easier for us to pay if hard-pressed with other financial obligations, but the credit card company is counting on the interest assessed against the unpaid balance—literally speaking.

• **Do not float your checks.** Floating is when you submit the check for payment, but the money won't be in the account until later. You risk the payee receiving the check, submitting it for payment, and the check getting bounced.

As of this writing, banks have successfully lobbied for new legislation, the Check Clearing for the 21st Century Act. One of the key provisions of this legislation is that a paper check is virtually cleared once the payee's bank cashes it. A digitized image converts and replaces the paper check in order to facilitate the exchange of currency.[51] Translation: Make sure 'yo money is there first, or you may incur a bounced check fee!

• **When sending in large payments by mail,** call and ask the credit card company customer service representative to make a notation to this effect on your account. I do this as a way of providing a "heads up" and for my own peace of mind!

• **When paying a credit card balance in full, call and request the accurate pay-off balance and a zero-balance statement.** Request an accurate pay-off balance coinciding with the timeframe the credit card company will actually receive the payment—remember, interest compounds daily! I've had both positive and negative experiences with this. When my husband and I were paying off debt, I called and asked two companies for an accurate pay-off amount so we could write the checks and say "good riddance!" to the debt. Company A took into consideration the date that the payment would be received by them (based on the date I said I would be mailing the check), and provided me with a pay-off amount that even resulted in a few cents credit. Company B gave me that day's balance, and that's the amount of money we sent in. Before the next billing cycle, I called Company B to make sure they received the payment and that our balance was zero. Seven dollars and change was, in fact, due on account of compounding interest. I basically said that if the seven bucks in interest was *reeeally* that important to them, I'll pay it, but they'd lose our business. I knew I had been very clear the first time around when I asked for the pay-off balance, provided the credit card company received our payment by such-and-such a date. Imagine—seven bucks surplus payment multiplied by hypothetically 500,000 people accumulates to $3.5 million. I don't know about you, but I work too hard for a living to help make a corporation richer...with my pocket change.

Once you have paid off credit card debt, be aware that a statement may not automatically be generated to this effect. And what about customers like me who want to see that nice big, fat zero to tuck away in my files? A statement may not be sent unless there is new account activity in the next billing cycle; otherwise, be sure to call and request it.

• **Avoid cash advances.** When you acquire a new credit card, don't even think about withdrawing cash advances at the ATM machine. Interest rates are usually a percentage of the cash advance amount with a pre-set minimum and capped maximum (e.g., 3% of the cash advance amount but not less than $X, and not more than $Y).

• **By all means, avoid payday loans,** most often offered by storefronts and on the Internet. It works like this: If you need a loan, you apply for it, but the interest rate is so inflammatory, it is designed to keep you paying on the sky-high interest rate without hardly touching the principal amount originally borrowed. When payday does arrive, you are still in the hole and indebted to these sharks. The lenders' logic is that people seeking payday loans are high-risk anyway, thus justifying the high interest rate. According to one television news report, a man paid $2,300 just to finally put a stop to the $800 he originally borrowed. Oh—and they obtain your social security number and banking routing number when you apply for the loan to make sure they know where to find you should you be late, miss a payment or default. Consequently, they have the ability to garnish your wages and plunder your bank account. We know people who applied for a payday loan over the Internet so they could supplement their mortgage payment and other household expenses. They urged me, as weary, browbeaten consumers, to put their warning in this book: *Steer clear of payday loans and loan sharks, or you'll be eaten alive (pun intended)!*

Balance Transfers

The advantage to making balance transfers is that you may be able to pay either 0% on credit card debt or an interest rate that is lower than your other credit card(s) during the specified period of time listed on the offer. Here are the key questions to ask when making a balance transfer:

- What is the balance transfer fee?
- When will the introductory, or teaser balance transfer rate cease?
- What are the terms and conditions?

I know that last question is hefty, but learn from our mistake: we have a credit card that required us to make two purchases per month in order to qualify for a 0% balance transfer for the life of the entire loan. So far, so good. But then again—as long as we make two purchases per month on the card.

An appropriate question for me to ask at the time I initiated the transaction would have been: *"We have a balance of $500 worth of charges already sitting on the card. If we make this four-figure, balance transfer amount first, and send in $500 later, will the $500 be applied towards the balance currently owed?* I didn't ask the right question(s) or know precisely what to ask. I later learned that the bank was making its money off of the interest rate applied to the two required monthly purchases. But they were also making money in interest upon the $500 balance that we were no longer making any headway in paying off because of the structure of the terms. So it didn't matter to them at all that they were *not* making any money off of the balance transfer amount; they were still getting paid. The only way for us to make a dent into the total amount owed would have been to make payments above the required minimum monthly payment. And if we dared ever make the mistake of failing to make two monthly purchases within the specific time period or were late with a payment, the interest would have immediately accrued on the *entire* credit card balance—including the amount transferred—Yikes! It would have been in our personal best interest to pay off the $500 balance already on the credit card before making the balance transfer to ensure that interest accrued only on the two monthly purchases. Even if those two purchases were candybars each month. Alas, if only we had asked the right questions. Does this make sense?

"It's easier to get into something than to get out of it."
~ William H. Swanson, CEO and President, Raytheon Company ~
(From Swanson's "25 UnWritten Rules of Management")

A desirable position to be in…or is it?
An important tidbit you need to know, from consumer-to-consumer, is that credit card companies like to "sweeten the pot" when you have a strong credit profile and little debt. It's their job to find a way to convince you to make a purchase. Sometimes it's your job to wait for the sweeter offer and enjoy it…but pay it back much more quickly than they'd like. Heh, heh. For instance, I currently have three offers from a major credit card company.

Offer #1 was sent to me in September encouraging me to write a balance transfer check at a 4.99% interest rate that must post to the account by October 31st. I did not respond to the offer, not because it wasn't attractive to my carefully trained eye, but simply because there was no debt to transfer at the time.

A month later, same company sent **Offer #2** congratulating and encouraging me to write a balance transfer check at less than a 1% interest rate and to hurry, Me'Shae! The charge must post by November 30th. I did not take advantage of that offer either.

Like clockwork, the very same company sent **Offer #3** in the mail a month later, this time at a 0% interest rate as long as the amount was posted by the end of December. By this time, my home office needed a major piece of office equipment and I considered taking advantage of the offer. How do they generate revenue off of me at a 0% interest rate? Because if I don't pay off the balance by May of next year, the interest rate will jack up to the prevailing variable interest rate. They are taking a chance that circumstances will interfere with our being able to pay off the entire balance by then. The point is, they would rather *gamble* on making some profit off of my account—whether it's at 4.99%, less than 1%, or 0% with a hidden catch—rather than definitely making no profit from my account at all. As for the congratulatory tone of the correspondence—it's just a gimmick!

Resources:
FREE resource from the Fannie Mae Foundation:
"Borrowing Basics: What You Don't Know Can Hurt You"
Download from www.fanniemaefoundation.org, or call
1(800) 688-HOME / 4663 – in Spanish, call 1(800) 782-2729

CardTrak (a credit card industry tracker) –
www.cardweb.com to research various credit cards and their offers/terms on your own

For more information regarding credit card usage, visit: Motley Fool at www.fool.com; includes a financial glossary

To obtain a comparative listing of credit card rates, fees & grace periods, contact: New York State Banking Department at:
www.banking.state.ny.us - 1(877) BANK-NYS / 226-5697

Credit Union National Association – www.cuna.org

CASE STUDY: DEBT ELIMINATION STRATEGY

Once you have committed to living a debt-free life, there are certain ground rules that must accompany your lifestyle in order to accomplish your goal. Ask yourself questions such as:

- How much money will my budget allow for me to pay down my credit card- and other debts?
- How can I accelerate payments?
- What lifestyle changes must I undertake in order to work towards debt elimination?

For example, if I have been charging my meals, then is it possible for me to bring more beverages, snacks, and food from home for when I'm out and about?

- Provided I stop using the credit card(s), how am I now going to pay for items I had been previously charging, so that I can avoid paying interest on the new charges, as well? More fundamentally, the question becomes: were said items needs, wants or desires (see section 5.6)?

Listen, all I'm saying is to **connect the dots** between *"I'm going to get out of debt,"* and the action required to do so.

If you have indeed found yourself drowning in credit card debt, then here is a credit card debt elimination strategy developed by Larry Burkett with Randy Southern in *The World's Easiest Guide to Finances:*

The Millers have over 8,000 worth of credit card debt, the average amount of debt Americans carry each year. Here is an itemization of those expenses:

Credit Card	Balance	Interest Rate	Minimum Monthly Payment
Visa	$5,500	10.5%	$110
MasterCard	$3,000	13.5%	$80
Discover	$1,100	18%	$65
Citibank	$750	9.5%	$35
Gas Card	$500	21%	$25
Department Store	$295	21%	$15

(Taken with permission from *The World's Easiest Guide to Finances* by Larry Burkett and Randy Southern, Northfield Publishing, copyright © 2000.)

1) The Millers have been paying the minimum monthly payments totaling $330.
2) The Millers do everything they possibly can to tighten the belt and save money.
3) After doing so, they've identified they can allocate an extra $150 per month towards eliminating credit card debt.

4) They call all bank card issuers and ask for the lowest possible interest rate.
5) The Millers then rank the credit card balances from greatest to least.
6) The Millers begin paying off the credit cards with the smallest balances and highest interest rates first.
7) They continue paying the minimum amount owed on all cards except for the first card on the hit list, the department store card—which gets the $150 in "found/saved" money.
8) Once the department store card is paid off after two payments, there is a great sense of satisfaction, achievement and encouragement.
9) The Millers then take the $150 in "found/saved" money they were paying the department store card and add it to the $25 minimum payment required for the next card on the list—the gas card—increasing their monthly payment on that card to $175. At this rate, the gas card is paid off in three months.
10) They repeat this cycle until the card with the highest balance, Visa, is paid off.[52]

Assuming the Millers are consistently making one monthly payment on all credit cards, it takes them approximately 31-32 months, or 2½ years to pay-off their entire credit card debt. In additon to having a steady income, the single, biggest, necessary factor in order for this method to work is to stop using credit cards, plain and simple. How do you think the Millers felt after all credit card debt was eliminated? What must it feel like to be free of all those monthly payments? Do you think they went out and plunged back into debt over more "stuff?" I don't think so! My guess is that they were able to breathe financially and redirect the surplus income towards savings, investments, kids' college education, and other things in life meaningful and important to them.

Resource: Crown Financial Ministries, 1(800) 722-1976
– www.crown.org

Once you get out of debt, STAY out of debt
by living as much as possible on an all-cash basis.
~ MBR ~

CHAPTER 9
CREDIT REPORTS & FICO SCORES

"The plans of the diligent lead to profit as surely as haste leads to poverty."
~ Proverbs 21:5 ~

Credit Bureaus

SINCE CREDIT IS SO CRUCIAL toward obtaining a home, auto, or personal loan, let's take a moment to examine a few pointers regarding credit bureaus aka credit reporting agencies. To order copies of your credit report, you must provide your name (including variations), address, social security number, and date of birth. If you have moved within the last two years, then you must also provide your previous address. The three national credit bureaus are as follows:

EQUIFAX
P.O. Box 740241
Atlanta, GA 30374
1 (800) 685-1111
M-F, 9 a.m.–5 p.m., EST
www.equifax.com

EXPERIAN P.O. Box 9701 Allen, TX 75013 1(888) EXPERIAN 1(888) 397-3742 24 hours/day, 7 days/week www.experian.com
TRANSUNION P.O. Box 2000 Chester, PA 19022-2000 1 (800) 916-8800 M-F, 8:00 a.m.-8:00 p.m., EST www.transunion.com

You are entitled to a free credit report from each of the three national credit bureaus once every twelve months. This amendment to the Fair Credit Reporting Act became effective on December 1, 2004 in the western states, and was phased in over a nine-month period, finally rolling out to the eastern states—including New York, New Jersey, Connecticut, and Pennsylvania—on September 1, 2005.[53] To order directly, simply contact:

ANNUAL CREDIT REPORT REQUEST SERVICE P.O. Box 105283 Atlanta, GA 30348-5283 1 (877) 322-8228 www.annualcreditreport.com

Under the Fair Credit Reporting Act, outside of your free annual credit report, other circumstances under which you are entitled to a free credit report include: adverse action being taken against you due to information contained in your credit report (e.g., being denied credit); a non-financial action such as being turned down for a job; if you are on public assistance; or if you are the victim of identity theft and have requested that a fraud alert be placed on your files[54] (see Chapter 11 on identity theft prevention and victimization). You are also entitled to a free copy of your corrected report. Whenever I report updates or corrections, the bureaus automatically send a report to me.

Positive information may remain on your report indefinitely. Types of information that may be removed from your credit report include outdated negative information more than seven years old; bankruptcy actions (the length of time it can be removed depends on the type of bankruptcy filed); or inaccurate, incomplete, unverifiable information. Bureaus have 30 days from the date of your notification to remove these types of information. If they cannot prove the information is factual, then they must remove record of the entire account from your credit file.[55]

It took my husband and I *years* just to clean up the following mistakes: mistaken identity between James and his father (my husband is a "Jr."); accounts with a zero balance showing up as "open" when we had in fact closed them; and accounts with adverse information over seven years old. In the latter case, we were in the process of purchasing a home, and blemishes from the early years of our marriage were still on our reports. The information was over seven years old and therefore, was removed after we presented the necessary proof and documentation. Yay!

Contact The Source Directly

If you have no such proof or documentation, contact the credit card company you had the account with, and request that they provide you with a copy of their records, as well as provide that same updated information to the credit bureaus. Before I became financially organized, I did not retain any information regarding a Mobil credit card. Why in the world I applied for a gas card when I did not yet own a car is beyond me! The card was still showing up as open credit on my report years later. I contacted Mobil directly, they located my record, and rectified the incorrect information on my credit report. You can also fill out and submit the credit bureaus' investigation forms to make corrections to your credit report.

You also have a right to write a 100-word statement to the credit bureau(s), providing an explanation of extenuating circumstances that may have caused delinquent payments, such as economic hardship.[56] That explanation will become a part of your record and help provide a story behind the numbers.

You might consider requesting that unauthorized inquiries be deleted from your credit report. Too many inquiries may be perceived negatively.[57] Your credit score is not affected when you check your own report.[58]

FICO Score: What Does It Mean?

The term FICO score (not Fido, as in the dog) is an acronym for Fair, Isaac and Company, Inc., the firm that developed the formula used to compute credit scoring. Your FICO score is a single composite calculation from the three major national credit bureaus, designed "to see how lenders see you". The three-digit score can range anywhere from 350 to 950, depending on the source calculating the score. The most important thing to keep in mind is that the higher the score, the better.

The very best rates go to people with scores in the high 700s or more. A consumer with a score around 720 is considered to be very good because the risk of default is statistically low. According to Experian's National Score Index website, the national average credit score hovers around 677-678.[59] According to Fair Isaac, "The median FICO Score in the U.S. is 723."[60] A respectable score of 620 is considered the dividing line between good and bad credit. A score below 620 is considered relatively high risk.[61]

Each score takes five types of information into account: payment history, amounts owed, length of credit history, new credit, and types of credit used. Each type of information comprises a percentage of the total score.[62]

There are numerous ways to find out your FICO score (for a fee, of course). The most direct way is to visit:

www.myfico.com or call 1(800) 319-4433
The "Credit Education" menu answers FAQs under the following two categories:

Credit Scores:

- What's in your score
- What's not in your score
- How scoring helps you
- Improving your score
- Facts & Fallacies

Credit Reports:

- What's in your report
- How mistakes are made
- Checking your report
- Average credit statistics
- Credit inquiries

Apart From Your Free Annual Credit Report

The last time I checked on the Internet, you may obtain your score for as little as $5 from Experian. Experian's credit report plus your FICO score is $14.50 (apart from the free annual report). As of this writing, the cost for all three reports plus a free score is as follows (you'll have to check or call for the latest yourself). If buying online through...

- Equifax – $39.95
- Experian – $34.95
- TransUnion – $29.95
- MyFico - $44.85 (3 scores and 3 reports)

In addition, each site offers fee-based credit monitoring services in order to guard against identity theft.

About Those "Open," But Inactive Accounts

If you have a zero balance on your credit card and are no longer using the card, do not, under any circumstances, assume that the card is inactive or closed. It is considered open until you close it. Perhaps like yourself, as a consumer I have heard two different viewpoints regarding whether or not to close open, but dormant credit card accounts, so I will relay the same information to you as I have learned myself from consumer specialists such as *New York Daily News* Columnist Asa Aarons:

It is perfectly acceptable to pay-down and cut-up credit cards so that you do not incur any more charges. However, go ahead and keep those accounts open. Put simply, older accounts help to demonstrate a longer credit history and increase the amount of your available credit, which in turn can boost your credit score.[63]

According to financial expert, television host, and author Suze Orman, the important thing to remember is that there is a correlation between your debt ratio, your FICO score, and your interest rates: when you pay down your debts, your FICO score goes up, and the interest rates you are eligible for go down.[64]

On the other hand, if for any reason you decide to close the account, then carefully consider the timing thereof: closing dormant accounts and decreasing the length of your credit history is not a good idea, especially when on the verge of making a major purchase such as a home.

FYI, it is important to keep in mind that a co-signer is responsible for repaying a loan if the applicant defaults (failure to pay back a lender on a loan). So think twice about co-signing for friends, family members, pets, outer space aliens, etc. It *will* affect your credit history.

Along with derogatory, but *accurate* information (i.e., you indeed racked up $6,000 on the department store's charge card and subsequently failed to make timely payments), allow *time* to clean up your credit history. The process will demand patience on your part, to say the least.

Resources:
You may read the entire Fair Credit Reporting Act by visiting the Federal Trade Commission's website at: www.ftc.gov/os/statutes/fcra.htm, or by visiting www.fightidentitytheft.com/fact_act.html

FREE resource from the Fannie Mae Foundation:
"Knowing and Understanding Your Credit"
Download from www.fanniemaefoundation.org or call
1(800) 688-HOME / 4663 - in Spanish, call 1(800) 782-2729

CHAPTER 10

PREPARE TO OWN WHILE YOU ARE RENTING

"Four things on earth are small, yet they are extremely wise:
Ants are creatures of little strength, yet they
store up their food in the summer"
~ Proverbs 30:24-25 ~

IT'S A CONCRETE JUNGLE OUT THERE. When I add up all of the rent from living in Park Slope, Brooklyn in the early 90's, Crown Heights, Brooklyn in the mid-90s to the early part of the millennium, and Spanish Harlem (Manhattan) until mid-2004, the grand total is over $76,410...and James and I had what we consider to be reasonable rent! This figure does not even include the two years' worth of rental fees we paid for storage space while living in Manhattan. (Tack on an additional $4,560 in case you are curious.) As one renter lamented after another recent hike on rent-stabilized apartments, *"I can't afford to stay, and I can't afford to move."* If you are a long-term renter and are wondering why should you consider owning, I have three words for you: E-QUI-TY. If we've heard it once, we've heard it a zillion times: James and I could have been investing 80 grand toward equity all of those years. Instead, we were helping to fatten someone else's pockets, send them on vacation in the Bahamas, or at the very least, helping to sustain their existence.

A Word Or Two To Renters

If you are currently renting, don't be too hard on yourself. It takes time and planning to prepare yourself for homeownership. Although you miss out on certain tax benefits, there are expenses associated with being a homeowner that you do not have as a renter (homeowner's insurance, heat, maintenance and repairs, etc.). However, if you do rent, please keep up your dwelling even though your name is not on the deed. Don't throw your chicken bones in the street, in front of your door, or leave whole cartons of pork fried rice on the sidewalk, ringing the dinner bell for the rats and their cousins. By now, I'm sure you're thinking, "She did *not* go there." Oh yes I did. There is honor in not worrying about what we don't have just yet in life, but maintaining and keeping clean what we do have. Be noble in tending to those responsibilities.

Renters: Adopt a Homeowners' Mentality

Regardless of where or when you plan to own, in the meantime, you can **prepare yourself right now** for homeownership by educating yourself on the following questions and scenarios:

- *How much* home can I afford?
- *What* real estate offices are located in the neighborhood I am interested in?
- *Who* is going to be on my team (real estate agent, attorney, inspector, mortgage lender)?
- Is the real estate agent acting as a *buyer's agent* (works for the buyer), *the seller's agent* (works for the seller), or a *dual agent* (works on behalf of both buyer and seller)?
- Is the property I'm interested in *appraised* at the asking price?
- *What types* of loan programs are available to fit my situation?
- *How much money* is required—and to whom—at closing?

If you are in the market for your first home, and you have the intent to actually live in it, as opposed to flipping it (that is, buying it just to refurbish it, increase its value, and sell or rent it for a profit), do not under any circumstances wait until you see *the home*, and then scramble to get your act together. There is too much information to digest, too many resources to tap into, too many homeownership seminars to attend, too many questions to ask for you to stand by like you're hanging out on the street corner until the property bumps into you. I am not an economist; I do not know if or when the housing market bubble is going to burst. What I do want to know is, if the opportunity **does** present itself to buy an affordable home, are you going to miss out because you did not take the time to put your financial house in order?

Trust me on this. It took years for me to clean up simple mistakes and to provide accurate updates to the credit bureaus regarding our credit reports. Purchasing a home is most certainly a time in life where you would want to be financially organized.

Homeownership occurs, in my opinion, when preparation meets opportunity. Have you heard of the expression, *"Work as if everything depends on you, and pray because everything depends on God?"* Preparation is not going to happen overnight. Now let's dig in.

Even though you may not own a home yet, know and understand that potential mortgage lenders inspect the following: [65]

1) Verification of current income/proof of current employment &/or job history.

   The lending institution will ask to see: your W-2 pay records (depending on the type of dwelling we were applying for, we were also asked to provide tax returns).

2) The size of your down payment (generally a minimum of 3-5% of the purchase price of the home; 20% to avoid PMI, or private mortgage insurance). At some point in the process, a mortgage lender will wanteth to see your bank statement(s) to determinith from whence the down payment cometh. What many potential homebuyers do not know, however, is that there are a variety

of homeownership programs and financing options available, since one size does not fit all! Consult an established, reputable mortgage lender to assess your situation for various financing options available.

The lending institution will ask to see: assets such as recent bank statements.

3) Your debt-to-income ratio (your debts in comparison to your income). This is another incentive for you to eliminate credit card debt.

The lending institution will order your credit report.

4) Your FICO score. Examine your *own* credit reports and learn what your *own* FICO score is beforehand. **Sitting in the chair at some big financial institution, playing peek-a-boo with your credit information is *not* the time to find out your own biz-ness.**

The lending institution will look up your FICO score.

In the interest of financial organization, I strongly recommend that you place the aforementioned data in a three-ring binder and label the tabs accordingly. Do you know that co-op boards of glitzy apartment buildings require such data in this same format? James and I also added to our binder proof (receipts) of on-time rent and utility payments, and homeownership seminar completion certificates so that it was easy to put our hands on the information at a moment's notice.

Singing To The Choir

The interesting, difficult thing about New York City is that once apartment #3-J in a high-rise building on Staten Island goes on the market, there is no "for sale" sign hanging out of the window. Units get advertised through whatever method or venue the owner(s) choose(s). The owner does not necessarily want 5,000 calls, and it is nearly impossible to know what real estate agency is going to have the listing.

It is not uncommon to go to an open house, and find potential buyers there along with their agent and attorney, pre-approval papers in hand, ready for a good old-fashioned bidding war as if it were a street fight. Remember the Sharks and the Jets in *West Side Story?* Recounting this urban legend certainly makes great fodder, watching the raised eyebrows and look of bewilderment on the faces of folks in rural and suburban parts of the country as they sit on their rocking chair on the back porch overlooking their parcel of land.

Like you, I **do** understand how it feels to be sniffed at by someone over the phone upon our revelation of the amount of money we had saved for a down payment on a co-op in Riverdale. I **do** know what it is like to scour the newspapers for a "needle in the haystack": property that doesn't look like it is going to fall over if you stare at it the wrong way but yet, requires thousands of dollars worth of renovations on top of the asking price.

So let me get the next question out of the way: *"Where am I going to find the down-payment I need for a home?"* Income is most certainly a major factor in the equation, but this book is primarily about your expenses. I do not wish to over-simplify the answer to your question, but re-read Chapter 5 for ways to drastically reduce your daily living expenses. Are these tips going to produce $75,000 for a down payment? Probably not, but is that embroidered leather jacket you are buying also hindering you from making progress towards your goal? Probably.

Real Estate Team

Your real estate team consists of a licensed real estate agent, mortgage lender, homeowner's insurance agent, home inspector, and an attorney specializing in real estate law. I will focus on the real estate agent and the mortgage lender. They are the ones my husband and I seemed to spend the most amount of time corresponding with. The insurance agent and attorney will let you know what they need from you: generally a bunch of paperwork! I cannot emphasize enough how important it is to develop a good rapport with your real estate team, although I know it is difficult because people have such a limited amount of time to spend with you. Beyond that, you have to know what to ask. How do you know what to ask? By educating yourself on the process, and by reading whatever you can get your hands on regarding homeownership...the questions will come naturally.

The single, most effective thing you can do for your real estate agent is to identify the criteria you are looking for so s/he is not looking all over Gotham on your behalf. First of all, where do you want to live? Corona Park, Queens? Bedford Stuyvesant, Brooklyn? How many bedrooms? Bathrooms? What kind of kitchen—full or eat-in? Does it have a combo living room/dining area? What about den/family room and patio/deck? Do you need a one-car or two-car garage? Do you want any other amenities, such as a doorman? (Although in a big city, some of the above criteria may count as luxurious!)

Below are sources for dwellings that you can also research for yourself:

- Realtor.com
- RealEstateBook.com
- Homes.com
- HomeStore.com
- JustListed.com
- MLS (Multiple Listing Service) Google search
- Your neighborhood realty offices
- FSBO (For Sale by Owner): www.gonehome.com
- HUD Foreclosures: firstpreston.com
- nyc.gov/hpd (NYC Dept. of Housing & Preservation Development's Homeworks program)
- nhsnyc.org (Neighborhood Housing Services)
- Other community-based neighborhood organizations

NEWSPAPERS

- Friday's *"New York Daily News"*
- Friday's *"Newsday"*
- Saturday's *"New York Post"*
- Neighborhood publications (i.e., *Amsterdam News, Gotham Gazette,* etc.)

REAL ESTATE AGENCIES
For a comprehensive listing of licensed real estate brokers in the area you are searching for, visit www.HouseValues.com, enter your zip code, click on "Licensed Real Estate Broker or Agent" at the bottom of the home page, click on the state, and viola! (NYC has over 250 alone.)

RESEARCH the various homeownership programs available!
~ MBR ~

Crunch The Numbers With Your Mortgage Lender
Pre-qualification is a very informal process. A loan officer develops an informal determination of how much money you may be able to borrow for a home based on information you provide him or her about your income, savings, and debt, etc. Pre-approval is a much more formal process. The mortgage lender does all of the legwork to verify income, credit, score, etc.[66]

The mortgage lender then hands you a pre-approval letter, good for a pre-set number of days (check with your mortgage lender for specifications), so long as you find the home of your dreams within that timeframe. A growing industry trend is to show homes to potential buyers only if they are pre-approved so as not to waste the seller's, real estate agent's, or buyers' time.

Obtain a pre-approval letter from your mortgage lending institution to present to the seller. It signals serious intent to buy, and it can give you the advantage over other bidders for a home. From consumer-to-consumer, bear in mind that a mortgage lender may very well pre-approve you for all the money you can afford on paper, but it is not examining your budget for other expenses, such as utilities, transportation, children's expenses, etc. Your personalized budget (see Chapter 2) will be able to provide a snapshot—through the lens of your current residential expenses—of what kind of mortgage amount you can realistically afford in relation to your other living expenses. If, for instance, you are making car payments, that will not necessarily disappear when you acquire the home unless you are consciously planning to pay-off the vehicle prior to purchasing the home. Otherwise, it must be reflected in your budget.

In addition, take into account that the asking price is not in and of itself the cost of a home. The components of a mortgage payment consist of: the principal (the cost of the home minus your down payment); plus interest; plus homeowner's insurance; plus property taxes.[67] **This is how people get into trouble: by failing to crunch the numbers and getting in over their heads financially.**

Two To Tango

Select a lender whose mortgage consultant/representative takes the time to explain basic facts to you. A home is the single, largest purchase you will ever make in your entire life. Do you not deserve the decency of your questions being answered without being made to feel like an idiot? Or like you are taking up the mortgage rep's precious time because they need to beat rush hour on the Verrazano Bridge? I am not saying that you should monopolize—or as we say in Indiana, hog their time—but have you looked on the street corners around the city lately? There are other banks in the sea. A bank has a long-term financial interest vested in *you* selecting *it.* A bank's job is in determining how much of a risk it can take on you paying back the loan. The income/down-payment/debt ratio/FICO score mentioned earlier in this chapter helps the bank to make that determination. Do not spend more time making selections at the mall than you do researching and investigating the lending institution you are going to have a long-term financial relationship with. *Touché*

As an astute consumer, inquire of your mortgage lender what various loan options are available to you. Request that all of your if/then scenarios be thoroughly answered. *"If I choose loan option A, then how much will my monthly mortgage amount be at the prevailing interest rate? If I choose loan option B, then how much will my monthly mortgage payment be?"*

On top of your other costs, closing costs are generally 3%-7% of the purchase price of the home. Do not forget to also budget inspection reports and moving expenses in the equation. Ahhh…this, again, is where your personalized budget comes in handy.

FREE resources by the Fannie Mae Foundation - Download from www.fanniemaefoundation.org, or call 1(800) 688-HOME / 4663 – in Spanish, call 1(800) 782-2729:

- "Borrowing Basics: What You Don't Know Can Hurt You"
- "Knowing and Understanding Your Credit"
- "Opening The Door To A Home Of Your Own"
- "Choosing the Mortgage That's Right For You"

Homebuying for Dummies, Eric Tyson and Ray Brown, IDG Books Worldwide, Inc., 1997.

Calculator Tools:
www.mortgage101.com (includes a financial library)

www.mortgage-calc.com
(Includes mortgage, financial and amortization calculators)

www.mortgage-net.com
(Includes consumer interest articles in their Reference Desk menu)

Real Estate & Homebuyer Expos every spring in the West 34th-street area with hundreds of mortgage lenders, brokers, real estate agents, inspectors, appraisers, etc.; periodically conduct a Google search for latest postings.
Home-buying seminars hosted by community-based organizations, real estate agencies, banks, churches, colleges and universities, etc. including but not limited to:

Neighborhood Housing Services
A not-for-profit organization offering free workshops and

seminars to help you achieve financial fitness in preparation for homeownership.
www.nhsnyc.org - (718) 230-7610
NHS also has 7 other centers throughout NYC: Bedford-Stuyvesant, East Flatbush, North Bronx, South Bronx, Jamaica, Northern Queens, and Staten Island.

NYC Department of Housing Preservation & Development
HPD conducts housing education courses; the website includes a template for homebuyers
www.nyc.gov/hpd - 311 (within NYC) or (212) 863-8830

Be Proactive During The Process

The pursuit of homeownership is an area where you just have to be proactive. How many times have I heard, *"Well, I called the real estate agent but she never called me back."* I pry: When did you leave the message? *"I left voice messages for the mortgage broker way back yonder during the Ice Age, but he never returned my call...he must be awful busy."* Ya think? Ladies and gents, do you want that house or not? If the folks on your team are holding up the process by not being responsive to your basic needs, then find a representative of a reputable establishment who will.

I was told of a case where the homebuyer showed up on the Seller's doorstep seeking insurance information because the Buyer's agent had not forwarded the information. (In the home buying process, all formal transactions and correspondence typically go through the attorneys and the agents.) However, the closing date was nearing and the Buyers needed insurance by the closing date. The Sellers provided the requested information early on in the process, but it never got to the Buyer. *Tsk, tsk.*

From consumer-to-consumer, you heard it here first: be aware that once you are in the process of purchasing a home, the will be a plethora of important faxes, e-mails, telephone calls, and appointments amongst the team in order to keep the process rolling along to ensure a smooth closing. This takes both time and resources (revisit Chapter 5, section

5.39 on administrative glitches and technological access/capabilities), so have the proper protocol in place: reachable daytime telephone number to keep the lines of communication open (i.e., inspector's visit); incoming and outgoing fax capabilities (i.e., documents requiring signature); e-mail for less formal correspondence (i.e., what time do I meet you there?). Some matters, of course, are time-sensitive. Keep the lines of communication simple and obstacle-free.

In our case, personally, we listed only one phone number for all real estate-related calls to come though: our home number, where I was usually working in the home office. Not our cell. Not my husband's work number. I shared all info with James. Whatever our decision, I called/faxed the appropriate party or parties, and promptly took care of the administrative side of the transaction on our end.

Do whatever works most efficiently, effectively, and administratively *for you,* but have a system in place. This is the nitty gritty stuff you are not going to read in the homebuyer's manual. Did someone say grits? Boy, do I miss Indiana.

Encore:
If you plan to own a home someday, now
is the time, while still a renter,
to position yourself financially for homeownership.
~ MBR ~

CHAPTER 11
IDENTITY THEFT, DEBT COLLECTION, AND BANKRUPTCY

"The rich rule over the poor, and the borrower is servant to the lender."
~ Proverbs 22:7 ~

DUMSPTER DIVING. SKIMMING. SURFING. PHISHING. These are:

a) Terms you should know before going fishing in Coney Island;
b) Something having to do with the NYC Sanitation Department; or
c) Ploys identity thieves use to get hold of your personal information in order to wreck havoc with your credit and finances by stealing your identity

Identity Theft: America's Fastest Growing Crime
I personally know people who have fallen victim to identity theft. Chances are, you do to. Beware: children and the elderly are particularly vulnerable because their lesser or diminished attention

to financial matters makes it less likely that suspicious activity will be caught early. The problem has become so prevalent, federal agents are now eliciting the knowledge and enlisting the help of—get this—convicted identity thieves to combat this growing epidemic that even the government is having a tough time getting a handle on.

According to an article appearing in *Newsweek,* the days of sticking up a bank have become *so* old school. The real pay dirt is struck by:

- hacking into the computer systems of banks, credit card companies, merchants, educational institutions, employers, data brokerage firms, DMV, federal agencies (yes, even the IRS), etc.; and then

- auctioning the information in underground chat rooms:
    - $200 will get you 300 credit card numbers without the security code printed on the front or back of the card;
    - 50 credit card numbers with the security code can be hawked at $200;
    - a mere $40 will fetch you a person's social security number and date of birth[68].

Thieves buy this information from the brokers in bulk like I buy eggs at the wholesale club. They then proceed to the nearest BMW dealership to purchase a car with your name and credit while you're still riding the A train. No exaggeration.

Dumpster Diving is when raiders dig through your trash looking for scraps of paper containing any kind of sensitive data—particularly credit card offers. They can fill out a credit card application in your name, but redirect the card to a different address under the guise that you have moved.[69]

Protect yourself from dumpster diving by shredding sensitive documents before placing on the curbside for sanitation pick-up.

Skimming is when a low-down, dirty crook uses an electronic credit card reader—a device called a skimmer—in concert with swiping the card at cash registers and credit card machines. The skimmer electronically gathers pertinent information that is encoded on the magnetic strip on the back of your credit or ATM/debit card: your name, address, telephone name, card number, and personal identification number. People who most often use these skimmers are waiters, waitresses or gas station attendants. Of course, not all waiters, waitresses, or gas station attendants engage in these illegal activities. But anyone who has the opportunity to take your card and swipe it elsewhere out of your view is capable of skimming it, as well. Criminals are standing by, licking their chops for the information to sell on the black market. Scary stuff.[70]

Protecting yourself from skimming is admittedly a challenge, because you take a risk every time you hand someone your card to take out-of-view. In the case of ATM machines, be picky about which ones you use. Even if you do use the ATM machine of a reputable establishment such as a bank, survey the area surrounding the ATM machine to make sure no bogus external device has been installed in order to capture information from your card. If you see something or even *someone* lurking suspiciously, immediately alert banking officials and the police.

Surfing

Remember when pre-paid calling cards reached the height of their popularity? We then saw news reports cautioning us to make sure no one was lifting our calling card number and PIN by memorizing our finger movements from afar. Telephone companies responded by installing wings on the left and right of the pay phone's keypad. These kinds of over-the-shoulder thefts is called surfing. Prying thieves can do the same thing while you are entering your ATM and credit card PINs at say, the supermarket.[71]

Protect yourself from surfing by heightening your alert level (in the words of the Department of Homeland Security) to orange or red—whenever entering your PIN. I am quite sure I look like the Hunchback of Notre Dame whenever inputting my PIN.

Phishing is when bogus e-mails are sent to your in-box with logo designs and letterhead very much resembling legitimate companies, requesting money from you or asking for your most sensitive information with the pretense that this info has been lost or needs to be verified by the company. Never click on such a link sent to you in an e-mail. I'm telling you right now: it is a scam. Conversely, make sure that when you log onto a website, use your bookmark or type in the correct address and not some fake that sets itself up with a similar appearance or web address as the legitimate website.[72]

Protect yourself from phishing by not responding under any circumstances to unsolicited e-requests for your personal information or for money, and by taking extreme care when visiting websites to conduct transactions.

Tip:
If using a publicly shared computer terminal,
de-select "remember me,"
and remember to log-off properly.

Here are some other preventative measures when going out in public:

- Keep unnecessary credit cards at home.

- Be conscious and aware of your personal belongings at all times.

- Be familiar with your credit card billing cycles, so that should you ever miss a statement, you can call the credit card company to find out where it is. Identity thieves are notorious for changing victims' billing addresses. Whether on the Internet or offline, **constantly** check your credit card statements for any unauthorized charges. When entering sensitive data over the Internet, make sure the website is secure, generally denoted by https:// (versus "http"). Better yet, install firewall protection before making transactions online. As a rule of thumb, I do not under any circumstances type in my social security number over the Internet. Armed with personal information such as your social security number, date of birth, mother's maiden name, credit card number, the three- or four- digit security code on the front or back of your card, and PINs, hackers and identity thieves can apply for credit in your name, and rack up huge amounts of debt (which, of course, they have no intent of paying off for you).

- Institutions such as healthcare conglomerates and higher education institutions are eliminating the use of social security numbers as the primary source of identification, substituting a numerical sequence for one's SSN. Prudent move. What if a student were to lose his/her ID containing his/her SSN on campus grounds, and it fell into the wrong hands? I once attempted to purchase a pair of shoes, and forgot my department store credit card at home. The cashier insisted that I enter my social security number in the keypad in the absence of the charge card. I refused and walked away. A pair of shoes was not worth it for me, personally, to punch my social into an ATM keypad.

- Avoid using guessable passwords and if possible, use a combination of capital and lower case letters, along with numbers. Change passwords/PINs periodically. The challenge, of course is keeping up with not only all of the passwords, but also the changes.

In the unfortunate circumstance that your purse/wallet is lost or stolen along with your social security number, ATM debit card, or credit cards, the Federal Trade Commission advises that you *immediately* (emphasis added):

1) Call 911 and file a police report; you will need the report to prove that your identifying information was stolen;
2) Contact the three major credit agencies (Experian, Equifax, and TransUnion) to place a free 90-day "fraud alert" on your records;
3) Notify your banking institution(s) and credit card companies; and
4) Close the tampered or compromised accounts[73]

According to the New York State Attorney General's Office, if you report a credit or ATM debit card lost or stolen before a thief uses it, you cannot be held responsible for repayment of unauthorized charges. Federal law limits your liability for unauthorized charges to $50 so long as you report it missing within 48 business hours. Your liability increases to $500 if you report it within 60 days. The liability is unlimited if you do not report it after 60 days or at all.[74]

Timing is essential: the sooner your report the loss or theft, the sooner you stop an identity thief in his or her tracks, the sooner you prevent him or her from doing any further damage from what they may have already done, and the lesser your liability.

Beware of cybercrime in your quest for entrepreneurship
In your quest to earn extra income, I must caution you not to fall prey to Internet fraud or any home-based business scam, for that matter. According to *USA Today,* cybercrooks recruit unknowing, innocent job-seekers to reroute and traffic ill-gotten goods across U.S. borders. Why go through all of this? So as to make their own trail cold by inserting "mules" in their deceitful web of trafficking pirated goods on the international black market. They are brazen enough to solicit employees on legitimate job websites.[75]

If communication with your employer is solely Internet-based, and you can't see or talk to him or her, beware. You do not want to be a party in using innocent victims' stolen identity for illegal commerce.

Resources:
Federal Trade Commission
www.ftc.gov - 1(877) IDTHEFT / 438-4338

U.S. Department of Justice
www.usdoj.gov for tele-marketing-, Internet-, and mortgage fraud

Internet Fraud Complaint Center (IFCC), a partnership between the FBI and the National White Collar Crime Center: www.ifccfbi.gov

To report fraudulent use of a social security number, contact the
Social Security Administration at 1(800) 269-0271
- or -
U.S. Postal Service – Mail Fraud Division
Chief of Postal Inspector Service
475 L'Enfant Plaza, S.W.
Washington, D.C. 20260-2181
www.usps.gov/websites/depart/inspect

Privacy Rights Clearinghouse is a nonprofit consumer information and advocacy organization protecting consumer privacy and assisting victims of identity theft
www.privacyrights.org - (619) 298-3396
(In case you are curious, you're calling sunny San Diego, CA)
PRC provides 33 downloadable fact sheets, including what this book has already covered on junk mail, telemarketing, credit reports, identity theft, and debt collection; but also renters' privacy rights, online shopping tips, employee monitoring in the workplace,

background checks on volunteers, medical information privacy, etc.

FirstGov for Consumers – www.consumer.gov

New York State Attorney General's Customer Help Line:
www.oag.state.ny.us - 1(800) 771-7755 (within NYS)
For the Hearing Impaired: 1(800) 788-9898

Debt Collection: Your Rights In A Nutshell

In one community in central India, the city's revenue department sets up bands of drummers outside the homes of tax scofflaws. The drums beat incessantly day and night until the accounts are squared away. The result according to Reuters? One week's worth of drumming cleared away 18% of the backlog.[76] It hasn't gotten to that point here in the good ole' U.S. of A., but close to it.

First of all, a creditor is a party to whom you owe overdue money. A debt collector is authorized on behalf of the creditor to collect overdue monies. The main reason debt collectors are able to get away with so much harassment and abuse is that they know consumers, by and large, do not know their rights. So here are those rights in a nutshell.

Under the Fair Credit Reporting Act, while a creditor has a *right* to collect monies owed to them, a debt collector in the process of collecting the debt cannot:

- call before 8 a.m. and after 9 p.m.
- fail to properly identify him/herself
- harass or threaten you; or use profane or obscene language
- make any sort of misrepresentations or false statements regarding the debt[77]

If your employer disapproves of a debt collector calling you at your workplace, then you can state this in writing and request that they stop calling you at your job. You can write a cease and desist letter, and the debt collector(s) can no longer contact you. If they need to take action against you, then they must do so in writing.[78]

You must understand that debt collectors are trained to invoke *fear* and/or *anger*: *"If you don't pay up, then we will take such-and-such action."* Getting you upset or angry plays right into their strategy of keeping you from being able to think straight about your true options.

Let's say you are cooking dinner for your kids when they call. Somewhere in the conversation, they may accuse, *"If you were a good Mother, you would pay off your debts"*. Bam! They hit the emotional button. Try not to go off on them like Mike Tyson in the ring. Keep calm, cool, levelheaded, and business like, keeping the topic at hand to the debt only. Do not offer any more information than is necessary lest you give the debt collector extra ammunition to fire at you. And don't go into detail regarding your personal circumstances. Bear in mind that they hear down-and-out stories every single day.

Be aware that they are typing into the computer everything you agree to do. Therefore, request that any agreements made over the phone be put in writing and sent to you. That way, if Bob calls you later on about owing a different amount, you have your correspondence by Sue verifying what the terms of the agreement were. Even if you send in $2, send it via certified mail, return receipt requested. They have their paper trail; you had better keep yours as well.

Be mindful that once again, the collector has a right to collect their debt, and so establishing dialogue, communicating, and being proactive is helpful to the process. What do I mean by being proactive? Share your written plan with the creditors and **stick with it.** This provides a great sense of satisfaction on your part, as opposed to feelings associated with a situation spiraling out of control; it also demonstrates to your creditors that you are serious about paying them. Perhaps you cannot realistically pay everyone *everything*, but pay *something* to your creditors. Negotiate partial or delayed payments (preferably penalty-free), but pay *something.* Did you know that bill collectors should relay the terms of your payment offer to their client—the creditor—as opposed to rejecting your offer cold turkey?

Just because you cut up your credit cards does not mean you are absolved from repaying your debts. Avoid resorting to shady means of getting out of debt, throwing good money after bad. For instance, do not take out cash advances at an astronomical interest rate, and then use the money to go gambling or to play the lottery with. That is like dousing a fire with a gallon of gasoline, and tossing a grenade into it for special effects. Eventually, you'll find yourself unable to pay for any necessities at all.

Below is a case study of how one family devised a debt management strategy–negotiated what they could afford to pay to the debt collector–conveyed it in writing with return receipt to the debt collector—**and** stuck to the plan.

CASE STUDY: THE JEFFERSONS

Before we take a look at the following chart, there are a few things we need to know about the Jeffersons. They are a Manhattan couple, and although they make a decent income and look very much middle-class from all appearances, the Jeffersons are up to their eyeballs in debt. Don't be fooled by appearances; the Jeffersons are desperate. They are having difficulty meeting their debt obligations, so much so that debt collectors hound them around the clock. The difference between this chart and the Bakers' Debt Elimination chart in Chapter 8 is that the Jeffersons' minimum monthly credit card payments exceed the amount of their take-home pay. Unlike the Bakers, who have a debt elimination strategy, the Jefferson's overdue payments are causing them to be hounded by debt collectors because other necessary living expenses are constantly interfering with paying their creditors. The Jeffersons need a way to take control of their desperate financial state, managing their circumstances so as to keep their head above water rather than drowning helplessly.

1) The Jeffersons' combined net/take-home monthly pay is $3,585
2) The Jeffersons' budget their monthly necessities as follows:
   RENT: $1,800
   FOOD: $425
   - Groceries: $250
   - Dining Out (as much as the Jeffersons would like to cook at home, their busy lifestyle deems dining out as an occasional, unavoidable expense): $175

   TRANSPORTATION: $152
   - Mr. Jefferson's monthly unlimited subway/bus fare: $76
   - Mrs. Jefferson's monthly unlimited subway/bus fare: $76

   UTILITIES: $206
   - Electricity - $50
   - Telephone (monthly unlimited domestic service through land line) - $70
   - Cellular Phone (Shared Plan) - $62
   - Internet Service Provider (Mr. Jefferson's job necessitates having access to the Internet) - $24

   MISCELLANEOUS: $852

(This miscellaneous category comprises figures including medical expenses—such as doctor visit co-payments and pharmaceutical—their toddler's daycare expense, insurance premiums, and pocket money for miscellaneous expenses, all estimated at approximately $852.)

TOTAL MONTHLY EXPENSES: $3,435

AMOUNT AVAILABLE FOR CREDIT CARD PAYMENTS: $150

However, because their total credit card debt has reached $18,700, just paying the minimum monthly payments on that amount, exceeds what is possible with $150.

TOTAL MINIMUM MONTHLY CREDIT CARD PAYMENTS: $398

It doesn't look good for the Jeffersons, does it? If they did not have credit card debt, they would have a small monthly surplus. However, their reality is that they barely have $150 a month—barring any other expenses or emergency expenses that pop up—to allocate towards debt reduction. But wait. There is a way to, at the very least, keep the debt collectors at bay.

Let's take a look at the following chart.

1) The Jeffersons have $18,700 of combined credit card debt. (That $18,700 is repeated at the top of each individual credit card column.)
2) The monthly minimum payments on their credit card debt totals $398 per month.
3) They list the credit card debt and assign a percentage of total debt as follows:

	Visa	MasterCard*	Discover	Dept. Store*
Total Debt	$18,700	$18,700	$18,700	$18,700
Individual Credit Card Debt	$2,400	$7,000	$9,000	$300
Percentage of Total Debt	13%	37%	48%	2%
Minimum Monthly Payment	$28	$145	$180	$45
Amount Available to Pay Down Debt	$150	$150	$150	$150
Monthly Allocation Towards Debt	$19.50	$55.50	$72	$3

*In the Jefferson's particular case, the department store credit card has a higher interest rate than their MasterCard.

The Jeffersons take the $150 pot of money remaining after budgeting necessities and apply it toward the total debt in allocations that correspond to the percentages owed to each creditor. (That $150 pot of money is also repeated in each individual credit card column.) For example, MasterCard's $7,000 total outstanding balance represents 37% of their total debt, and so the Jeffersons' plan to pay MasterCard $55.50 (or 37% of their $150 available monthly amount to pay down debt) until the balance is paid off. The Jeffersons write a letter accompanied by a written plan to each creditor indicating how much of their debt they are *able* to pay for and on what timetable...and honor that commitment. This is not a perfect solution, but it is better than sinking towards financial doom. It will become clear to everyone involved that the Jeffersons are managing as best as they can, until some change in circumstances allows them to alter their strategy from Debt Management to that of Debt Elimination.

A reminder from Chapter 8's section on a Debt Elimination strategy: in addition to maintaining a steady income, the other necessary factor in order for this financial management strategy to work is to stop accumulating new debt, pure and simple. It is important to note that the preceeding strategy will not get the Jeffersons out of debt; paying less than the minimum required monthly payment will never get anyone out of debt. But what it does accomplish is the cultivation of effective habits of financial management in the Jeffersons' lifestyle, as well as creating a structure of repayment that will allow them to more easily switch to a debt elimination strategy when unexpected blessings and favorable changes in their circumstances finally allow them to achieve freedom from financial bondage.

There Is Money To Be Made In Old Debt

Did you know that the business of companies buying old debt is booming? The problem occurs if the old debt was indeed paid off, or arrangements were made between creditor and debtor to wipe the slate clean or to settle, and yet, the old debt note ends up being bought for pennies on the dollar years later. Unless records of these old records are accurately maintained, the new debt collector can come after you! This is another reason to keep certain old records until your credit reports accurately reflect old debt repayments. If at any point in the future you are contacted about an old debt that was indeed settled, you have *your* records to back you up. Under federal provisions, you cannot be sued for debt beyond the statute of limitations. In NY and NJ, the statute of limitations is generally six years, depending on whether the debt was oral, in writing, or a promissory note.[79]

If you are contacted about old debt, just be careful about how you reply to the caller. If you commit to any payment amount, the clock can start ticking on old debt all over again and the statute of limitations is out the window.[80]

Credit Counseling and Debt Consolidation

As with anything, examine the pros and cons, and research the track record of any credit counseling center or debt consolidation service (non-profits included) before proceeding; even then, exercise great caution in deciding whether or not to use these services. Credit counseling services must offer financial education along with their counseling services.[81] Debt consolidators negotiate with creditors on your behalf. Both can offer the convenience of consolidating one's debts to be repaid at a specified rate of interest. When the situation reaches critical mass, all the credit card company wants is its money. How will debt consolidation affect your credit score? Look at it this way: it is likely that your score is already compromised due to late, unpaid debt. Assess how taking this route may bode financially for you in the long-run if, for instance, you plan to go out and apply for more credit or buy a diamond ring or a yacht after entering the program. (To learn more about this very delicate subject matter, visit www.Answers.com, skip the sponsored links, and conduct a search for "credit counseling and debt consolidation".)

The New York State Attorney General's Office recommends that the credit- or debt counseling service be non-profit and licensed by the New York State Banking Department.[82] Request full disclosure regarding the service's fees. Beware of for-profit, unethical or illegal debt consolidators who take advantage of your situation by charging exhorbitant fees, or usury rates, for use of their services. I suggest that you take it a step further and look the organization up on Better Business Bureau's website (www.bbb.org). Finally, probe whether or not the service examines your entire financial picture, and not just the credit card debt snapshot.

Bankruptcy: Only As A Last Resort

If at all possible, declare bankruptcy only after you've tried all other options. Not only does bankruptcy protection remain on your credit for 7-10 years, but federal laws are also making it increasingly difficult for debtors to legally declare their inability to repay their debts (definition of bankruptcy). In fact, in an effort to crack down on the number of petitions filed, a mandatory provision made effective in October 2005 is that filers must attend a Department of Justice-approved credit counseling/debtor education program both before and after declaring bankruptcy.[83] Reach out for assistance by enlisting the help of a non-profit consumer credit counseling service (see resources below).

A primary difference between Chapter 7 liquidation and Chapter 13 repayment plan lay in *who* is creating a written, workable plan to pay off your creditors, presenting that plan before the court, and executing the plan for you (such a plan sounds awfully similar to a personalized budget to me, but who am I to say?). Anyway, both types of bankruptcy filings allow certain debts to be forgiven.

In a Chapter 7 bankruptcy filing, your assets are frozen and a court creates your repayment plan for non-dischargeable debts. Certain assets are exempt from seizure or liquidation so that you may live reasonably and modestly; others are not exempt. A trustee is an appointed attorney who can represent you. A Chapter 7 bankruptcy filing remains on your credit report for ten years.[84]

A Chapter 13 bankruptcy filing provides more flexibility by allowing you to create your own repayment plan for non-dischargeable debts, subject to the court accepting your plan. A court-appointed trustee monitors your situation and distributes your payments—made to the court—to your creditors. You are allowed to retain personal property. A Chapter 13 bankruptcy filing remains on your credit report for seven years.[85]

Interestingly enough, the most surprising thing about bankruptcy is that creditors **do not** wish to tie up time and resources dragging debtors into court. Declaring bankruptcy does no good in the long run if you do not analyze the circumstances or examine the habits that led you to that place to begin with. What steps are you going to take to end bad habits? Otherwise, if you are not careful, you may easily end up in the very same position even after declaring bankruptcy protection.

Resources:
You may read the entire Fair Debt Collection Practices Act for yourself by visiting: www.ftc.gov/os/statutes/fdcpajump.htm

National Consumer Law Center
(617) 542-8010/9595 (Publications Office)
www.consumerlaw.org or www.nclc.org
Call NCLC's publication department or review links to "What You Should Know About Debt Collection," "Tips on choosing a reputable credit counseling agency," "What you should know about debt collection," bankruptcy, student loans, protecting seniors, etc.

National Association of Consumer Advocates
(202) 452-1989 – www.naca.net

Consumer tips are also available on The New York State Attorney General's Office website (www.oag.state.ny.us); conduct a search for "Debt Collectors".

To locate your state's Attorney General:
National Association of Attorneys General
(202) 326-6000 – www.naag.org

The following are a few organizations approved as a bankruptcy counseling provider in order to provide personal financial management instruction for the U.S. Department of Justice:[86]

Association of Independent Consumer Credit Counseling Agencies (AICCCA)
www.aiccca.org - 1(800) 450-1794 for referrals nearest you

Association for Financial Counseling & Planning Education (AFCPE)
www.afcpe.org - 1(800) 388-2227 for referrals nearest you

National Foundation for Credit Counseling,
www.nfcc.org - 1(800) 388-2227 for referrals nearest you

Where else can I get help?
Consumer Credit Counseling Service:
www.cccsatl.org - 1(800) 251-2227

CHAPTER 12
BEYOND FOOD, SHELTER & CLOTHING: BEING GRATEFUL

"Praise the Lord, O my soul, and forget not all his benefits"
~ Psalm 103:2 ~

EVER SINCE I WAS A LITTLE GIRL, my family would bow heads and give thanks to God for the food on our table. I could be engaged in a pre-dinner squabble with one of my sisters. We'd pause, bow our heads to thank God for our food, and resume our picking with each other.

This carried with me into adulthood (the act of praying, not the strife, of course). Even though I had not witnessed it first hand, I knew that in other far-away parts of the world—and even in America for that matter—there were children starving. I saw them on milk cartons at the school cafeteria while I ate the homemade sandwich carefully packed by my Mom. I saw them on Sunday morning infomercials. Eyes sunken in. Stomachs swollen and protruding. Bones showing through their skin. Flies swarming around them. As a child growing up in a lower-middle income household, I knew I had a lot to be grateful for—food, shelter, clothing, a two-parent household, and the opportunity to get a good education.

Throughout most of my childhood, I grew up in a two-bedroom home in a residential neighborhood in my hometown of Anderson, Indiana. My parents made a conscientious decision to hold off on the 4-bedroom, 4 bath beauty that they eventually did acquire in order to put all five children through parochial school, at least through the 8th grade.

With five children, Mom put things on lay-a-way at KMart, a 'step up' for us from the clothes we found at the Goodwill. With the exception of my only brother and I—with me being the oldest—my sisters primarily wore hand-me-downs. The most important thing was that we were clean and presentable, and that our hair was combed neatly. I admit: it was hard getting on the morning school bus during those adolescent years seeing other kids wearing fashionable clothes, and enduring the taunts and jokes being hurled about me from the back of the bus: *"Yo, listen up! Her jeans so high..."* Chorus: *"How high are they?"* Reply: *"...So high, she look like Noah preparing for the flood!"*

Fast forward to twenty years later. Even though I'm in a position to buy nicer clothing than when I was growing up, the concept of delayed gratification has stayed with me. For instance, until I'm able to scrape together the money for the real Italian stuff, I try to look as cosmopolitan as I can in my black **pleather** jacket. You know—plastic leather from the 99-cent store![87] Seriously, though, being a Special Events professional has allowed me to partake of the best cuisine New York City has to offer, so at times I find myself in situations where there is an abundance of sweet and lucious fruits, *hors d'ouevres,* turkey and roast beef carving stations, beverages served in sparkling glasses, fine silverware and bone white china. I look around and see no one bowing their heads and giving thanks. A couple of nibbles here and there, and large portions of the food are discarded. This saddens me. Remember the scene in the movie *Castaway* when Tom Hanks' character had returned to the states after having been on a deserted island for years, catching fish and whatever else he managed to make edible? Everyone thought he had perished in a plane crash, and the company he had worked for prepared a lavish banquet upon his surprising return. He just stared at the buffet in utter disbelief.

There are people in other parts of the world for whom employment and career opportunities are phantom dreams. Just trying to eat or find clean water for that day, or preventing loved ones from being raped, beaten or killed is considered a good day.

But by the grace of God, there go I. (Come on, now, you intelligent city folk, we have to identify *who* we are giving thanks to. If we are rendering thanks, there has to be a recipient of our thanksgiving, right?) I just so happened to be born in one of the United States in America. I could have easily been born somewhere else if God had ordained it.

So let us look at our blessings beyond food and shelter. Did you or do you...

- have the opportunity to get a good education, or an education, period?
- use not just one, but various modes of transportation choices—car, bus, plane, or train?
- enjoy modern conveniences, such as a toaster? Can you press a button and your car window goes up or down? Do you have caller ID? A VCR? These things alone place you ahead of half the world's population.
- have the financial ability to go on a vacation?
- enjoy clean air, fresh water, green grass and trees? (No, you don't have to fly to New Zealand; we still have Central Park and the Brooklyn Botanic Garden)
- exercise the right to vote? Some countries do not allow women and certain citizens to vote.
- appreciate freedom of speech and religion? The same freedom that allows a Nazi skinhead or KKK member to express their beliefs allows me to practice Christianity. I recognize that my life is not threatened when I go to church

or utter the name of "Jesus" like Christian converts and missionaries in other countries are.
- have good health? Just ask a chronically ill person what being sick is truly like.

Being blessed with the aforementioned is not meant to detract from anyone's plight, but the bottom line is, someone in this country can be considered "poor" and still materially have more than a person in a developing country. I hate to say this, but we are not, by-and-large a grateful nation. Even the hungry in this country have places to go to for food (I know—I used to work for and volunteer in food pantries) and believe me, those bulging Thanksgiving and Christmas grocery bags rivalled anything in my refrigerator. And that's the way it should be. Those with more should share with those who have less.

"Our desire is not that others might be relieved while you are hard-pressed, but that there might be equality. At the present time your plenty will supply what they need, so that in turn their plenty will supply what you need. Then there will be equality..."
~ II Corinthians 8:13-14 ~

According to a *Time* Magazine cover article by Jeffrey Sachs, the World Bank defines three degrees of poverty: extreme or absolute, moderate, and relative. Extreme or absolute poverty, which exists in developing countries, is defined as earning an income of less than $1 per day. The most fundamental needs to human existence are virtually absent: food, clean water, shelter, clothing, sanitation, healthcare, and education. Such poverty is, according to the World Bank, "the poverty that kills." Moderate poverty is defined not too much differently than absolute poverty; earnings are $1-$2 per diem. Basic needs are *barely* met. Relative poverty is being poor, but not as poor in relation to someone experiencing extreme or moderate poverty.[88] I dare add that even the poorest of the poor in America can only be considered to be in relative poverty compared to people in countries like Haiti, Armenia, Honduras, or Zambia.

In the West, we all have much to be grateful for, whether poor, middle class, or wealthy. I know it is hard, because each level in our society tends to focus "up." The poor want to be able to go on a nice vacation. Middle-class citizens covet the salaries of the wealthy. Those fortunate to be born into wealth, want power to go along with it. I am no exception. Even though I am a homeowner, I curiously survey other people's home and interior decorations (Don't look at me that way—you know you do the same thing). All of us are mesmerized by the fame and fortune of celebrities and sports stars. It's human nature. But carefully watch some of those TV interviews. The constant pursuit of more, more, more doesn't fill the hole in our soul. No point in having a lavish house full of expensive toys while we are clinically depressed, our marriage is about to fall apart, or our children have run rampant and wild.

Even wise and wealthy old King Solomon concluded that in the end, the accumulation of wealth is meaningless because *"Those who love money will never have enough. How absurd to think that wealth brings true happiness! The more you have, the more people come to help you spend it. So what is the advantage of wealth—except perhaps to watch it run through your fingers!* (NLT)*"* (Ecclesiastes 5:10)

Whew! I wonder if King Solomon was inundated with credit card offers. Did he have to choose the next Apprentice to run his empire? Moving on...understand, it is not money in and of itself that is evil. The Bible distinguishes in I Timothy, chapter 6 verse 10 that the *love* of money is *a* root of all kinds of evil (emphasis added). The Good Book goes on to warn the rich not to be arrogant or to put their hope in wealth, which is uncertain, but to be rich in good deeds (I Timothy 6:17-18).

I say this to everyone, including the woman in the mirror: let's stop complaining and start being more content and grateful with what we have. To myself, I quote Proverbs 30:7-9:

> *"Oh God, I beg two favors from you before I die...give me neither poverty nor riches! Give me just enough to*

satisfy my needs. For if I grow rich, I may deny you and say, "Who is the Lord?" And if I am too poor, I may steal and thus insult God's holy name. (NLT)"

I cannot begin to describe how it so blesses my heart when my nieces sing, in a way that only a way precious little girls do, this simple prayer:

Our dear Father
Once again
Thank you for this blessing
Amen

~ If you are sponsoring or hosting an event, be sure to make pre-arrangements with a local food pantry to pick-up the food after the event is over. ~

~ Lenscrafters' Give the Gift of Sight charitable program accepts your old eyeglasses and cleans, repairs, classifies and delivers them to beneficiaries in developing countries who need eyeglasses. Lenscrafters issues a receipt for tax purposes. ~

Resources:
Red Cross - www.redcross.org -
1(800) HELP-NOW / 435-7669

The Salvation Army - www.salvationarmy.org -
1(800) SAL-ARMY / 725-2769

United Way - www.unitedway.org - 1(800) 892-2757
Habitat for Humanity - www.habitat.org -
1(800) HABITAT / 422-4828

www.chooseyourcharity.com - 1(800) 515-5012
(Includes a section on volunteerism)

Volunteer Match - www.volunteermatch.org - (415) 241-6868

www.give.org - (703) 276-0100
(The Better Business Bureau's Wise Giving Alliance to check out the record of a charity)

Do you want to make sure the money you're donating is actually going to charity and reaching the intended benefactors? Then visit www.charitywatch.org, sponsored by the American Institute of Philanthropy (773-529-2300)

Robin Hood Foundation - www.RobinHood.org,
(212) 227-6601
(100% of every donation is allocated toward programs combatting proverty in New York City)

If you are a City of New York employee, you can choose from over 950 non-profit organizations listed through the Combined Contributions Municipal Campaign, and donate through automatic payroll deductions. It is administered by the Department of Citywide Administrative Services (DCAS), and the United Way of New York City is the Campaign Manager. www.nyc.gov and visit the DCAS's homepage.

The Downtown Learning Center (adult literacy program) and King's Kids program at the Downtown Learning Center:
www.brooklyntabernacle.org/about/project.cfm

Is there a local cause or charity that may not be nationally known, but is near and dear to your heart?

If you are a Christian, remember to tithe 10% of your earnings to help your church to meet its mission and its expenses.

CHAPTER 13
GIVING, SHARING, BORROWING & LENDING

"Give, and it will be given to you. A good measure, pressed down, shaken together and running over, will be poured into your lap. For with the measure you use, it will be measured to you."
~ Luke 6:38 ~

Giving and Sharing: The Great Paradox

YOU MAY HAVE HEARD THAT YOUR NET WORTH is the difference between what a person owns and what they owe. Assets minus liabilities equals net worth. All of this is fine and dandy, but when it comes to giving and sharing, it doesn't always work out that nice and tidy because, you see, there are several ways to give. We can give...

- philanthropically, such as when a wealthy person underwrites a grant out of abundance to a charitable organization;
- sacrificially, when giving is actually inconvenient, constitutes self-denial, or creates a deficit on the part of the gift-giver;
- in-kind, aka non-monetarily, such as when we donate canned goods to a soup kitchen instead of money;

- talent-wise, such as painting the backdrop, gratis, for the school play; or
- of our time, such as taking the time to listen when a friend calls us.

Contrary to popular belief, you do not have to have Oprah's money to be a philanthropist. No one is asking you to give away 300 Pontiacs or trips to Disney World. You can make the world a better place by giving and sharing in accordance with what you have. It never ceases to amaze me that whether one subscribes to Hinduism, Buddhism, Islam, Judaism, Catholicism, or evangelical Christianity, a common tenet fundamental to these beliefs is "what goes around, comes around." If one is an athiest, the laws of science dictates that you reap what you sow. Plant bad seeds into the ground, the crops will falter. Plant good seeds into the ground, and they will yield a harvest.

Case-in-point: One day, the office supply store sent me a coupon for $10-worth of free copies at the office supply store as a result of the frequency points I accumulated. I knew I wouldn't need it, and wondered, *"Who can I pass this along to who might need it more than I and will actually use it?"* I called up a friend who's in the midst of a major project and offered to send the coupon to him. As we got to talking, he mentioned that he would be meeting with someone who is prominent in the field that I am in. In fact, the woman he was referring to was on my list to contact. Long story short, my friend would be meeting with the woman that week, and offered to hand my correspondence to her directly. After that conversation, I marveled, *"Gee, this valuable contact is about to be made just because I thought to give someone a coupon!"*

Let us examine the motivation for giving. We don't give to in order to get. We give (and do so cheerfully) because God is a giving God, and we are created in His image. Therefore, *not* to give is contrary to how the Creator designed us. If we give with the right motivation, we experience a particular kind of peace of mind and a whole lot of joy. Even if what is given is non-material, it's the gift that can keep on giving. Did you realize that this is what God intended for us?

Unfortunately, man's greed has gotten in the way of what is best, thus creating the inequality between the haves and the have-nots.

Of course, use wisdom when giving and sharing. Do not be "foolishly" generous, assuming the liability of others without making sure your own needs or those of whom you are charged with supporting are also taken care of. I once saw a young lady on television explaining how she consistently pays car fare for her boyfriend in Queens to visit her in Staten Island and yet, she is deeply in credit card debt. Not wise. If you are the beneficiary of someone's generosity, be a gracious recipient, and be careful not to take him or her for granted or take advantage of their kind-heartedness—they have feelings, too!

Conversely, how many times have we encountered a homeless person on the subway? *"What if he uses the money I give him or her to buy drugs?"* we hesitate. Instead, offer to buy him or her a cup of coffee or food. Ask God for discernment and if per chance you still made a bad judgment call, God sees all in the end.

"A generous man will himself be blessed,
for he shares his food with the poor."
~ Proverbs 22:9 ~

Borrowing and Lending: Don't End Up On Judge Judy

If you are lending, make it crystal clear that the money lent is indeed a loan. If you are borrowing, ask for a receipt when paying the money back, *especially* with cash. Do not under any circumstances put the lender in an awkward situation by having them to track you down, looking for you to pay back the loan. The borrower should be the one to take the initiative to seek out the lender to pay back a loan. You sought them out to borrow the money, did you not? And by all means, don't end up on Judge Judy just because the whole arrangement was "fuzzy," "ambiguous" or unclear as to whether the money in dispute was a gift or a loan.

"A righteous man...returns what he took in pledge for a loan"
~ Ezekiel 18:7 ~

Encore:
Giving doesn't always have to be monetary;
we can give of our time or our talents.
~ MBR ~

CHAPTER 14
HOW TO BUY A CAR WITHOUT GETTING RIPPED OFF

"Listen to advice and accept instruction,
and in the end you will be wise."
~ Proverbs 19:20 ~

WHEN JAMES AND I FINALLY CAME TO THE POINT OF PURCHASING OUR FIRST CAR, a friend offered to hook us up big time. We took a bus from the Port Authority to Rockland County, NY. Little did we know at the time that we ended up at the wrong dealership. We strolled in hand-in-hand, excited, because we had waited so long for this. Visions of the #2 train to soon become a distant memory. As we inquired about the whereabouts of our friend—an experienced salesperson who was going to meet us at the dealership—six salesmen circled us, each claiming to go "way back" with our friend. Each offering their services. Each salivating for a commission. My husband describes the eerie feeling of being the helpless carrion for a horde of vultures.

A vehicle is typically the second largest purchase in your life (next to a home), but the largest purchase that depreciates in value. Here are a few pointers to guide you through the process.

Before You Even Set Foot Inside The Dealership...
Determine your criteria for a car—decide on the desired **make** (e.g., Honda or Ford); **model** (Honda *Accord* or Ford *Taurus*); and **year** (1998 Honda Accord or 2007 Ford Taurus). An additional criterion to consider is the vehicle type, i.e., sedan or SUV, 2-door or 4-door, etc. A tip: If you are attracted to a particular type of vehicle, determine if the manufacturer produces a lesser expensive alternative, or if another manufacturer makes a model with similar features. For instance, did you know that Toyota is the maker of Lexus vehicles?[89] If you do not have "Lexus money," might you be willing to take a look at one of its lesser-expensive Toyota cousins?

Conduct your research on the following websites so you will know what the market bears for your desired set of wheels:

- Kelley Blue Book at www.kbb.com
- Edmunds at www.Edmunds.com
- National Association of Automobile Dealers (NADA) at www.nada.com
- Consumer Reports at www.ConsumerReports.org

Consider the pros and cons of the following:

- Purchasing new? *(You'll have a shiny new set of wheels with a clean record; vehicle begins to depreciate as soon as it is driven off of the lot, and takes a hefty depreciation during its first year life span)*
- Purchasing used? *(You do not pay depreciated value as if the car were new; get certified pre-owned vehicle to research record of reliability)*
- Buying vs. leasing? *(You own the vehicle, as opposed to the dealership; consider buying vehicles coming off of a lease)*
- Leasing vs. buying? *(Requires very little down payment up front; the vehicle is not truly owned by you; for all intents and purposes, leasing is equivalent to renting the vehicle; it is an expensive way to finance and operate a vehicle because you could end up being penalized for exceeding the prescribed mileage, or for excessive wear; an ideal*

circumstance for leasing is if you want or desire upgraded models for business purposes)

Consider the car dealership:

- What kind of reputation does it have?
- Decide on a brand-name dealership (e.g., Nissan); a non-brand name dealership (e.g., Mickey's Land of Automobiles); purchasing FSBO (for sale by owner); or purchasing from a leasing company.
- Don't limit your options to just one dealer; visit more than one dealership.

Once You've Decided On The Car Of Your Dreams...

In the case of a new car, determine the invoice price, which is the price the dealership paid the manufacturer for the car. Negotiate a price between the invoice price and sticker price aka MSRP, or Manufacturer's Suggested Retail Price. (Understand that the destination charge, or the amount that the manufacturer charges the dealer to deliver a new vehicle is non-negotiable). Include a reasonable profit for the dealer. [90]

In the case of a used vehicle, determine the blue book, or trade-in value of the car by visiting www.kbb.com. You can also research the history of the vehicle by visiting www.carfax.com. You must first have the car's VIN—Vehicle Identification Number in order to do so. Although James and I paid around $20 for our Carfax report, we later learned that we could have obtained it for free with serious intent to buy at our dealership. Oh, well. Next time we'll know.

Financing—How Am I Going To Pay For This?

- Determine how much your budget can afford on monthly car payments and correspond that to the price of a vehicle.
- Arrange your own separate financing through a credit union, bank, or some other financial institution, ideally before you even walk into the dealership.

If you opt for the dealer's financing options, keep in mind:

- 0% financing is advantageous if you have no money to make a down payment. Determine whether the terms of the loan are short, or if the note will be long-term; and what monthly payment amount this translates into. Compare the dealer's interest rate with that of other financing options (depending on your FICO score).
- Cash rebates: simply calculate the amount of the cash rebate vs. potential savings on the loan rate/monthly payments.
- Inquire about any special dealer incentives.
- Whether you finance through the auto dealer or an outside financial institution, make sure you have no loan pre-payment penalties.

Trade-ins:

Treat this as a separate transaction. Once you've negotiated the price of a vehicle, then and only then bring a used car to the table to be deducted from the agreed-upon price.

Day of purchase:

- The best deals are a) when interest rates are low; and
  b) during the last week or day of the month, and September of every year, because dealers are expecting new inventory and do not wish to pay interest to the bank on unsold vehicles.[91]
- Do not appear excited, even if you are.
- Keep it short and simple.
- Ask straightforward questions, as any educated consumer would.
- Bring a calculator. Not only will you need it, but in my opinion it signals to the salesperson that you're an astute client.
- Avoid any unnecessary add-ons—they drive up (pun intended) the price of the car.
- Do not sign any papers without reading them first; remember, a car is the second largest purchase next to

a home; it deserves the appropriate amount of care and attention.

- Fully understand the terms of the financing arrangement; you're going to have to live with the payments for the next 24-60 months.
- Lock-in your rate if you see your desired set of wheels one day and yet, you plan to pick-up the car later.
- Last but not least, put as much cash down as you can. **Do not, under any circumstances, arbitrarily pull this figure out of a hat…the unpaid balance rolls on over into the financing!** Case-in-point:

  —If a vehicle hypothetically costs $13,500. By the time the dealership adds on accessories, service fees, taxes, license and registration fees, inspection fees, etc. totaling $2,013.78, the price of the car is really $15,513.78.

  —Let's say you pay a mere $300, bringing the total down to $15,213.78

  —Assuming an APR of 4.5%, the dollar amount that financing the vehicle will cost you is $1,804.02 extra, on top of the car's purchase price.

  —The amount you will have paid after making all monthly payments as scheduled equals $17,017.80

  —This is $3,517.80 over the sticker price of $13,500! Granted, the typical fees were included, but you still pay almost two grand over the sticker price due to the minimal cash down payment.

Resource:

www.Consumer.gov (go to "Transportation," and then click on "Automobiles")

~ Credit Unions (in addition to AAA) often partner with a network of independent, participating dealers for no-hassle, no-haggle deals. ~

Encore from Chapter 10 on Homeownership:
Sitting in the car dealership's chair,
playing peek-a-boo with your credit information,
*is **not** the time to find out your own biz-ness.*
~ MBR ~

CHAPTER 15
ORGANIZING YOUR MOVE WITH EFFICIENCY

"The noble man makes noble plans, and by noble deeds he stands."
~ Isaiah 32:8 ~

NEW YORKERS ARE TRANSIENT. When my husband and I moved from Brooklyn to Manhattan, the process took a great deal of organization and financial prudence. Despite the fact that we only moved from one borough to another and that financial organization is my area of specialty, the move nonetheless took an unexpected bite out of our savings. On top of that, moving takes a tremendous amount of coordination. Here are some tips to consider as you plan *your* next move.

Compare Moving Company Prices

When we were newlyweds moving from our Park Slope studio apartment into a more spacious apartment in Crown Heights Brooklyn, all we did was dump what few possessions we had in boxes, call our friends, thank them with pizza and away we went! Six years later, after having established a home with real furniture and significant possessions, we needed professional assistance for the move from Crown Heights into our Manhattan apartment. Hence, we searched for a moving company.

We called three companies. One was a national franchise, the other was a local "mom and pop," and the third was a referral. The first two gave me a quote over the phone. The latter company took the time to visit and provide a free consultation. According to the friend that provided the referral, the third moving company was economical, provided courteous service in addition to complimentary boxes, and even called the next morning to welcome them into their new home! We were impressed. Combined with the friend's recommendation and the fact the third moving company quoted the lowest price, the deal was sealed for us.

Resources:
If you are moving in-state, research any complaints regarding your designated moving company at:
Better Business Bureau - www.bbb.com

NYS Consumer Protection Office
www.consumer.state.ny.us - 1(800) 697-1220

If you are moving interstate (across state lines), research possible complaints regarding your moving company at:
U.S. Department of Transportation Federal Motor Carrier Safety Administration (FMCSA)
www.fmcsa.dot.gov - 1(888) DOT-SAFT / 368-7238

The American Moving and Storage Association provides a moving referral service that lists moving companies that agree to abide by the association's rules, as well as an arbitration service.
www.moving.org - (703) 683-7410

Insist that a representative from the moving company come to your home in person to physically assess your belongings rather than merely giving you an estimate over the phone. Having a conversation over the phone about the weight of all of the items in your entire household is just not gonna cut it. Obtain an estimate in writing so that there are no major discrepancies on the day of the move. Press for "fixed-price" or "not-to-exceed price" bids from moving companies so you are not in for the shock of your life when the movers hand you the bill upon arrival at your destination. Don't put yourself in a situation where your moving company holds your goods hostage until you pay them what they want. In-person estimates also provide the moving company with the opportunity to scope out whether your residence is a walk-up or has a freight elevator, etc. Inquire about freebies, and obtain receipts for anything you pay for upfront. Make sure the terms of the contract are clear and adequately communicated between the estimator and the movers contracted for the big day.

Why do I say all of this? The Managing Supervisor for the moving company came to our home for the free consultation, provided the estimate, and gave us free boxes. I prepaid for the wardrobe boxes, but the movers were not aware of this, as it was not noted on the invoice. Had I not presented *my* receipt, it might have been a hassle, causing unnecessary stress on the day of the move.

Change-of-Address Notifications

Fill out the free change of address cards with your local post office or on the Internet at www.usps.com. Until the original parties' changes take effect, the post office will forward first class mail to your new address. The USPS recommends 30 days prior to your move date. I recommend filling out one card for each household member, including name variations, even if it takes a few more moments to fill out each card individually. My surname is formally "Brooks-Rolling," but some mail appears as "Rolling." For the sake of thoroughness, I filled out two cards for myself, and one for my husband. You do not want sensitive documents—such as credit card offers—ending up in the hands of the next occupant of your old dwelling place.

And if those new occupants are not as financially astute as you are at this point about calling the OPT-OUT # and shredding sensitive documents (Chapter 3), they just might toss it in the trash for an identity thief to get their hands on, and then you'd have to place a fraud alert on your records (Chapter 11)...so get the address change card filled out, OK?

Send out move notifications as soon as you know the new address. Unless circumstances dictate otherwise (e.g., your new dwelling is still occupied by someone else), I recommend sending out move notifications about 1½ to 2 months before the move in order to account for the time it takes for the database management personnel in various companies and organizations to update their records.

Decide the best methods for notifying family, friends, acquaintances, business associates and places from whom or from which you regularly receive mail. Should you use a post office move notification card? A stationery store's move notification card? E-Mail? Fax? A telephone call? A combination of some or all of these methods?

For instance, calling mail order companies might be a good idea because 1) it is efficient and cost-effective and 2) it generally takes anywhere from one to upwards of five or six more mailings before the updates take effect because magazine labels are often pre-printed several months in advance. The method all depends on what is the most effective communication method to the intended party without your having to make multiple efforts to change your address with each party.

In our case, we did not want certain parties in possession of our e-mail addresses; we were willing to spend only so much money on postage; and I, as the "Domestic CEO" of the household, had more time on my hands than my husband to make the notifications. Therefore, I e-mailed family and friends in addition to sending them cute little "I'm moving" cards from Hallmark; I also called the places that sent us mail regularly, such as our professional and alumni associations, and mailed notices to the remainder.

Also, take the opportunity to notify organizations from which you no longer wish to receive mail. And do not assume that the national headquarters of an association is going to alert its local counterpart.

Notify both. For instance, Meeting Professionals International, of which I am a member, has a local chapter, as well as a magazine for its members. I notified national headquarters, the local membership officer, and the magazine subscription office of our new address. Keep extra move notification cards on hand for old mail that trickles to your new address.

Alert your credit card companies. Unlike mail order companies, the changes take effect immediately. These companies do not want you to miss a payment deadline and of course, will be more than happy to make whatever accommodations necessary to expedite your paying on time. Call and check off the "change of address" box on your statement. Time it such that both you and your next credit card statement are physically at your new address at the same time.

Avoid overlaps in utilities. If you know when you are moving, turn on/off utilities at the proper time so as to avoid overlaps in billing. For instance, if you are moving on the 15th of the month, make sure the utilities (gas, heat, water, electricity, phone, cable) are turned off at your old residence on or around the day of the move, and that utilities are turned on at your new residence *by* the first night of occupancy. Make sure the bills are prorated; that is, you're paying only for the time up until you vacate the old residence and not until you occupy the new residence. The utility company will not automatically know this information unless you communicate it to them.

Address Change Notifications

There is an entire list of entities that you should remember to provide a change of address notification to directly, using one of the aforementioned means. In select cases, you may opt to forego providing a forwarding address, but let the entity know nonetheless that you will no longer be at the address (so that your private mail will not end up in the hands of the next tenant).

Remember to time sensitive address change notifications. You do not want your credit card bill preceding you at your new address, or your bank statements still arriving at your previous address. Here is a checklist you might refer to:

- Family and Relatives
- Friends and Neighbors
- Banks and Financial Institutions (i.e., Investments & Retirement)
- Credit Card Companies
- Credit Reporting Agencies
- Utility Companies (i.e., gas, electric)
- Phone company, Cell phone company
- Government Agencies (i.e., DMV, Voters Bureau, Veterans Administration)
- Place of Worship
- Gym & recreational franchises
- Daycare providers
- Educational Institutions (i.e., Alma Mater)
- Professional Associations
- Human Resources/ Personnel/ Benefits Administrator
- Healthcare agencies
- Business Associates/Clients
- Professional Service providers (Doctor, Lawyer, Insurance Agent)
- Vendors (i.e., Salon)
- Magazines & Subscription offices
- Mail Order Catalogs
- Frequency Rewards Partners
- Airlines, Hotels and Car Rental

Watch Your Budget

Beware. Extraneous expenses can easily creep up on you. To help control your budget, take inventory of all of your possessions and calculate the number of boxes you will need, as well as the various types of boxes. I was amazed to find that U-Haul sold boxes specially made for TV/DVD/VCR, microwave, wardrobe, kitchen utensils, glasses, etc. Don't forget packing supplies, such as duct tape, rolls of bubble wrap and rope. If the moving company provides complimentary supplies, take advantage!

Packing and Labeling

Make signs bearing the name to the rooms of your new residence in big, bold readable letters (typing the signs on a computer is more preferable, if you can do so). Proceed to make several copies of each sign to tape to the boxes. You can even color-code them if you like (i.e., "Bathroom" signs are all yellow). As you are packing, write the contents of the box on each sign. For instance, the sign may read "Kitchen". Write "pots and pans" on one sign. Write "utensils" on another Kitchen sign, "glasses, cups and mugs" on another, and so on and so forth. That way, the movers can place the box into the kitchen, but you know which box contains pots and pans as you unpack *several* kitchen boxes.

Reserve one set of signs you have made to affix to the doors of each room in your new residence as a guide map for the moving crew. For instance, tape the "Bedroom #2" to...guess which door? This is so you will not have to move boxes around from room to room once you get settled in; that is what you are paying the movers to do! Label boxes with delicate items with the caution "Fragile—handle with care."

Finally, as you unplug all of the plugs, extension cords, adaptors and modems, write where the items belong to on masking tape with a black marker; wrap tape around the cord. For instance, as you unplug the VCR, label the cord "VCR," and wrap the tape around the cord. Designate a box specifically for "electronics". When we last moved, knowing to which appliance each of the cords, plugs, adaptors and modems belonged was a pure timesaver, and kept me sane.

Resource:
To locate a Professional Organizer who can assist in packing your apartment for a move, contact The National Association of Professional Organizers at
www.napo.net - **(847) 375-4746 (national headquarters)**
www.napo-ny.net - **(212) 439-1088 (within NYC)**

What To Do With Throwaways

Moving is an excellent time to shred papers and to give items away. There are at least four ways to go about this. You can:

1) Throw out pure junk (clearing the clutter away).
2) Give away clothes to the Salvation Army or the Goodwill (tax-deductible).

3) Give away nice items to family and friends (promotes goodwill).
4) Sell to consignment shops (extra cash in the pocket).

Hey, you can also have a yard sale. The thing about throwaways is that one person's junk is another's treasure. I remember giving expensive candle votives that my husband thought were ugly to a family member who happened to be a "candle person." She loved them!

What To Keep With You

Keep sensitive documents such as social security numbers, credit cards, checkbooks, passports, pertinent financial and legal info, insurance policies and wills within your possession at all times. My husband (the one who hated the candle votives) went so far as to insist that the computer hard drive travel with us during our move. Make plans for these items to travel with you and you alone to your new destination.

On The Big "Day Of"

Make provision to eat breakfast. Even if other people are moving you, it still takes a lot of energy on your part, so be sure to eat nutritiously. Have a suitcase already packed with personal effects, night clothes, and a change of clothes so that once the day's moving is over, you can get a good night's sleep without fumbling for toiletries such as toothpaste.

Storage Considerations

If you absolutely must go the storage route, evaluate affordability, cleanliness and accessibility. Storage was once a foregone conclusion for us, as our new Manhattan apartment was smaller than our previous Brooklyn apartment. We did not own a car at the time, so storage locations outside the borough of Manhattan were out. When I visited one storage facility with the lowest price, it looked downright scary. It was located in an old warehouse and was dark, dank and dingy—I thought a bat would fly at my throat at any minute!

We ultimately chose a well-lit facility with attentive customer service on Manhattan's Upper West Side, and the price fit our budget. Avoid basement storage units, where vermin and mice like to hang out, and look for signs of leakage or damp smells in your unit before you lock those precious belongings behind closed doors. You don't want any nasty surprises! Assess accessibility times—the best prices in town won't help if you cannot gain access to your items at times most convenient to your schedule.

Once You Arrive...

If you are moving to a new locale as a direct result of a job offer or relocation, be sure to keep all receipts for either reimbursement or tax purposes. Finally, have someone to help you with unpacking—the sight of all of those unopened boxes can be overwhelming. But if everything is labeled, you can put everything in its proper place.

As you can see, moving is not a task to be left for the last minute. It is a process. The steps outlined above can help to eliminate stress. Mazeltov, and happy moving!

2 more moving tips by MBR:
~ If you have the opportunity, sweep and
mop prior to moving furniture in.
It's hard to mop floors once the furniture has
been moved into your new residence. ~

~ When getting settled in, it is easy to become overwhelmed.
Focus on first things first: Bathroom-Kitchen-Bedroom.
Resist the urge to buy new furniture and appliances
immediately. Get by with what you already have. ~

CHAPTER 16
EARNING YOUR KEEP IN THE CITY: THE ENTREPRENEURIAL MINDSET & SPIRIT

"If a man will not work, he shall not eat."
~ 2 Thessalonians 3:10b ~

I AM NOT YET A MOMMY MYSELF, but you may have noticed in the Acknowledgments of this book, I dedicate this book to Moms. Many of my friends and family members are either single or married stay-at-home Moms. Regardless of marital status, most women find themselves in a quandry: to work in order to support their household and place their child in someone else's care, or to stay at home to invest in their children's lives while sacrificing much-needed income. Recognizing that you cannot save and organize money until you have first earned it, I am including the next three bonus chapters on entrepreneurship.

My Inspiration

In their book, *Rich Dad's Cashflow Quadrant,* Robert Kiyosaki and Sharon Lechter's sequel to the bestselling *Rich Dad, Poor Dad,* the authors advocate moving away from being an Employee or even being Self-Employed; rather, they explore the benefits of becoming a Business Owner and an Investor.[92] As I interpret it, the difference between being self-employed and being a business owner is that in the latter case, a system is in place and employees are running the business for you. In the former case, all functions depend on you; if you're not there, it doesn't get done.

These books provided the initial inspiration to my venturing into consulting and eventually, toward becoming an entrepreneur. Something resonated within me and my heart began to beat with excitement with the turning of each page, amidst the car sirens outside of our apartment. *'Give me a "B" for business! Give me an "I" for investor! Give me an "E" for entrepreneur! Rah! Rah! Rah! Go Team!*

Scratchin', Scrapin', Scrimpin', and Survivin'

I personally know more men and women who are *unhappy* in their jobs than I know who are happy and content in their professions. Those who are a good fit for their company or organization and are comfortable with their level of compensation, often exchange that good salary for a piece of their soul because they are not able to spend enough time with their families. Or they:

- are working to provide bread and butter on the table, but at jobs they were not cut out to do (I'll address this issue later);
- have a job that pays the bills, but they are not challenged mentally or creatively—the brain cells are just kinda' sittin' thar, takin' up space;
- expend a tremendous amount of emotional energy navigating office politics;
- face institutionalized racism or sexism everyday on the job;
- commute long, draining periods of time in and out of the city in order to enjoy suburban living;
- dodge threats of being laid off, outsourced or downsized; or, or, or...

I personally think New Yorkers and other urbanites would make worthy *"Survivor"* contestants.

No job is totally secure nowadays. It didn't matter that my federal government colleagues had seniority. When Washington, D.C. headquarters decided to close shop, some were a month away from their pension, and did not receive it (see Chapter 20 "Our Tale"). Which, by the way, is a cautionary tale for not making your job your all. Your entire existence. Your reason for breathing. Spend—no, *make* time now for your family and friends. Curtail your spending and consumption, and start saving money you earn from your job, so you can spend your time doing some of the things more important than earning money.

Resource: Could you use a fresh, new perspective after having been laid off? Then read *Downsized Up: Trusting God Through Your Layoff* by Lillie J. Cameron (2003). Pleasant Word.

The Case for Entrepreneurship While You Keep Your Day Job
One reason: unfortunately, the society in which we live too often places negative emphases on the very same diversity of thought, ideas, and experiences that makes innovation possible. Being an entrepreneur transcends whether you're polka dot, purple, or orange—so long as your product or service is *good* and in demand. Clients either salivate for your baked goods, or they don't; it doesn't matter what you look like. Patrons will either commission you to do a painting, or they won't; it doesn't matter what accent you talk with. Customers are either in the market for the cactus you sell, or they're not; it doesn't matter that your cactus "greenhouse" currently occupies your dining room in the projects. Your livelihood is not dependent upon whether or not the supervisor woke up on the wrong side of the bed that morning or worse yet, "has it out for you." All that matters is that you are able to meet or create a demand for quality goods and services, and do so at an affordable price. The customers will find you.

You might do well to adopt the mindset Stephen M. Pollan and Mark Levine explain in their book, *Live Rich* (also the authors of *Die Broke*)—that of a mercenary. They encourage workers to adopt a mercenary attitude on their current jobs: continue doing your best on your job (arrive on time, produce quality work, watch out for those office politics!), but adopt a mentality that the job is not the end-all, be-all for the duration of your professional life. After leaving that 9-5 job, go home and work out a business plan that encompasses your entrepreneurial dream.[93]

The reason I speak of a "mindset" is because, as Robert Kiyosaki and Sharon Lechter observe in *Rich Dad, Poor Dad,* we have been programmed to go to college and get a 9-5 job.[94] In other words, we have been programmed to fit into the machine, not to invent a new machine.

Even billionaire Donald Trump was intrigued by the notion of college-educated vs. non-college educated; so much so that "The Donald" divided the two competing teams accordingly in season three of *The Apprentice.* So here is my weigh-in: While I advocate entrepreneurship, I also believe that having a college education in our society is essential. Why? Speaking from personal experience, my level of education automatically makes me eligible to apply for certain higher salaried positions. Unless you have a rich uncle, or were anomalously groomed for entrepreneurship, you still need to be able to obtain the money from *somewhere* in order to begin funding your dreams.

I grew up in a small factory/residential town in Indiana. Back in the day, folks who graduated from high school could immediately make upwards of $14-$20 per hour (pretty good for the '60s and 70's huh?) assembling auto parts for Guide Lamp and Delco Remy, divisions of General Motors at the time. Throughout the years, these factory jobs became more and more scarce. As consumers began buying more and more foreign-made vehicles, the factory workers' choice was to either move to Detroit or Flint, Michigan or to get laid-off.[95] With no advanced education to fall back on, the person who was blue collar and laid-off meets the person who was white collar and downsized in the shrinking corridors of possibility. The difference in the color of the collar no longer mattered. The concept is the same: some of those folks never rebounded because they were dependent on one company and had all of their eggs in one basket. Unfortunately, *if* coupled with the mismanagement of personal finances *while* employed, it can spell financial hardship or disaster. The point is to prevent yourself from being dependent on one stream of income. Heaven forbid, if some sudden, unforeseen circumstance were to affect your primary bread and butter, is it possible to position yourself to tap into other revenue sources?

We've already taken a peek in Chapter 5 at how millionaires profiled in Dr. Stanley and Dr. Danko's bestselling book, *The Millionaire Next Door,* described themselves. Three out of four are self-employed professionals or entrepreneurs.[96] Further, they describe their businesses as down-right dull (e.g., pest controllers, stamp dealers, rice farmers.)[97] But four out of five are also college-educated, and invest heavily in their offsprings' education.[98]

My late father was a mortician, and my mother, a cosmetologist and a beautician who gave up her beauty shop to become a stay-at-home Mom after the second child was born. Being a funeral director is not for everyone, to say the least, but my father was very good at what he did. He came from a lineage of funeral directors, and he took great pride in servicing the community in this manner for 38 years. It was often said of my father *"When Mr. Brooks made you up, you looked better dead than when you were alive! Yessiree."* Both my mother and my father—who made sure we were college-educated—encouraged my siblings and I that "regardless of how many degrees you have, consider using your skills and training as a vehicle to own your own business, and you'll never go hungry." It's like integrating the philosophies from the classic thinkers Booker T. Washington and W.E.B. Du Bois; one advocating the benefits of a learned vocation, the latter advocating the special responsibilities that come with a higher education. It doesn't hurt to have both philosophies in your hip pockets, as long as you don't ignore all of the potential possibilities, rewards…and, yes, risks…of entrepreneurship.

"Be very careful, then, how you live...making the most of every opportunity..."
~ Ephesians 5:16a ~

Think Outside Of The Box

Have you ever thought about earning residual or passive income transitioning into non-traditional niche markets that you've scarcely heard of or considered? If mortuary science is not your cup of tea—I totally understand. But I was flipping through a business magazine one day, and spotted an ad for a training manual on how to own and operate a freight brokerage business. How about owning a billboard and renting advertising space? Storage facilities? Parking lots? A laundromat? How about ice, anyone? The owner of the ice-making company down the street from the house I grew up in made a lot of money off of my family, especially during summer barbeques!

Of course, no parent indoctrinates his or her child to think in this manner. When a child is asked, *"What do you want to be when you grow up, little Jimmy? A Doctor? A Lawyer? President of the United States of America?"* What do you think the reaction would be to: *"I want to own and operate bubble gum machines all over the nation, Mommy and Daddy!"*

I have yet to meet a small business owner or consultant who—barring normal start-up challenges—expresses dissatisfaction with what they do, unless he or she missed his or her calling to begin with. I once met a garage-door opener salesman (no disrespect, but I'm not quite sure what to call him). Though he isn't occupying the corner office suite on the 60th floor of a high-rise Manhattan office building, he seems perfectly satisfied installing garage door openers for homeowners. And few other people were doing it.

Does this mean I am against a "9-5"? Of course not! But do I advocate having a little sumpthin' sumpthin' on the side? You bet. Take the cases of two acquaintances who have kept their day jobs and operate a hobby-turned-into-a-catering/restaurant business on the side. The one from "da Bronx" indicated to me that she is waiting for the business to grow and expand to the point where she can help sustain her family's current standard of living sans the day job (which, by the way, happens to be in training and management information systems at a huge New York City bank). God forbid, in these days of downsizing, lay-offs and uncertainty, the moment either of them receives a pink slip...they can slip right on into their own business full-time! Until such time, they have more than one source of income.

"Work hard and cheerfully at whatever you do..."
~ Colossians 3:23a (NLT) ~

Find Your Niche

It may take awhile for you to identify your niche, as it did for me; sometimes the clues have been right before you all along. A key question is: what are you naturally inclined to do? Dan Poynter is an expert on self-publishing who just so happens to be a feline lover. In addition to authoring—no—publishing books (Hello!) and speaking around the country on self-publishing, he attends—get this: Cat Conventions. He gets paid for speaking at those feline conventions. That's who he is...he loves cats. And that's not all. Mr. Poynter is a skydiver. Attorneys call on him from time to time to serve as an expert witness on hanggliding and parachuting accident cases.[99] If you don't believe me, to see for yourself, visit his website at www.ParaPublishing.com.

- Are you an Auto Mechanic who knows how to design websites?
- Are you a Teacher or a Salesperson who loves gardening?
- Are you a Librarian who loves to travel? How about writing a travel guide and marketing it to visitor and convention bureaus?
- Are you a Cook who is talented to make films?
- Are you an Event Planner whose passion is teaching Financial Literacy to others?

Then discern, narrow and excel at your niche...find a way to make money at it...and the money will come. What I mean by narrowing is to define your particular segment within a broad field. The field of medicine, for instance, encompasses: pediatrics, surgery, ER, nursing, radiology, administration, etc. Don't make money the object. The object is to discover what you would do even if you were not paid for it, and then turn around and find a way to get paid for it. Got it?

Resource: For a theological perspective on earning a living, read *Your Work Matters To God* by Doug Sherman and William Hendricks (1987). NavPress.

You may have to brush up on your marketable skills. Despite my advanced degree and credentials, I attended a "Writing, Publishing and Promoting Your Book" seminar at The Learning Annex (taught by Dan Poynter, incidentally) to learn about this area.

Entrepreneurs are visionaries and risk-takers. They have a vision and are driven to see it to fruition. Entrepreneurs also march to a different drumbeat. They just do not necessarily want to be 47 years of age, and in a position where the boss-man is watching his Swiss watch, arms crisscrossed, tapping his fingers and toes, bushy eyebrows furrowed, to inspect whether or not s/he is in his/her cubicle at zero nine hundred hours.

Regardless of how talented you are, think like a businessperson. There are creative folks who do not necessarily know how to run a business, and businesspeople who aren't creative enough to market their goods or services. Business savvy and creativity do not have to be diametrically opposed. Learn how to harness, focus, and convert your creativity into business sense. You either have to know how to do both yourself or hire someone who does. If/when you hire employees, personnel issues bring to bear a whole new dimension. Your training, experience and certification won't amount to a hill of beans if your business is not run in an organized, fiscally sound fashion, or if your product or service isn't marketed effectively.

While You're Still Holding Down The Day Job

If you have a full-time job, do not insulate yourself—establish and cultivate alliances outside of the walls of your company or organization! By the way, is there a skill you are adept at or are currently learning that can be applied towards entrepreneurial pursuits? Being a Special Events Planner (see "Our Story" in Chapter 20) has taught me sensitivity to timelines; running events has taught me the nuances of daily organization. To this day, being organized and meeting deadlines is essential to running my business.

Transfer the "40 ways to save money" tactics from your personal life into your business practice. Do not allow your business to falter due to improper financial management and disorganization. *"I don't have enough energy at the end of a long, hard day to do all of this, especially with young'uns crawling all over me,"* you stretch and yawn. One of the first rules of professional organizing is to take a large task and parcel it down into smaller tasks. Conscientiously set aside after-work or weekend time to setting up your small business. Weekend #1: Fill out the papers for your business name. That's it. You don't want to become overwhelmed. Next Wednesday after work: apply for Tax ID #. Next Saturday: conduct domain name search for your website. In two months: develop marketing flyers to post and distribute; and so on and so forth. Progress builds momentum, as well as confidence and encouragement.

Pssst: Just as we find the money to spend on those things in life we *r-e-a-l-l-y* want to buy; we also make time for activities we *t-r-u-l-y* want to devote time to.

~ *"Dream small dreams. If you make them*
too big, you get overwhelmed and
you don't do anything. If you make small
goals and accomplish them,
it gives you the confidence to go on to higher goals." ~
John H. Johnson, Founder & Publisher
Johnson Publishing Company
Ebony and *Jet* magazines

Finally, do not be surprised if you find yourself devoting more and more of your time to entrepreneurial pursuits because your dream is taking off like an airplane off of the tarmac; consequently, you will have to manage your time more and more effectively (see Chapter 18 for more tips on running a business that you will not necessarily learn in school).

"To do a common thing, uncommonly well, brings success."
~ Founding principle of Heinz Ketchup,
established in 1869 by Henry John Heinz ~

Resources:

The 1995 What Color is Your Parachute? A Practical Manual for Job-Hunters and Career-Changers, Richard Nelson Bolles, Ten Speed Press, 1995

There are a number of personality tests used to help assess skills and abilities, along with personality type. The Myers–Briggs Inventory is one of them.

U.S. Small Business Administration
www.SBA.gov - 1(800) U-ASK-SBA / 827-5722

Example SBA publications that you can download from the website library:

- *Guia Para Obtener Prestamos*
- Pricing your products and services profitably
- Problems in managing a family-owned business
- How to start a quality child care business
- Trademarks and business goodwill
- Managing employee benefits

Kudos to the San Francisco Small Business Development Center for providing free, quarterly business classes (e.g., marketing) specifically tailored for artists.

SCORE®, Service Corps of Retired Executives
www.score.org - 1(800) 634-0245
(A resource partner with SBA; offers free counseling advice to small businesses)

New York City Department of Small Business Services
www.nyc.gov "Small Business Services"
311 (in NYC) or (212) NEW-YORK / 639-9675

Visit www.nylovesbiz.com, and click link to "small and growing businesses, where you will find New York State's Division of Minority- and Women-owned Business Development (MWBD) or call the Empire State Development at 1(800) STATE-NY / 782-8369

Entrepreneur Magazine's Bookstore sells "how to start" manuals on all kinds of businesses ranging from: how to start a business on eBay; hair salon & day spa; gift basket business; coin-operated laundry; wedding consultant; cleaning service, staffing service, car wash, and many more! Each manual costs $69 plus shipping and handling.

Visit www.smallbizbooks.com to see view a complete listing and tables of content. Call 1(800) 421-2300 to order. Small Biz Books even offers state-specific business start-up guides including—well what do you know—New York and New Jersey for only $10 + S&H.

CHAPTER 17
STEPS TO STARTING A SMALL BUSINESS

"His master replied, 'Well done, good and faithful servant! You have been faithful with a few things; I will put you in charge of many things.'
~ Matthew 25:21 ~

MY HOME OFFICE IS THE "NERVE CENTER" of our home. It is where calls are made, bills are paid, and commerce takes place. The purpose of this chapter is to provide the building blocks you must consider as you start a small business—you are urged to further research the components necessary to develop your business for optimal efficiency. Let's start with the basics, shall we? Here are items you'll need off the bat:

- a designated space
- adequate lighting, heating in the winter, and air conditioning in the summer (I learned this the hard way as perspiration interfered with my concentration, and so I had to get ventilation while in the midst of inspiration while writing this book)
- a desk and an ergonomic chair

- a desktop or laptop computer; (basic software: word processing, spreadsheet capabilities, financial software) *PC or Apple Mac? I'm not touching that debate!*
- a fax machine, scanning and copying capabilities, whether a stand-alone, multi-functional device or software on your computer
- floppy or zip disks, or flash drive; CD-R or CD-RW compact disks
- a printer, copy paper, ink cartridges, mouse, mouse pad
- an ISP (Internet Service Provider) and e-mail address(es)
- a calendar, address book (whether in hard or soft form)
- a phone with answering machine or voice mail capability and quite possibly, call waiting, caller ID and three-way calling (personally, I multi-task by using speakerphone if being placed on hold; however, when my party answers, I either switch off of the speaker or ask them if they are comfortable conversing with me over the speaker, assuring the caller that it's just me and him/her so s/he will not feel self-conscious about privacy)
- pens, pencils, markers, highlighters, paper clips, stapler, tape, scissors, a letter-opener, ruler
- a calculator
- a wastepaper basket, shredder
- envelopes, business cards, stationery
- filing cabinet or mobile file caddy/bin; file folders
- bookcase(s) for books, magazines, and periodicals; crates may be used as an inexpensive, alternative substitute
- Optional: artwork. I bought a pastel-colored, attractive-looking abstract print for $15 years ago from KMart to hang up in my home office, although my husband, who is a visual artist, reminds me that I can hang up his work for *free*
- access to a nearby post office or alternative means of sending and receiving your mailings (e.g., courier, private mailbox)

This is by no means an exhaustive list but of course, will help get you started until you are financially ready for growth and expansion components, such as a website.

Listen up: all of this costs money, honey, and so that is all the more reason to save money, particularly if you already have a job. Surplus income can be allocated towards small business start-up costs.

~ A couple of home office hints: set your default printer on "Draft" mode as opposed to "Normal" or "Best" mode. It lengthens the life of the ink cartridge. Also, print non-important materials on scrap paper, and save the clean paper for final review and presentation. But remember to remove all staples first! ~

Resources:
New York Ink Jet – www.NewYorkInkJet.com - 1(800) 699-6292
Sells Toner/Ink Cartridges (both originals and remanufactured), office supplies and office furniture

Office Depot, Office Max and Staples are the major office supply stores in the city. They all have some type of frequency rewards program. Be sure to provide your rewards number when making a purchase. Contact the following for details regarding shipping and handling policies, and to find the location nearest you:

www.officedepot.com, 1(800) Go-Depot / 463-3768

www.officemax.com, 1(800) 283-7674

www.staples.com, 1(800) 333-3330

Devise A Business Plan
A business plan is the blueprint for your business, and is also a document that a lending institution will require you to submit for review for consideration to underwrite a loan. A business plan includes many of the aspects outlined below. The key components of a sound business plan are: Introduction, Executive Summary, Mission Statement, Company Description, Description of the Product(s) and/or Service(s) offered, Marketing Plan, and Financial Analysis.[100]

Online resources that can assist you in developing a business plan include: www.Allbusiness.com and www.BPlans.com

Your Creative Niche...What Is It That You Are Providing?
Decide on the type of business: are you providing a **product** or **service?** Is there an existing demand for the product or service, or will you have to work to create that demand?

What Is The Name Of Your Business Going To Be?
Is the name you are considering already in use by another entity? Where do you have to formally file the name? With your municipality? Your county? Your state?

Tax/Legal Structure...How Is Your Business Going To Be Set Up?
Determine your business structure; options include Sole Proprietorship, Partnership, Corporation, Sub-Chapter S Corporation and Limited Liability Company, or LLC. Each structure employs its own set of tax and legal implications. One place where definitions of these structures may be found is...

www.nolo.com, or call 1(800) 728-3555 for business descriptions; proceed to consult with your attorney *and* accountant for the structure that is best suitable for your situation.

Don't forget to obtain your EIN, or Employer Identification Number from the IRS (www.IRS.gov). A bank will require an EIN in order to establish a business account for you.

Pssst...from consumer-to-consumer, when contacting the IRS, specificy whether your routine inquiry is individual or business-related, so that you may be connected to the appropriate representative.

Brand...What Kind of Image Do You Wish to Project?
Determine how you wish for your business to appear on your business cards, website, press kit, promotional materials, voice mail, etc.

Marketing & Promotion...How Will They Know You Exist?
How are you going to spread the word as to what goods and services your business provides? Who is your **target market?** How are you going to promote your business and attract the intended audience? Are you going to use free publicity and/or paid advertising? Here are the six "Ps" of Marketing 101: Product, People, Place, Price, Plan, and Promotion.

Referral Network...Where Are You Going To Go To Attract Clients?
Establish connections and develop relationships within and outside of your industry, as well as through business-oriented affiliations. *Organize* your internal and external contacts; it's often not who you know, it's who *they* know...

- past &/or current clients
- past &/or current co-workers
- professional associations
  - in your area of expertise
  - outside of your area of expertise
- alumni groups
- friendly competitors
- family & friends
  - peers & friends of friends
  - neighbors
- members of your church, synagogue or place of worship
- local vendors
- *your* personal service providers (i.e., hairdresser, accountant, dry cleaners)
- travel encounters
- peer networking at conferences & workshops
- acquaintances at community & civic groups
- other small business-owners like yourself
- journal ads in non-profit publications you support
- local chamber of commerce & business-oriented organizations
- hobby buddies
- acquaintances made at sporting and entertainment events

Administrative/Operations...How Will You Go About "Takin' Care of Business?"

How is the infrastructure of your business going to be set up? Determine how day-to-day operations (i.e., phone system, fax, cell, e-mail, snail mail) will be most efficiently handled (particularly, initially as a one-person operation).

Business Meetings...How Will You and Your Clients Connect?

Will clients come to you, or you to them? Personally, I hold my complimentary Client Consultation meetings at a restaurant and pay the tab. I conduct subsequent client meetings on their turf, but ninety percent of my clients' work is done in my home office.

Billing...What Are You Going To Charge For Your Product and/or Service?

What is the current market for your product or services? How are you going to charge—Flat fee? Hourly? Per Diem? Commission? A combination? What are acceptable methods of payment—Cash? Check? Credit card? Establishing a store account? How are you going to handle overdue payments?

Accounting System...How Will You Keep Track of Revenues and Expenses?

Keep personal and business financial records separate. Devise an orderly system for tracking revenues and expenditures. I highly recommend Quicken®, Quickbooks®, or Microsoft® Money (see Chapter 3). Remember that a portion of your home office expenses can be tax-deductible if the space is used solely for business purposes. Check with your Certified Public Accountant for details on this and on quarterly tax filing.

Resource to order FREE tax guides for your small business: www.irs.ustreas.gov, or 1(800) TAX-FORM / 829-3676

Legal Assistance...Watch Your Back!
Retain the professional services of an attorney (e.g., for document and contract review).

Insurance...Protect Yourself!
Consider obtaining liability insurance (i.e., errors & omissions policy).

Benefits...Take Care of Yourself!
Don't forget to factor in benefits (that you used to have at your full-time job) such as health coverage.

Mentorship...Extremely Valuable!
A mentor is a trusted counselor who can show you the ropes for professional mobility or advancement. S/he can help guide or navigate you through various situations, the handling of which is not necessarily taught in school. They may be a seasoned professional whose opinion you trust. Find ways to show your appreciation to such a person. Oh—and don't forget to become a mentor yourself one day!

Resources:
Chamber of Commerce – (202) 463-5560 - www.USChamber.com

National Association of Female Executives – a nice mix of women professionals and business owners (headquartered near Grand Central Station) www.nafe.com. The cost of *NAFE Magazine* is included in the cost of the low annual membership of $39, one of the lowest rates around for membership in a professional association. NAFE's parent company is Working Mother Media at www.workingmother.com. 1(800) 927-6233 or (212) 351-6400

Black Enterprise Magazine – www.blackenterprise.com - 1(800) 727-7777

Entrepreneur Magazine - www.entrepreneur.com - 1(800) 304-6388

Inc. Magazine – www.inc.com - 1(800) 234-0999

Money Magazine - www.money.cnn.com - 1(800) 633-9970

Smart Money Magazine - www.SmartMoney.com - 1(800) 444-4204

Small Business' www.StartupJournal.com - The Wall Street Journal Center for entrepreneurs (This is a website from Dow Jones & Company; includes real-life case studies)

"Coming up with CREATIVE IDEAS for your business is one thing; being ORGANIZED transforms those ideas into ACTION PLANS, and being thorough converts action plans into CONCRETE GOODS AND SERVICES."
~ MBR ~

NOW THAT YOU HAVE YOUR BUSINESS STRUCTURE ESTABLISHED, here are eight steps toward earning the business of a prospective client.

1) Consider a professional or trade association membership affiliated with your area of interest or expertise. You can also pay the non-member rate to attend meetings and cocktail receptions.

2) You might also consider professional or trade affiliations outside of your area of expertise. One of the best pieces of advice given to me was not to just join groups in my field of interest or expertise, but to also join groups outside of my genre. For example, as an Event Planner, it is perfectly all right to attend gatherings where other Event Planners frequent, but why not attend a museum art exhibition where art connoisseurs gather, thereby reducing the chance of there being other Event Planners present in the room? Plus, if you just so happen to be particularly interested in the subject

matter, you can be conversant with the other guests at the function. This has worked like a charm for me.

3) Carefully screen conventions/conferences/seminars/ workshops, speakers, topics, and the relevancy thereof; take advantage of the Early Bird Registration.

4) Make sure your name badge is clearly easy to read; if provided the opportunity forgroup introduction, devise a catchy, memorable introduction of yourself.

This is very important, as I've gone to many a networking reception and simply because my name badge was spelled wrong and written in tiny print, I got:

Potential client: *"So you're Masha (as in mashed potatoes?) from Rollins Consultants."*

My response: *"No, it's Me'Shae, like paper mâche, of Rolling—like rolling-a-ball—Consulting. Uhhh, please allow me to get the ball rolling on your next project."*

After that intro, I felt like whatever confidence I walked into the room with was quickly zapped away. Finally, I decided that rather than the usual intro, I would convince people to hire me as their Financial Organizer by standing up and visually demonstrating as follows: *"If your important papers are organized like this* (manila folder with a bunch of messy papers falling out), *but you need them like this* (a neatly labeled color file folder)*, then call me."* It's one sentence, but a picture is worth a thousand words. I've had to manage prospective interest after an intro like this like celebrities ducking from the paparazzi.

5) It is more important to obtain prospect's business card than it is for them to obtain yours. Why in the world do I say this? Because now that you've read this book, I trust that you have become an organized individual. Oftentimes, people misplace and lose business

cards. My own personal approach is predicated upon being a follow-up person. A typical example of what I might write on the back of someone's business card while my memory is still fresh would be:

> *"Met Lena Smith on 5/14/05 at Black Enterprise Conference in Dallas, TX; requested James Rolling's book on African-American Art for Children"*
>
> When you return to your office, organize, catalog, or input prospects' contact info into whatever manner or system suits you. If I have not successfully reached the prospect after attempting to make contact once or twice, then I conclude that what the prospect and I were excitedly discussing in an intimate setting over the gala awards dinner was not as high of a priority on their radar screen the next day as it was at that moment in conversation. It's okay to move on to other prospects.

6) If you have made contact and the prospective client expresses interest in further information about your product or services, send him/her an info/promo kit with a personal note attached. Components may include:

A. business card
B. bio
C. flyers
D. press coverage
E. articles you may have written
F. upcoming appearances

7) Follow-up this mailing with a telephone call or e-mail inviting the prospective client to a free, no-obligation consultation (relieves pressure on them).

8) This complimentary consultation has a two-fold purpose:

a) To convince the prospective client how retaining my services can provide value-benefit to their particular circumstances in a competitive marketplace; and

b) To assess the prospective client *as a person,* as well as his/her situation before agreeing to go forward; this is the appropriate time to decide whether or not **you truly want to work with this client.**

One of the reasons I went into business for myself is so that I can have the flexibility to work with people I enjoy. After talking to other small business consultants, I hear over and over again how they screen and size-up potential clients to the same extent that they are being assessed so they don't end up with "psycho" clients. That's one of the advantages of being in business for oneself...having some measure of control over who you work with.

If a prospective client does not wish to proceed, graciously thank him or her and ask to be kept in mind for future referrals, perhaps offering an incentive such as a gift certificate for each referral. If prospective client is not ready for your services, be patient and mark your calendar for a follow-up contact at time convenient to their schedule. If they want to work with you, commence work!

Keep in mind that sometimes contacts do not germinate until later, perhaps much later. Once you get the word out through family, friends and business associates that you are starting a business, they themselves may not require your services right then and there, but perhaps later on they or someone they know may be in need of what you have to offer.

Networking is all about building relationships;
meeting the needs and/or expectations of clients is
about adding value to those relationships.
~ MBR ~

Customer Satisfaction...Guaranteed?

There is nothing more damaging to a growing business than attracting new business, but not being able to keep up satisfactory client relations once you have earned the client!

Exercise attentive customer service once you retain a client's business. I've never really understood the logic or concept behind indifferent customer service, as if the product or service provider is doing *you* a favor by servicing you for products or services that *you* are paying for.

Personally speaking, I purposely maintain a small client roster because I do not wish for my quality to decline in case my volume increases. But that's just the nature of my business. Point is, obtaining a good client is half of the battle. Properly and courtesously servicing clients produces long-term effects, such as referrals to other potential clients whom they know.

I once attended a homeownership seminar and subsequently called one of the mortgage representatives. I could not get hold of her. It's like she fell off the face of the earth and yet, she had passed out her business card to the whole class. Wouldn't it have been more efficient to have mechanisms in place to handle the potential volume of calls after making such a public presentation?

Providers of goods and services are constantly soliciting new clients. More customers. More money. The pitfall is whether or not they can properly, efficiently and courteously service existing clientele due to the increasing workload. Protocol must be established to service the increasing demand.

For example, if you purchase a new home or vehicle and have never had one before, how do you know what is expected of you? Inspections. Deadlines. Paperwork. Grace periods. Yet, if your insurance agent does not keep you abreast and involved in the process and yet, fully expects and demands your payment in full and *rightfully* expects your payment to clear on time, don't you also have a right to good customer service?

Nowadays, if we are going to have a long-term relationship with a service provider, I get on the phone with the owner or manager and make especially clear, as politely as possible:

a) My husband and I rely on your knowledge and expertise.
b) If you feel you cannot service us for whatever reason, we have no problem moving on. No harm done.
c) Service above and beyond the call of duty yields glowing recommendations from us.

Case in point: we wrote a summa cum laude letter of commendation to the boss of one of our long-term vendors and put every credential behind our names because she:

a) took time with us...made us feel as if we were the only clients she had, although I know her plate is full; and
b) answered numerous questions without a hint of *"Oh brother, you guys again"* nor did she make us feel like any question was stupid.

We are not pesky clients at all, bothering folks at the drop of a hat (this works both ways, you know, and can backfire if a vendor feels s/he is spending an inordinate amount of time with you).

Customer service expectations are commensurate with the caliber of the product or service you are purchasing. Of course you don't necessarily expect a high level of service from the guy squirting ketchup and mustard on your hot dog bun at the Penn Station concourse. Although, that *would* be nice. But you *do* have every right to expect it of your attorney, accountant, insurance agent, financial advisor, real estate broker, physician, hairdresser, general contractor, auto mechanic, consultant and others whose businesses are financially benefiting from a long-term professional relationship with you, regardless of what city you live in.

Merchants in NYC (not all of them, of course) feel they can get away with bad service because they figure if they lose you as a customer, there will be 100 more customers to replace itty bitty you. But New Yorkers, just like any other living, breathing, human being on the planet desire good service, too. Even then, aren't you more likely to return to that particular stand if the guy hands you your hotdog with a smile and says thank you—even if his hotdog costs a little more?

During the beginning of my career as I was trading in college sweats for my professional wardrobe, I shopped at a particular store in 5 World Trade Center. Not once, not twice, but several times, as I went inside of the store with my pumps and briefcase, I was followed around by security guards when my Caucasian counterparts were not being treated in the same manner. Yet, I was handing over the same green dollar bill as everyone else standing in line. Racial profiling, by the way, is documented by numerous undercover hidden camera investigations. One day, I had had enough. Rather than ignoring the situation or ceasing to shop there, I made it a point to let the owner/manager know that unless his security guards underwent sensitivity orientation and training, and either altered their behavior or behaved equally toward everyone, then I would no longer shop at his store. You see, how will he know why he lost my patronage if I don't tell him? He apologized, and I gave him a chance to ameliorate the situation. But since the security guards' behavior continued, I then promptly called my female friends (both Caucasian women and women of color) and they joined me in boycotting the establishment simply by no longer shopping there. I let the manager know this, as well.

Some may consider this approach too radical. Too aggressive. Listen up, folks: Aren't you already dealing with office politics? An overlong commute? An inadequate salary? Conversely, don't you have a right not to be treated like a dog when you spend your money? (And metropolis canine lovers even treat their dogs better than some merchants treat their clientele.)

I once gained 3,000 complimentary frequency points just for calling a complaint into a hotel chain's corporate headquarters. I was not seeking rewards at the time; but if you were a business owner, wouldn't you want to know if there were glaring problems at your establishment, or would you rather people gossip behind your back about your shoddy services?

A vendor I do business with has one main criteria: that he is the first to know if there is a problem. There's one thing I learned about New York: despite her millions of people, the six degrees of separation makes her akin to a small town in certain respects. You never know who's talking to whom about you.

Resources: Better Business Bureau, www.bbb.org
New York City Department of Consumer Affairs advocates on behalf of consumers and "educates New Yorkers about their legal rights to a fair deal and high business standards" To voice a complaint about a business, call 311, or visit www.nyc.gov/html/dca

"I didn't start a business to get rich—I started a business to provide a service and to improve myself economically. I think it's a mistake to set out to get rich."
~ John H. Johnson, Founder & Publisher
Johnson Publishing Company ~

"Being an entrepreneur is about patience and persistence, not the quick buck..."
~ Reed Hastings, Founder, Netflix ~

CHAPTER 18
OFF THE RECORD

If you need wisdom—if you want to know what God wants you to do—ask him, and he will gladly tell you. He will not resent your asking."
~ James 1:5 (NLT) ~

THERE ARE THINGS ABOUT RUNNING A BUSINESS that you're not necessarily going to learn in the classroom, at a workshop, or in a seminar. The book of Proverbs (chapter 3, verse 15) compels us to above all, seek wisdom because *"...wisdom is more precious than rubies; nothing you desire can compare with her."* Where does wisdom come from? I believe wisdom comes from the Lord because God is omniscient. He knows all things past, present and future. He knows what is going to happen before it happens, so I have learned the hard way that it is much better for me to consult with Him first so He can steer me clear of the potentially damaging consequences. Information is a tool. Think about it: people plunk down big bucks for the information they receive at conferences. But knowing how to apply and utilize it properly requires wisdom.

The Electricity Bill Has To Be Paid

Small companies cited the category of accounts receivable as the largest cash-flow concern, according to a survey conducted by American Express.[101] Do not be afraid to discuss the terms of compensation before commencing work! In a typical situation, no one begins a new job without knowing what their salary or wages will be. Or starts out as a small business owner with the intention of ending up as a debt collector. Likewise, product consumers do not buy merchandise in the store or over the Internet without paying for it. I do not know for the life of me why being a service provider is perceived as being any different. Why anyone thinks my light bill has a different due date on it than a person with a steady job is beyond me. I must have missed that course in my Business Administration class.

Particularly if you are a service provider: 1) make sure you're dealing with the financial decision-maker in your client's organization; 2) agree on the parameters or scope of the assignment; 3) thoroughly negotiate compensation, assignment due dates, and payment schedule; 4) commence work and do an excellent job; and 5) get paid. It's that simple. Anyone with whom I have contracted to perform a service knows that the first words out of my mouth are: *"How much will/do I owe you and when?"* (I am fortunate that my clientele thinks the same way.) This is one of the best ways to build a solid business relationship.

Also consider bartering for non-monetary compensation. One of my clients is a restaurant owner. If I am servicing his business, obviously I'm not at home preparing dinner in the kitchen. In such circumstances, a meal from my client's establishment is more valuable to me than the money. The bottom line is, you don't want the arrangements to be murky from the beginning, and then you're looking to get paid later like a scavenger prowling around. (Conversely, don't put others in that position.)

Be Patient, My Dear Child

I admit that I recently attended a financial seminar with a bit of skepticism. The speakers were highly motivated individuals, and I agreed with much of the information they were disseminating. I found, however, that I had to go home, cool my head off, and simmer down because they had me so pumped up that I was ready to sprint a 400-meter dash around the track at Brooklyn's Boys and Girls High School. I needed time to process the information and separate the wheat from the chaff, instead of acting in the moment (which is what they wanted me to do), and walking into a mound of debt. The seminar was packed with information based on the speakers' knowledge, and information is capital; but wisdom said to pluck the free golden nuggets of information and filter out the irrelevant.

Has this ever happened to you? The salesman or woman invites you to apply for the store's credit card on-the-spot? And before you know it, you have ten department store charge cards that you don't really need?

Don't Slap Slop Together...or You'll Blemish Your Reputation

I needed a logo to brand my company's identity, business cards to promote my company, and a website to increase exposure. I wanted that logo, business card, and website, and I wanted them right now! *Wah! Wah! Wah!* Wisdom said to earn the capital resources first so as to have the cash on hand and zero debt accruing as I established my infrastructure (no bank or government loans for me, thank you very much). Remember—that web hosting fee is setup to hit your debit or credit card account *on time* every single month, whether the money is there or not! After my tantrum, I carefully **researched** graphic and web design costs *while* earning revenue. One potential vendor weeded herself out of the running simply because she didn't respond to my request-for-proposal (RFP). How much of a waste of time and money do you think it would have been on down the road had I contracted her company out of impatience?

*If there is anything I have learned about starting my own business, it is that it is a process that **demands** patience.*
~ MBR ~

Never Waste Valuable Contacts

Wisdom also said it was a waste of time and money to stick my business cards in any 'ole person's hand at a networking function. My business card doesn't belong at the bottom of a wastepaper basket. I use discretion and carefully scope out prospects. Even more importantly, I get *their* business card because I know myself...I am a follow-up person. This is a more targeted approach that yields greater results *pour moi.*

Conversely, if there is a VIP *you* wish to meet and have the opportunity to do so say, after a dinner reception, carefully think about what you wish to convey. There are times when I am so "star-struck" with the VIP I am meeting, that I fumble in this area. Be courteous and polite, and make the most of your face time with him/her without monopolizing his/her time while other guests are standing in line to meet him/her.

Mixing Business With Friendship

Do you want to save yourself some migraines and agony? This is what I've found—when conducting business with those you don't know, and *especially* with those you do know, establish a set of **clearly defined expectations**...friend or not. Colleague or not. Fellow congregant or not. Nice doesn't matter here. (In fact, nice people are the hardest to work with because they're well, so nice!)

My experience has shown that any difficulties that arise usually revolve around issues of **time** (when will you be able to get me the first draft?), **money** (how much of a deposit will I owe you and what are the intervals for the down payment and the balance?) and **communication**.

Let's face it: life happens, but ongoing communication can ameliorate misgivings and misunderstandings. (*"I know we agreed tomorrow we'll discuss such-and-such, but can we postpone it until Friday afternoon? My son sprained his ankle, and I have to go to the doctor with him."*) Consider the opposing scenario: **No communication** about why the draft was not sent in on the agreed-upon date, **failure** to make payments on time, voice mail oblivion or screeners taking calls and messages on behalf of the person delivering the product or service, and **bad feelings** ensuing. Now, the problem affects both business **and** the friendship. Address and adhere to the aforementioned suggestions **from the start** so that both business and friendship remain intact. This way, you will also **preserve mutual respect.** I will go as far to say this: anytime I feel that business is interfering with a friendship, the other party and I mutually agree preliminarily to drop the business arrangement like a hot potato because the friendship is more important to us.

Label Your E-mails Appropriately and Effectively

Avoid subject lines like "Re: Re: Fwd: Fwd: Read this". Label or rename that baby before launching it off into cyberspace: "New Year's Sponsorship Request for Toys"; "Tim's reply to Karen re Toy Request" so that even if the recipient auto-replies, you have a specific subject matter to refer to amidst numerous e-mails. Sometimes I even insert the recipient's name in the subject line (i.e., "Barbara, let's meet for lunch"), because we all pause when we see our name in writing. That's just the way it is.

Resource: Google offers Gmail, a free, experimental webmail with lots of storage space that organizes your e-mails into conversation format; must be invited by a current user

Prioritize Your List of Tasks

As a Special Events professional, I learned to prioritize my "to do" list in the interest of efficient event management, particularly where the success of an event depends on team effort. The secret? Before doing anything else, put in a request for tasks that you are reliant upon others to do, first. Do not underestimate the time it takes other people to access their voice mail, play phone tag, read their e-mail, get back to you; and then plan and execute the completion of their portion of the overall task. Plus, you don't want to approach people at the last minute. For example, on a normal work day, my "A.M." hours are reserved for reaching out to others. I spend my afternoons trying to do deskwork; even so, someone will inevitably e-mail, or someone who is getting back to me will ring the phone. Speaking of calls...

Return Them!

As a professional courtesy, if someone has been attempting to reach you for a while, don't blithely neglect to return the call—particularly if you have maintained a cordial relationship with the individual. I've had my own personal experiences where people I (thought) I had a mutual understanding with regard to "the next action step"; and they totally, unequivocally, unapologetically, disappeared into the intergalactic wormhole. If it's plain 'ole busyness preventing you from making contact, then set up an e-mail auto-responder or have an assistant call the person on your behalf, but have some type of system in place. Sometimes the recipient understandably has every intention of returning a call, but is waiting for some information to come through, but the caller won't know that unless it is communicated.

Here is a sample script:

> *"I know we agreed to talk on Wednesday, John, but I don't have an answer for you yet. I'll contact you when I do, Okay? Thanks for your patience. I truly appreciate it."*

Technology is such that you do not even need to be sitting next to your landline, chewing bubblegum and filing your nails, to know that someone has contacted you. In this day and age of text messaging, remote access, call forwarding, e-faxes, hand-held devices, publicly-shared computer terminals, etc., it's awfully hard to justify non-replies (to those in your universe, that is). For more on communication etiquette, and netiquette, revisit sections 5.18 and 5.39 in Chapter 5.

Technology: Is It Helping or Impeding Your Communication?

Is it possible that the technological gadgets we rely on are actually preventing us from communicating with each other? Or is it that *because* technology is designed to make us more efficient, we feel we can multi-task anything; hence, taking on more responsibility and committing ourselves to more activities without ever realizing we're taking on more than we can effectively handle?

One of my best clients—a real mover and shaker—has **no** e-mail and fiercely protects his cell number as if he were a pit bull (this Type A personality will count this as a compliment). We have our standing appointment, and he calls me if there are to be any changes in the schedule. I don't feel trepidation in calling him while he's in the middle of screaming *"you moron!"* at the neighboring taxicab driver. This relieves me from any awkward moments or uncomfortable feelings of interrupting him. There are people with electronic calendars, five e-mail accounts, home voice mail, work voice mail, cellular phone, electronic Internet fax—and I still can't reach them half of the time! I admit that calendar software is great for pop-up reminders for my husband to get a haircut. By the way—whatever happened to looking in a mirror?

Before Verizon, Samsung, Yahoo, and other telecommunication Goliaths write 'lil ole David a letter, allow me to qualify my comments by stating that it's up to you how to most efficiently use the plethora of technological resources we have available to mankind in the 21st century. Reach out and touch someone, okay? Better yet, kindly send them a handwritten note.

Establish and Maintain a Regular Schedule

Once you are up and running with your business or consulting, establish a system and maintain a regular schedule. Bear in mind that you are administering the everyday details of your life alongside running your business. One of the biggest challenges I initially encountered as a new consultant was getting people to understand that even though I had autonomy over my schedule, that I did in fact maintain a schedule.

For me, it's enjoying coffee or tea (no different than an office worker); and then making calls and sending e-mails in the morning. I've learned it takes folks awhile to get settled in, take care of *their* priorities, and then reply to their correspondence. I make lunch around noon (again, no different than an office worker), and oftentimes work **way past** 5 p.m. (My payback for having a 30-second commute). The assumption has been made that because I work out of my home office,

I have the luxury of lounging around in my bathrobe and comfy slippers, eating popcorn and watching Oprah. Well...my mid-day break coincidentally happens to be around 4 p.m., okay?

Meetings, breakfasts or luncheons that involve travel take me out of the office for a whole day. Therefore, I spend time doing two things: organizing and doing the preliminary planning for tasks so they don't pile up on me upon return. I pre-set my e-mail "away" message if I'm going to be out of the office for an extended period of time. I rarely give out my cell, because I don't like conducting business while I'm bagging my groceries, and I utilize telephone remote access capabilities when out-of-town. I am cognizant, however, that such a schedule is not so cut and dry if you are a parent.

Honor RSVP deadlines—you never know what time-sensitive obligations the hostess or event planner must fulfill.
~ MBR ~

Guard Your Time and Protect Your Solitude

Setting aside time to hear yourself think is essential, even if you're one who thrives on adrenaline. Eliminate distractions that hinder you from your vision. How many times have I said "yes" on the spot to something, only later to find that the commitment would somehow create a self-imposed inconvenience? We sometimes prematurely commit verbally because our hearts say "yes," but our calendar was not privy to that discussion. Make a list of what areas in life are important to you (e.g., domestic/household affairs, family and friends, church and community service, business and career, recreational activities, etc.). Hey—stop peeking at my list and go devise your own! Tonight, for example, I am attending a Toastmasters meeting. This is going to help me hone my presentation skills as I jet all over the globe to teach the masses how to become financially organized, thus igniting a financial revolution in homes, communities and churches! (I'm allowed to dream big, aren't I?)

If you are invited to the unveiling ceremony of the latest spaceship at the Kennedy Space Center, and the trip is in alignment with your goal of becoming an astronaut, then go for it! If meeting Lieutenant Worf at the Star Wars convention is part of your networking plan for upward mobility, then don't let me stop you. The point is, build parameters around your time. If a bunch of little activities here and there are all lining up, just itching to affix themselves onto your calendar, but are not conducive to your prescribed categories and overall goals, then the answer is unequivocally "no." Avoid suffocating your schedule; allow breathing room for a last-minute invitation to dine with a friend or some other quality-of-life activity.

Resource:
Visioneering by Andy Stanley (1999). Sisters, Oregon: Multnomah Publishers, Inc.

"I only volunteer and commit my time to that which I feel I can give my best to."
~ MBR ~

"If you don't intend to make a concerted effort to follow through on it, then don't verbally commit to it!"
~ MBR ~

CHAPTER 19
TEACHING OUR YOUTH FINANCIAL LITERACY

"In everything set them an example by doing what is good.
In your teaching show integrity, seriousness and soundness
of speech that cannot be condemned..."
~ Titus 2:7,8a ~

I DO NOT UNDERSTAND FOR THE LIFE OF ME why I was not taught financial literacy in school, along with English, math, and science. I speak English everyday, but I cannot honestly say that I interface with science to the degree that I do with personal finances. Not a day goes by when I do not have to negotiate how I handle money. Do I want a small, medium, or large? Which bills have to be paid today? Do I need to refill my subway/bus card? Does the car need gas? Do I really want to spend extra for sausage and pepperoni on my slice of pizza? What are we going to do this weekend, and how much will it cost?

When I was a teenager, I worked odd jobs helping my Daddy at the funeral home by helping out during calling hours aka wakes, driving the funeral hearses, and spooking my younger sisters by playing the organ. In the dark. Next to the casket. (But I didn't get paid for that). I also sold Avon products, had a newspaper route, and was handsomely rewarded by my clients with tips. I worked so hard earning it, I was the type of person who thought long and hard before spending it—I had to be convinced to spend it even on my favorite "blue moon" flavor at the ice cream parlor. Even to this day, my husband balances me in this area. Though he too, is a financially responsible person, James is more likely to say *"Let's lighten up and have some fun, you tightwad. Dear."*

Young people must be taught how to handle their finances—this cannot happen by osmosis. Many have summer or after-school jobs and stay home rent-free. There is nothing wrong, of course, with our youth using money they earn to buy some of the things they want. However, they must also be taught how to save and spend wisely, or we will end up with a financially illiterate generation. Unfortunately, this is already happening. But you can go against the tide.

Start by setting an example in your own household. It starts with an allowance. One family I know uses the envelope system described in Chapter 3, and includes the children's allowances in the envelopes. All of the family members, including children, participate in the managing of those envelopes. Once an envelope is depleted, everyone understands that they will have to wait until the next replenishment. This helps children to learn how to pace their spending.

Do not make children feel self-conscious, however, about what they may not have. How many of us "grew up po' and broke," but did not feel it because there was so much love and mutual support in our home? Allow your children to designate a charity to volunteer their time to. Trust me—your child will not end up kicking, screaming, hitting and biting on *"Nanny 911"* if they are passing out toys to children with lesser economic advantages during the holiday season. By doing so, you are also passing on a legacy you can be proud of.

~ Credit card companies have a vested interest
in cultivating debt in young people.
I recently purchased paraphernalia at my alma
mater's university bookstore, and
numerous credit card offers were also stuffed
in my bag of merchandise. ~

Resource: New York Financial Literacy Coalition (NYFLC) conducts a financial literacy certification test and a personal finance program called Banking on our Future, provided by Operation HOPE. Operation HOPE focuses its efforts on economically underserved communities. Download lessons at www.bankingonourfuture.org. Help your children learn basic financial education and literacy.

Misdirected Talent

I was standing on the train platform one day when a young male approached me about buying a T.D. Jakes' *Woman Thou Art Loosed* DVD. Mind you, he also had several pop stars on hand, as well. But he profiled me as someone who might choose T.D. Jakes, probably based on the way I was dressed, the day of the week (Sunday), and my demeanor. I wasn't interested in purchasing pirated goods, but this young man could nonetheless do quite well in sales and marketing. You see, he tailored his pitch to his target market: he approached me in brisk, but mannerly way. He had his CDs and DVDs all lined up in an orderly fashion. Are you advertising and marketing executives, small business investors, and government economists out there listening? The energy and ingenuity of our youth can be tapped into if groomed in an entrepreneurial direction.

If you are a young person reading this book, please use the talents God gave you to add to and not to subtract from. To build up, rather than to tear down. To help, rather than to hurt. Think about negative activities you may be engaged in right now. **How can those *very same* talents, skills and abilities be channeled to even more productive use?**

Kudos to the New York City Department of Consumer Affairs for devoting a page on their website for young people, since our country's adults haven't been doing all that great a job managing the nation's debt: www.nyc.gov/html/dca and click on "consumer resources"

Kudos to Tiger Woods for founding a 14-acre, multi-million dollar hi-tech learning complex in Anaheim, California, right next to the golf course on which he learned to play golf. There are a great many philanthropists who have preceded him; may his generosity inspire many more to follow suit.

CHAPTER 20
OUR TALE

"I know what it is to be in need, and I know what it is to have plenty. I have learned the secret of being content in any and every situation, whether well fed or hungry, whether living in plenty or in want."
~ Philippians 4:12 ~

IF I TOLD YOU SOMEONE DID SOMETHING and I failed to acknowledge the person, wouldn't that be a negligent oversight? Well, it would be an oversight if I did not tell you that God helped my husband, James and I. But what does God have to do with our finances, and why would we be so transparent? You might ask. All valid questions.

The answer? I am compelled to share exactly what He did for us in order to encourage you. We all need encouragement sometimes. James and I are no better or any more special in God's eyes than you are. What He did for us, He can also do for you.

James and I have been married for 13 years. We met at Syracuse University in the summer of 1989. He, from the neighborhood of Crown Heights in the borough of Brooklyn in New York City, was studying for his Masters degree in Fine Arts. I arrived in Syracuse,

New York on a Greyhound Bus just one month after graduating from Anderson University in my hometown of Anderson, Indiana. I had migrated to the East Coast to pursue my Masters degree in Public Administration. We were both blessed to be Orangemen on fully funded fellowships. I was there during the basketball play-offs between the Hoosiers and the Orangemen, but my nose was in a book, so please don't ask me who I was rooting for.

I worked as a graduate intern at a municipal agency starting out at $7/hour, and then received a $2/hour raise once I earned my degree. Because I was blessed with an unbelievable break on rent, I paid off my **undergraduate** school loan (which amounted to less than $2,500) with my $9/hour wages, and just enough left over to spare for groceries. True story.

In the fall of 1991, I moved to New York City after being recruited by a top federal agency (Unfortunately, the building my agency was housed in was later destroyed by the September 11th attacks).

While my roommate-to-be—who was also a Syracuse colleague and a Queens native—was scouting for an apartment, I specifically prayed for an apartment with the following characteristics:

- that it not have a long commute to the World Trade Center in Manhattan
- that the rent would be reasonable, whatever that meant for New York City
- that there would be no rodents
- that the apartment would be near my intended place of worship
- that it would be located someplace where my fiancé would not have to travel extensively to visit me

By now, you must be saying, *"In your dreams, honey!"* Say what you will, but I lived in a studio apartment in Park Slope, Brooklyn that met each and every one of the criteria above!

- My commute to work was no more than half an hour.
- There were two of us splitting the rent on a studio apartment.
- There were no roach or mice problems.
- The apartment was around the corner from The Brooklyn Tabernacle, located at the time on Flatbush Avenue.
- James' visits from Crown Heights (where he moved back to upon graduation from Syracuse) was 15 to 20 minutes, tops!

After getting married in August 1992, my new hubby and I moved into an identical studio apartment next door that miraculously became vacant. Same rent. Same landlord.

I wish I could tell you that we newlyweds lived happily ever after, but there is more to our story.

Between absorbing wedding costs, furnishing a newlywed's home made convenient by credit cards, adjusting to daily living expenses, and making payments on James' undergraduate student loans, we found ourselves deep in debt. I will never forget the times we'd shop at the neighborhood grocery store and have to place half of the food back on the shelves, because we got to the cash register and found we could not afford everything we needed! I also remember when we'd pool together the last nickels and dimes in our dresser drawer just to buy a token to get to work. Ahh, tokens. Remember them?

We questioned ourselves relentlessly: *"Do we not earn enough on our respective jobs?" "Do we spend too much?" "Are our expenses higher than the norm because we live in New York City?"* After all, my parents reminded me that the mortgage on their 4 bedroom, 4 bathroom home back in Indiana was **less** that the monthly rent on our tiny studio apartment.

Regardless of the underlying reason, we felt something was wrong with this picture. As Christians, we truly felt that this was not the way God meant or intended for us to live—with the constant stress and duress of debt hovering over our heads. We went to the Word of God, the Bible, and discovered that there are literally hundreds of verses addressing the issue of finances.

We immediately made it a goal to get out of debt. We made a commitment to tithe (set aside 10% of our earnings to the church) no matter what. We scrutinized each and every expenditure in our household to "plug the leaks". For example, I cut down on the phone bill by calling my family back home less, or only during certain hours, or with a calling card or special prefix numbers. Remember, the early 1990's did not have as many communication choices as we have today. We read everything we could get our hands on to educate ourselves financially. We also developed a personalized budget sheet (see Chapter 2 and Appendix A) that we use to this very day.

In the summer of 1995, we were blessed with lower rent and larger space in Crown Heights, just in time for me to be downsized—along with about 100 or so other people—from my federal agency. I went from a federal salary with performance-based and annual cost-of-living increases, straight to the unemployment line.

You see, by this time, I had been with the agency for almost four years. I began to suspect that there was a mismatch between my interest and skills when I got more of a thrill out of making sure my work team's itinerary was coordinated down to a "T," than I was grilling high-ranking government officials on their expenditure of taxpayers' dollars, which is what I was hired to do.

One unsuspecting day in early Fall 1995, office workers were summoned into the conference room, where it was announced that Washington, D.C. headquarters was closing the New York Regional Office. You could hear a pin drop during the long moment of stunned silence. Needless to say, this news was a devastating blow to those who had invested years of sweat equity into their profession. For me personally, however, the circumstances provided the opportunity to make a career change.

It was by happenstance that I was Chairperson of the Social Committee at my job at the time the news broke, and so my committee was responsible for the farewell dinner on Governor's Island. Following the program, my colleagues were so pleased with the occasion that many of them approached me afterwards and emphatically remarked, *"Me'Shae, you should seriously consider Special Events Planning."*

This admonition resonated within me since I had enjoyed planning, organizing and coordinating events for as long as I could remember. The federal government paid for my retraining in Special Events at New York University, and James and I used my severance compensation to pay off a loan we had taken out early on in our marriage. Using the adage *"you have to crawl before you can walk,"* I took entry-level jobs in the special events field paying (despite my Masters degree) under $15 per hour.

I worked on odd special events jobs ranging from helping to plan and execute the Macy*s Thanksgiving Day Parade, to temping in FORTUNE Magazine's Conference Division, to assisting on the launch of a Wall Street media project. Due to my career change, for the most part, it felt like two people trying to make it on one income. Money debates in our household focused not so much on paying the bills, but rather, *which* bills demanded priority. It was not uncommon for us to pay Con Edison only a portion of the total electricity bill due until next payday.

Despite our financial struggles, in the fall of 1998, we paid off the last of the credit card bills and student loans. Being debt-free was one of the most wonderful feelings in the world: to be under no obligation to pay anything more than the basic monthly necessities of rent, transportation, utilities, and groceries. No credit card companies. *Nada.* To be able to eat out, and pay k-a-s-h for it. To be able to give extra money to church and charity. To be able to help family and friends in need, as well, without feeling like it is a big, huge, dramatic sacrifice. The downside to all of this was that we also broke even:

money that was coming in was also going out at almost the same rate due to living expenses alone.

Around this time, James had completed his Masters degree in Education at Teachers College, Columbia University, and was eventually accepted into TC's Art Education doctoral program. His desire was to excel in the general area of education so as to employ that knowledge as a complement to his studio arts specialization.

By the end of the 1990's, the careers of my husband and I took off—he, the Director of Academic Administration for the Department of Curriculum & Teaching at Columbia University and me, an Event Coordinator with The Office of the Mayor of the City of New York during Rudolph W. Giuliani's Administration. We resolved, with the help of the good Lord, never to apply for another student loan but rather to pay his tuition between our salaries and his scholarships and tuition exemption employee benefits. James simultaneously worked full-time, in various part-time jobs, and attended school part-time, but still maintained an A+ grade point average. We did what we had to do to make it.

We also resolved that in spite of the increases in income, we would live based on the lessons learned from our years of struggling. **We did not increase our spending habits just because our incomes increased substantially. We maintained the same level of expenditures as if the salary increases were not a factor.** Consequently, we saved like gangbusters. We learned that along with abundance came the increased responsibilities of stewardship, giving, and sharing, as well.

I wish I could tell you that we became prosperous philanthropists, able to establish a foundation, but that is not what happened.

In early 2002, we learned that the house we were renting an apartment in was going to be sold, and we did not wish to remain under new ownership. James' subway commute to Columbia University turned into 1½ hours following the September 11th attacks anyway, and he wanted to move closer to Columbia's campus to finish out his last year of schooling. Manhattan's rents scared me to death, and although we were saving for a car and home, we did not feel in a position to purchase either just yet. Friends from our church who owned homes were generous by inviting us over for dinner and sharing with us how they became homeowners. God bless them.

Once again, I went to what Christians call "the throne of grace" after hearing an encouraging sermon by my Senior Pastor. Here is the prayer I wrote in my journal later that Sunday afternoon:

> *"Lord, housing is a need, and your Word says that you will supply all of our needs according to your riches and glory. You also said that we have not because we ask not, and sometimes when we ask, we do not receive because we ask with the wrong motives (based on James 4:3). Well Father, this is what we are humbly asking for: housing near Columbia University, and once again that it be clean with no rodent problems, that the landlords are accessible and attentive, and even though we're realistic that there will indeed be a rent increase, that it be as reasonable as can be. You are the same yesterday, today and tomorrow. You did it for us in 1991 when I first came to New York; You did it for us in 1995 when we needed to move into a bigger place; and now we trust that you'll do it again as we prepare to make another move."*

James researched prospects, and I made the initial call and point of contact. We looked at no more than four apartments between Spanish/East Harlem and Harlem, the neighborhoods bordering Columbia University. One apartment in particular seemed too good to be true:

- It was a top-floor apartment in a brand-new gated townhouse community; therefore, its occupants would be the first-ever;
- James' commute was to be 15-20 minutes, tops;
- The landlords, owner of the townhouse, lived downstairs;

- Though our rent tripled, it was still considered a "reasonable" amount for Manhattan; and
- it just so happened to be down the street from Central Park!

We acquired the apartment as one would a home: The real estate agent ran a credit check on both of us, took our bank statements & W-2s and screened us. We were the first to see the apartment that day and there were 30 people waiting in line behind us to see the apartment, so we had to make a quick decision. I truly believe that that morning, the Holy Spirit prompted me to bring the checkbook, which we did. We wrote a deposit on the spot in order to secure the apartment.

God came through again.

Well, I wish I could tell you that we happily sang *"There Is A Rose in Spanish Harlem,"* accompanied by acoustic guitar, but wait—there is more.

I experienced unemployment once again around this time, but God in His omniscience knew that James and I would experience the move, illnesses and the death of an immediate family member all in the same summer. Therefore, it would not have been an ideal time for me to hold down a full-time job, too. With the post-9/11 national and municipal economy going into a recession, and unemployment rates skyrocketing, I had applied for positions but despite my credentials, there were no takers, not even temp agencies or part-time jobs! I figured that would be as good a time as any to begin consulting and venture into entrepreneurship. (Books I had been reading on consulting and entrepreneurship had a profound impact on me). Plus, becoming a consultant would be an ideal starting point for me with an eye toward motherhood.

By 2003, I had acquired a small clientele for whom I performed both Special Events Management and Financial Organizing services, the latter of which involved helping individuals and couples to establish a budget, set up a filing system, and engage in ways to save money in everyday city life. You may legitimately be wondering, *"Where in the world did Financial Organizing come from?"* I know it seems out of the blue, but you see, in addition to being a Special Events Manager, my other specialty happens to be what I like to think of as the cousin of special events planning—Professional Organizing. You have probably seen some of us on *Oprah*, organizing people's clutter, closets, home offices, mounds of paper and—yes, special events. My specialty within the realm of professional organizing is financial organizing, born out of my passion to see people financially literate and savvy with their money. Got it?

I no longer earned what I used to, nor with the same frequency as one does with a 9-5 job, and therefore, felt it was primarily my responsibility to monitor household expenses like a hawk. Between my husband's income and my consulting revenues, all of our needs were miraculously met. I say miraculously because as you know by now, I'm a big proponent of tracking one's expenses on financial software. Let me tell you something: the figures showed that our expenses consistently exceeded our income during that time period! I've never seen so much red in my life. We were grateful that the rent was paid on time and we still had life's basic necessities. The struggle and the challenge, however, was in trying to maintain debt-free living by penny-pinching, meeting the higher rent, maintaining our savings (which was really earmarked for a car and home down payment); and doing all of this on one and a fraction of an income. We decided that one of the elements in this equation that needed to change was the issue of homeownership.

I must conclude that God helped us to keep our heads above the water and stay afloat financially *in spite of* the raw figures in black and white. I do not mean to use colloquial expressions, but He made a way out of no way.

After an eight-year journey, James earned his doctoral degree in Art Education and graduated from Teachers College, Columbia University. He also came home one day with the "baby" he had been working on for years—his first book, titled *"Living Sacrifices: For*

Those Dying To Rise To A Life Worth Giving," (Pleasant Word), based on the 12th chapter of the book of Romans in the New Testament of the Bible. A year-and-a-half later, he was approached by a representative from Lickle Publishing to write *"Come Look With Me: Discovering African American Art for Children."* James asked me to help promote his books since I have an undergraduate degree in Marketing (you see, none of one's talents go to waste).

Here's another example for you: Although I am inherently shy by nature, I used to be in the Clown Ministry at my church. Go ahead, get it out of your system. Laugh. That's all right—I was a clown for a little over a decade so I'm used to a chuckle or two. To this day, I cannot believe some of the humor that inadvertently creeps into my lingo and rolls off of my tongue when discussing, of all things—finances! (Dude, I **know** you aren't wearing a pair of designer sneakers when you've got books and tuition to pay for! *Ka-pling! Boink!*) Finances is no laughing matter, mind you. But humor allows people to digest new information in a way that they don't normally associate with a subject matter that is often considered, shall we say, deathly sterile. The point is, even the most absurd of one's experiences do not go to waste.

Back to James' books. At that point, I faced a professional identity crisis: How can I be an Event Planner, Financial Organizer, and Book Promoter? You know, *"jack of all trades and good at none?"* I had even gone as far as obtaining the highest credentials one can attain in the special events field (my CSEP, which stands for Certified Special Events Professional, as conferred by the International Special Events Society). Does engaging in one of these areas mean that I am abandoning another? Or are there elements of all three that somehow tie in together? It got to the point that when people asked me what I did, I stuttered and pleaded the 5th because I wasn't quite sure myself! More about the resolution later.

I attended homeownership seminars but faced a rude awakening: our neighbor to the west—Harlem, was one of the toughest nuts to crack in terms of homeownership in all of New York City! Despite excellent credit, a decent income, and savings, there was no way James and I had the down payment required for a co-op, condo or a brownstone. We scoured Brooklyn, Manhattan, a section of the Bronx I had never heard of in my life—Spuyten Duyvil (will somebody pronounce that for me, please?). And we could forget Westchester County and Long Island...the property taxes were ridiculous.

Now that he had earned his terminal degree, my husband had opportunities to apply and interview for professorship opportunities out-of-state. We're talking upstate New York and the Midwest here, where due to the housing market, homeownership would absolutely not be an issue for us. One of our Pastors encouraged us to make sure we had exhausted homeownership options here in the metropolitan area before totally moving away.

New Years Day. 2004. A friend of a friend called us out of the blue because he heard through the grapevine that we were looking for a home. He invited us to come look at his inventory of homes. Now I must admit, we had overlooked New Jersey because whenever we passed through, all we saw were the industrial smokestacks and prematurely concluded that this was not the place for us, our future family, or our lungs. However, after taking a tour of a neat little community, the Garden State was lookin' pur-ty good. We saw a house, *the house*, but didn't realize at first that it was *the* house because James was interviewing in other states, remember?

Fast forward to Spring 2004. We camped out in a Holiday Inn in NJ during James' spring break, and it all happened so fast: we saw more houses, revisited *the* house, and got pre-approved—well, actually approved for a loan due to our very high FICO scores, among other factors (see Chapter 10). What we did not know at the time was that an offer was previously made and accepted on *the* house, but that deal had fallen through. The sellers subsequently accepted our offer—accompanied by our mortgage lender's approval letter. Needless to say, we felt exhilaration. But guess what? Around this time, we were also sent letters of invitation to apply for the brand-new condo and co-ops being built on Madison Avenue in East Harlem and on West 148th Street in central Harlem. When we compared the square footage, cost, etc., we decided that the home was the better choice for us, personally.

Wait, I'm almost done. Professionally, my event planning background is utilized to promote all *three* of our books in conjunction with: book signings, art exhibitions, speaking engagements, and financial literacy seminars. (Why should I hire someone else to plan these events?)

And as for my auditing experience just out of grad school? It has become extremely beneficial in analyzing my clients' expenditures, as well as that of my own household. I can spot money unnecessarily spent a mile away! The oil deliveryman is downright scared to come to our home, as I hover over the nozzle of the hose monitoring every drop of oil they pour into our tank at over 2 bucks per gallon. That extra crispy fried chicken in the bucket may as well have dollar signs attached to its wings, as far as I am concerned. Let me stop! My husband-who consumes the heat and the chicken anyway-has learned to ignore my obsessive compulsive disorder. James equally enjoys teaching art education and writing, writing, writing. And editing. (Thanks, honey!)

Does this mean that the struggles we experienced were a waste? Absolutely not! **God is oftentimes more interested in working out the process in us, before we ever get to the end-result.** And when we do accomplish our goal and reach the finish line, we know that it was Him, and not our intelligence, or our money, or the headhunter, or the "right agent", or anything else. Case-in-point: What do you do when a seller is deadlocked between choosing you and another prospective homebuyer? Your competition's FICO credit score is just as high as your FICO score? However much money you put down, the other bidder can match or exceed? The wind could literally blow in one direction or another as the seller is making his or her decision. What do you do? Personally speaking, we prayed to the Lord and asked for mercy, grace and favor. And if it was not meant for us, we would yield to the knowledge that God knew something that we did not know about the deal and move on until He engineered and revealed what He had in store for us—which may very well be better than what we desired in the first place.

That is not the end of our story, but it will have to do for now until the sequel, "How To Save Money and Organize Your Finances: Tales of a Suburban Mom" (wink, wink).

" And we know that in all things God works
for the good of those who love him,
who have been called according to his purpose."
~ Romans 8:28 ~

CHAPTER 21
FINAL THOUGHTS: YOUR TALE

"Do not be afraid, for I am with you..."
~ Genesis 26:24b ~

BY NOW, YOU HAVE LEARNED OVER 40 WAYS TO SAVE MONEY on a daily basis. There is a difference, however, between being cheap and being frugal. Being cheap means you are saving money at the expense or detriment of other individuals. Being frugal means you are cautious about your spending habits so that you save money in your pocket toward fulfilling your real needs. Being frugal means that you benefit those you love and desire to care for, while keeping your money out of the pocket of entities that do not truly need your money.

For example, when dining in a restaurant, being frugal is ordering water instead of the $3 non-refillable small or regular soda, and instead redirecting that same $3 towards refilling your subway or bus transportation card, which is probably a need. Being cheap is receiving good service at the restaurant and leaving less than the appropriate tip—or perhaps not even paying your fair portion of a shared check.

Read To Learn. Yearn To Learn.
Read whatever you can get your hands on regarding business, finance and consulting books, as well as books in your fields of interest. If you are interested in culinary arts, in addition to reading up on the culinary arts field, read books on business management, as well. It doesn't have to cost you big bucks to do so. Glance at the business section of a newspaper. Read the consumer advocacy columns of local and national newspapers.

I highly recommend *USA Today's* Money section, and Asa Aarons' New York City-specific "Ask Asa" consumer reports column featured in *The New York Daily News* on Mondays, Tuesdays, Thursdays, and Fridays. Also catch *The Suze Orman Show* Saturday nights on CNBC. For a **quality** reality show that doesn't require participants to digest gigantic cockroaches, catch Michelle Singletary's new show on personal finances, *Singletary Says*, currently airing on the satellite cable channel TV One on Wednesday nights. This *Washington Post* syndicated columnist gives financial makeovers to distressed and debt-ridden individuals and couples. There are hundreds of books, magazines, websites, workshops and seminars for you to take advantage of. New York is the business and finance capital of the world, and every major city has its own wealth of resources! C'mon, shake a leg!

Resources:
The Learning Annex is located in nine major cities: Atlanta, Boston, Chicago, Dallas, Los Angeles, Minneapolis, New York, San Diego, San Francisco – www.LearningAnnex.com (New York – 212-371-0280)

Financial Literacy & Education Commission
www.mymoney.gov - 1(888) my-money / 696-6639

Do you novices really want to challenge your brain cells? Then go to www.marketwatch.com, or read Inc., FORTUNE, or Forbes magazines, or The Wall Street Journal.

Top search engines:
www.Google.com; www.Yahoo.com; www.msn.com;
www.askjeeves.com
Type in your financial-related question; I was simply amazed to type in a question from a consumer viewpoint—not a just a phrase, but a question—into Google, and be able to pull up results (i.e., Can a late utility payment affect my credit score? Why do small businesses fail?)

Would you believe there's even a website named www.Answers.com?

Getting A Raise

If you are blessed with a raise, by all means, maintain the same standard of living, or learn to live on less. Oftentimes, people increase their expenses when getting a raise and consequently, the amount of the raise either becomes nil or they flat-out end up deeper in debt. Create a surplus by spending the same or lesser amount of money than you did prior to the raise.

2 for 1

Our lives go through various financial phases. If you are a two-income-earning newlywedded couple, try and discipline yourself *now* to live on only one of those incomes (eliminating debt, saving, and investing the second). God forbid, if one of you gets laid off one day, or chooses to stay home with the baby and has no choice but to resign or reduce the work week, financially speaking, you won't feel like you've been side-swiped by a yellow taxi and didn't know what hit you.

Remember, three key ingredients in making joint personal finances work seamlessly are: communication, coordination, and administration.

Be Innovative

Use your imagination and exercise creativity. One day as I was about to purchase a pricey wooden tea chest, the idea struck me to use a beautiful jewelry box that was tucked away, unused, for that purpose instead. My guests haven't seemed to care—or notice. Until they read this book and discover that they've been horribly deceived. Are there things you want to buy, but do not have the money yet? Then look around your apartment or home for suitable substitutes.

Stewardship—Not Just The Tangible, But The Intangible

Every time someone passes away, it makes me stop and reflect on my own life. Funny how death makes you think about life. Bottom line: I can't take it with me. Someday—on an appointed day and time that only God knows—I'll go six feet under with only one set of clothes on. My flesh and bones will eventually deteriorate. My bank account and whatever is left in it will be left behind. People will remember how I was as a person, and not what kind of house I lived in or how many degrees I had behind my name. Was I mean-spirited? Or will they have good things to say at my eulogy? The best I can do is carefully tend to my relationships and manage my time, talent, money and possessions while I'm still alive, don't you think? How can God bless me financially if I use that which I am a steward over in ways or on vices displeasing to Him?

I count it a blessing to have a stream of income. I know what it is like to be on both sides of the fence. Did my alarm wake me up this morning in order to go to the job? God ordained that I wake up. Does the boss like me? If so, that is called favor from above. Do I count myself exceptionally talented? Let's think about that for a minute—have you ever been awed by majestic mountains, a beautiful sunset, or crashing waves on the seashore? We are all God's creations, and God imparts those giftings to us to engage in good, and not evil acts on this earth. You are a part of a masterpiece in the making. Are you with me?

Stewardship includes evaluating how we spend our time. I stopped watching all of those 7-8 p.m. daily entertainment shows. It dawned on me one day that there I was watching people making gazillions of dollars and doing whatever they can to keep their name in the press so a hungry viewing audience can eat up more of their celebrity—so that their latest album or movie sells. I could be using that same time slot to grow my own business. Or I could spend it writing a book to help educate people.

A relative shared a poignant revelation with me one day: she made a conscientious decision to stop buying gangsta rap CDs because she felt that she was bringing filth into her house to fill her child's innocent ears. On top of all of that, as a struggling single mother, she felt she was helping to fund the bank account of people who don't deserve her money. What sense does that make? There is a Bible verse that cautions us, "I am allowed to do anything—but not everything is beneficial." (I Corinthians 10:23b)

Unfortunately, society's priorities get mixed up when we practically throw open the bank vault to people in professions we place on a pedestal; meanwhile, others like teachers, social workers and nurses are not compensated nearly as much as they ought to be. Did you know that the salaries of some U.S. movie stars, corporation heads, and sports figures could run the entire economy of some countries in the world? Yeah...it's a free enterprise. They made theirs. Are you earning and retaining yours?

What If I've Done All I Can Do?

If you are able to live a debt-free life in The Big Apple or any other metropolis and do not use credit cards, hi-five! But what if you are at a place where you have done all you can? Perhaps you make a decent salary. Not six figures, but you're not at poverty level, either. Those student loans and car payments are killing you. You've cut corners. You don't go to see $10 movies. You go without so the kids don't have to. You just cannot seem to get ahead. The savings account is anemic or nil. Unless you put consumables on the credit card and stockpile more debt, the cupboards remain empty. You have no choice but to resort to credit card usage until the next payday rolls around. Your FICO score is so low, you've been denied credit. It's an endless, black wormhole.

I've been there myself. Money comes in, and despite my best efforts to watch how we spend it, still we either break even, or have more month at the end of the money.

What if it's more dire than that: simple, basic household needs are not being met? What if you are a pretty good money manager but you just don't have enough to manage? These are tough questions, but here are a few suggestions:

First, let's recap (these ten suggestions are also for young people just starting out):

- **Double-check** that your net pay is accurate;
- **Make a commitment to curtail unnecessary spending** ***right now*** by implementing the 40 ways outlined in this book;
- **Avoid borrowing** *any more money* and racking up *any further debt;*
- **If credit card abstinence is nearly impossible,** then is it possible to simplify by streamlining down to one, low-interest credit card in order to preserve cash flow in your household?
- **Become financially organized** so that you can locate your files, records and documents;
- **Create a personalized budget** so you know exactly what is coming in, what is going out, when, and to whom;
- **Begin saving for an emergency or contingency fund** so the next time unexpected emergencies happen, you have *your own money* to be able to tap into;
- **Establish financial goals** and create mini-steps to reach those goals (which is likely to entail future revisions);
- **Incorporate principles** of giving and sharing into your life (both monetarily and non-monetarily); and
- **Consider entrepreneurship** and ways to bring in additional income; or even multiple streams of income.

When faced with seemingly insurmountable debt, develop a written plan. You need to be able to see the numbers in black and white, with all chips on the table; all hands on deck. Develop a long-term budget that addresses the needs of all parties involved, including yourself. What I mean by that, is to make certain your housing, necessary utilities, necessary transportation, and food remain in the budget. Have a calendar nearby so that you can devise a budget in coincidence with your future paydates.

Do not let balances accrue or pile any more debt on top of that which you already have. A smaller hole is easier to dig out of than a larger one—even that minimum credit card payment. Call and ask the credit card company to refinance to a lower interest rate so that the balance isn't accumulating more interest than it has to. The worse they can do is say *"No."* In these cases, it's helpful to let your improving habits to speak for themselves. So make sure you develop a history of on-time payments.

Sometimes pinpointing the problem is elusive…so you'll have to dissect your expenses on the autopsy table and identify the pathology in your financial household (remember, I'm an undertaker's daughter). If you find yourself in the red at the end of every month, is it that your lifestyle constantly calls for the accumulation of debt? Do you need more training, skills, and education to increase your earning power? Granted, you may very well have to consider consumer credit counseling; pursue additional sources of income; get a raise; or work harder to reduce daily expenses. I hate to tell you this, kiddo, but have you ever considered that you may need to move to a region with a lower cost of living? Sure, your salary and wages may very well be lower, but your daily living expenses are likely to be lower, as well (taking into consideration how much debt you carry with you and depending on where you move, of course). Exercise wisdom.

Ask Lots of Questions

Personally, I thrive on information. The more information I have, the more I can make an informed decision. Likewise, if you have a question about your finances (credit card, a bill, financial aid), pick up the phone, call the appropriate party, and ask questions so you can proceed accordingly. Do not make assumptions.

I hope you see the point I am making. It doesn't matter that you start with nothing or next to nothing. Keep practicing the habits that stretch nothing into something. If you've gotten this far in the book, then you've already started. Don't stop!

Do not neglect your spiritual, mental, emotional and physical health and well-being in the process of achieving financial freedom! Don't be ashamed to pray about your situation. Ask God to help you. God knows already. God hears. God helps. The sun will break through the clouds eventually.

DON'T SACRIFICE THE FUTURE FOR THE PRESENT. Don't forget the big picture in the midst of short-term needs and present-day demands. Preparing your own hot beverages, for example, can serve as an everyday reminder that your ultimate goal is to redirect and apply funds you're saving towards long-term goals. One of my financial regrets is not contributing to a retirement account in my formative professional years, rationalizing that "I need that money *now*." Now that **you** have the foundation you need for saving money and organizing your finances, I am going to leave you in the hands of competent pros. Your...

> **Accountant**...to help you engage in sound taxpaying practices and capture those legitimate tax-deductible expenses;
> **Financial Representative**...to advise you on investing and saving for college and retirement;
> **Benefits Administrator**...to furnish you with information on health and job-related benefits available to you;
> **Attorney**...to provide guidance in instituting a business structure if you plan to go into business for yourself and to help you devise a will;
> **Real Estate Broker**...to aid you in finding a home to purchase;
> **Mortgage Lender**...to grant you a mortgage loan with terms most suitable for your situation;
> **and your Insurance Agent**...to provide asset protection for your home and auto, and to help you establish life and disability insurance.

"I have fought the good fight, I have finished the race, I have kept the faith."
~ 2 Timothy 4:7 ~

How shall the rest of your financial tale be written? Hey, I'm just asking—from one consumer, to another.

From consumer-to-consumer, I wanted to know where to go to find out about topics to educate myself. Well, here they are:

ME'SHAE'S FAVORITE RESOURCES

Asa Aarons, Consumer Reporter on WNBC-TV, Channel 4 News (metropolitan New York market). *New York Daily News* Columnist (*Ask Asa*) appears on Mondays, Tuesdays, Thursdays and Fridays.

Michelle Singletary's *Singletary Says* on TV One on Wednesday evenings (check your local listings).

The Suze Orman Show on CNBC on Saturday evenings (check your local listings).

FREE, downloadable booklets by the Fannie Mae Foundation, www.homebuyingguide.org or at www.fanniemaefoundation.org These books are available in Chinese, Korean, Haitian Creole, Russian, Polish, Portuguese, Spanish, and Vietnamese:

- *"Borrowing Basics: What You Don't Know Can Hurt You"*
- *"Knowing and Understanding Your Credit"*
- *"Opening The Door To A Home Of Your Own"*
- *"Choosing the Mortgage That's Right For You"*

For all languages, including English, call 800-688-HOME (4663) or the Consumer Resource Center during normal business hours at 1(800) 732-6643; for Spanish, call 1(800) 782-2729

ME'SHAE'S TOP BOOK PICKS (IN ADDITION TO THE BOOKS IN THE REFERENCE/BIBLIOGRAPHY SECTION)

Larry Burkett, *Using Your Money Wisely: Biblical Principles Under Scrutiny*, Moody Publishers (1990).

Mary Hunt, *The Complete Cheapskate: How To Break Free from Money Worries Forever, Without Sacrificing Your Quality of Life,* Broadman & Holman Publishers, (1998). Mary Hunt is also the Founder & Publisher of *Cheapskate Monthly.*
Visit www.cheapskatemonthly.com for details.

Robert T. Kiyosaki with Sharon L. Lechter, CPA, *Cashflow Quadrant,* TechPress, Inc. (1999).

Robert McKinley and Marc Robinson. *Managing Credit: What You Need To Know To Boost Your Buying Power,* Dorling Kindersley (2000).

Austin Pryor. *Sound Mind Investing: A Step-By-Step Guide to Financial Stability & Growth*, Austin Pryor (2004).

ME'SHAE'S TOP 5 WEBSITE CHOICES

Federal Trade Commission's website at www.ftc.gov
Why? Because it covers the gamut of consumer interest topics: Identity Theft, Debt Collection, Telemarketing, Bankruptcy, etc.

Fair, Isaacs & Co. at www.MyFico.com
Why? Because it helps take the mystery out of your credit score.

U.S. Small Business Administration at www.sba.gov
Why? Because it's a comprehensive source on how to start and operate a small business, and includes a tax section.

MSN's money central at http://moneycentral.msn.com
Why? Because the articles address everyday situations such as saving money on heating bills, purchasing a car, coping with gas prices, etc.

Nolo at www.Nolo.com
Why? Because it explains business management structure in user-friendly terminology.

OK...I'll make it 6:
Consumer Reports at www.consumerreports.org
Why? To get the low-down on the stuff we buy; plus, Consumer Reports doesn't accept paid advertisements, which helps to keep their consumer products test results unbiased.

ENDNOTES

Preface

1 The Associated Press (n.d.). *Housing costs lift rents out of reach, study finds. Retrieved December 30, 2005, from* http://realestate.msn.com/Rentals/Article.aspx?cp-documentid=159225>1=7474.

2 *The most expensive U.S. cities for renters.* Retrieved February 22, 2006, from http://realestate.msn.com/Rentals/Article.aspx?cp-documentid=262175.

3 TV One. (2005, November 20). *Sharp Talk* (Gentrification) [Television Broadcast]. TV One, LLC.

4 T.B. Brooks (personal communication, December 3, 2005)

5 Mish, Frederick C., et. al. (1997). *Merriam Webster's Collegiate Dictionary* (10th edition). Springfield, MA: Mirriam-Webster, Incorporated. p. 249.

6 Ibid, p. 1154.

Chapter 3

7 Harris, Diane. (2000, April). *Five Steps to Simpler Record-Keeping.* (Real Simple.com). Retrieved October 19, 2005, from http://www.realsimple.com/realsimple/content/0,21770,688976,00.html.

8 Ibid.

9 LeBlanc, Heidi and Rowe, Barbara R. (2003, June). *Are You Drowning in Personal Finance Papers? What To Keep And What To Toss.* (Utah State University Extension). Retrieved October 19, 2005, from http://extension.usu.edu/files/publications/ff21.pdf.

10 Harris, Diane. (2000).

11 LeBlanc, Heidi and Rowe, Barbara R. (2003).

12 Harris, Diane. (2000).

13 Ibid.

14 LeBlanc, Heidi and Rowe, Barbara R. (2003).

Chapter 5

15 Stanley, Thomas J. and Danko, William D. (1996). *The Millionaire Next Door: The Surprising Secrets of America's Wealthy.* New York, NY: Pocket Books. p. 12.

16 Ibid, p. 9.

17 Ibid, p. 10.

18 Ibid, p. 11.

19 Ibid, pp. 9-10.

20 Bach, David. (2002). *Smart Women Finish Rich* (revised edition). New York, NY: Broadway Books. pp. 100-102, 176.

21 H&R Block (2000-2005). *Most Overlooked Deductions* (Tax Advice 101). Retrieved November 1, 2005, from http://www.hrblock.com/taxes/fast_facts/articles/overlooked_deductions.html.

Wall, Ginita CPA, CFP. (1995-2006). *Can We Deduct Our Preschool Payments?* (iVillage.com). Retrieved February 10, 2006, from http://home.ivillage.com/homekeeping/homefinance/0,,nwmm,00.html.

22 Eisenson, Marc. (1984). *The Banker's Secret.* New York, NY: Villard Books.

23 Thottam, Jyoti (with Paige Bowers, Stefanie Friedhoff & Sean Scully). (19 December 2005). "War on the Water Front." *Time,* p. 60.

24 Petrecca, Laura. (2005, October 7). "Fast Food Restaurants spruce up coffee." *USA Today,* p. B1.

25 Bach, David. pp. 93-95.

26 AMC Theatres. (2005, June 21). *AMC Entertainment Inc. and Loews Cineplex Entertainment Corporation to Merge.* Retrieved November 19, 2005, from http://www.investor.amctheatres.com/ReleaseDetail.cfm?ReleaseID=166601.

27 Fiona Phillip (personal communication, June 15, 2005)

28 Ibid.

29 Verizon. "Telephone Sales Calls—Know The Facts." (2005, August). [Newsletter]. Verizon. p. 1.

Chapter 6

30 U.S. Department of Labor – U.S. Bureau of Labor Statistics. (2005, June). *Consumer Expenditures in 2003.* Retrieved October 21, 2005, from http://www.bls.gov/cex/csxann03.pdf.

31 Furman, Phyllis. (2005, June 2). "Stressed out by finances." *New York Daily News,* p. 33.

Chapter 7

32 Roha, Ronaleen. (2001, August 8). "Debit or Credit: Which Card is Safer?" *Kiplinger's-Personal Finance.* Retrieved February 28, 2006, from www.kiplinger.com/personalfinance/columns/fitness/archive/2001/ff20010808.htm?

33 Graham, Jefferson. (2004, March 26). "The check is **not** in the mail." *USA Today,* p. 3B.

Chapter 8

34 Discover Card. (2001). *How Credit Cards Work – Some Helpful Thoughts from Discover Card* [Brochure]. Discover Bank. pp. 39-41.

35 Weston, Liz Pulliam. (n.d.). *The truth about credit card debt.* Retrieved October 21, 2005, from http://moneycentral.msn.com/content/Banking/creditcardsmarts/P74808.asp.

36 Soriano, Cesar G. (2005, December 22). "Credit card debt catches up with Britons." *USA Today,* p. 5B.

37 Federal Reserve Board. (2005, October 7). *Consumer Credit.* Retrieved October 21, 2005, from the Federal Reserve's Federal Reserve Statistical Release. Access: http://www.federalreserve.gov/releases/g19/current/default.htm.

38 Kadlec, Daniel (with Jeremy Caplan, Sarah Sturmon Dale, Greg Fulton, Rita Healy & Adam Pitluk). (2005, December 12). "The Mind of a Shopper." *Time.* p. 49.

39 Lee, Evelyn. (2004, September 27). "Schumer slams student credit cards." *metro,* p. 9.

40 Citi Customer Service Representative (personal communication, November 14, 2005)
Discover Financial Services Customer Service Representative (personal communication, November 14, 2005)

41 Ibid.

42 Ibid.

43 Citi Customer Service Representative (personal communication, February 2, 2006)
Discover Financial Services Customer Service Representative (personal communication, February 2, 2006)

44 Citi Customer Service Representative (personal communication, November 14, 2005)
Discover Financial Services Customer Service Representative (personal communication, July 13, 2005 and November 14, 2005)

45 Citi credit card customer service representatives (personal communication, November 14, 2005 and November 15, 2005)

46 McKinley, Robert & Robinson, Marc (2000). *Managing Credit – What You Need To Know To Boost Your Buying Power.* New York: Dorling Kindersley Publishing, Inc. pp. 31, 46-47.

47 Ibid, p. 31.

48 Ibid, p. 22.

49 MBNA America Customer Service Representative (personal communication, January 14, 2006)
Citi Customer Service Representative (personal communication, January 14, 2006)

50 Verizon. (2005, August). "Your Credit Scores and You" [Newsletter]. Verizon. p. 4.

51 Commerce Bank. *Check 21-Check clearing for the 21st Century Act* [Pamphlet]. Commerce Bank.

52 Burkett, Larry (with Southern, Randy). (2000). *The World's Easiest Guide to Finances.* Chicago, IL: Northfield Publishing. pp. 390-391. Used by permission of Northfield Publishing.

Chapter 9

53 Privacy Rights Clearinghouse. (2004-2005). *FACTA, The Fair and Accurate Credit Transactions Act: Consumers Win Some, Lose Some.* Retrieved October 15, 2005, from http://www.privacyrights.org/fs/fs6a-facta.htm.

54 Federal Trade Commission. (n.d.). A Summary of Your Rights Under the Fair Credit Reporting Act. Retrieved October 21, 2005, from http://www.ftc.gov/bcp/conline/pubs/credit/fcrasummarty.pdf.

55 Ibid.

56 McKinley, R. and Robinson, M. (2000). p. 51.

57 Ibid, p. 19.

58 MyFICO-a division of Fair Isaac. (2001-2005). *Credit Inquiries.* Retrieved October 9, 2005, from http://www.myfico.com/CreditEducation/CreditInquiries.aspx.

59 Experian (2005). Retrieved November 15, 2005, from http://www.Experian.com.
Experian (2006). Retrieved February 10, 2006 from http://www.nationalscoreindex.com/USScore.aspx.

60 The Credit Scoring Site. (n.d.). *What is a good credit score?* Retrieved October 11, 2005, from http://www.creditscoring.com/pages/bar.htm.

61 Ibid.

62 MyFICO-a division of Fair Isaac. (2001-2005). *What's In Your Score.* Retrieved October 9, 2005, from http://www.myfico.com/CreditEducation/WhatsInYourScore.aspx?fire=5.

63 Aarons, Asa. (2005, July 1). "Keeping paid-off accounts open can lift credit score." *New York Daily News.*

64 Twentieth Television. (2005, October 8). *The Suze Orman Show* [Television Broadcast]. CNBC.

Chapter 10

65 Fannie Mae Foundation. (1998). *Opening The Door To A Home of Your Own.* [Brochure]. Washington, D.C.: Fannie Mae Foundation, pp. 4-10.

66 Tyson, Eric and Brown, Ray. (1997). *Homebuying for Dummies.* Foster City, CA et. al.: IDG Books Worldwide, Inc., p. 105.

67 Fannie Mae Foundation. (1998). *Opening The Door To A Home of Your Own.* [Brochure]. Washington, D.C.: Fannie Mae Foundation, pp. 11-13.

Chapter 11

68 Levy, Steven & Stone, Brad. (2005, July 4). "The Scary New World of Identity Theft-Grand Theft Identity" cover article *Newsweek,* p. 46.

69 Ibid, p. 44.

70 Ibid.

71 Ibid.

72 Ibid.

73 Federal Trade Commission (2005). *Your National Resource about Identity Theft - If you think you identity has been stolen. Here's what to do* (consumer-identity theft). Retrieved October 17, 2005, from http://www.consumer.gov.idtheft/.

74 Office of New York State Attorney General Elliott Spitzer (2003). *Identity Theft: What To Do If You've Been Victimized* (consumer issues). Retrieved

September 28, 2005, from http://www.oag.state.ny.us.consumer/tips/id_theft_victim.html.

75 Acohido, Byron & Swartz, Jon (2005, July 11). "Cybercrooks lure citizens into international crime." *USA Today,* pp. 1A, 4A, 5A.

76 Parade. (2005, December 18). "Worst Late Penalty." p. 11.

77 Office of New York State Attorney General Elliott Spitzer (2003). *Credit & Lending issues: Debt Collectors* (consumer issues). Retrieved September 28, 2005, from http://www.oag.state.ny.us.consumer/tips/debt_collectors.html.

78 Ibid.

79 Credit Info Center (n.d.). *Statute of Limitations on Debts* (Rebuild/Repair – Find Out the Statute of Limitations for Judgements in your State). Retrieved September 29, 2005, from http://www.creditinfocenter.com/rebuild/statuteLimitations/shtml.

80 Weston, Liz Pulliam (n.d.). *Zombie debt collectors dig up your old mistakes.* Retrieved August 18, 2005, from http://moneycentral.msn.com/content/Savinganddebt/Managedebt/P74812.asp.

81 Aarons, Asa. (2006, January 12). "Don't get taken for a ride in search for debt advice." *New York Daily News.* p. 23.

82 New York State Office of Attorney General Elliott Spitzer (2003). *Consumer Tips: Debt Collectors* (consumer issues). Retrieved June 9, 2005, from http://www.state.ny.us/consumer/tips/debt_collectors.html.

83 U.S. Department of Justice (2005). *U.S. Trustee Program Begins Approval Process for Budget and Credit Counseling Agencies, Financial Management Instructional Courses.* Retrieved July 1, 2005, from http://www.usdoj.gov/ust/bapcpa/ccde.htm.

84 McKinley, R. & Robinson, M. (2000). pp. 66-67.

85 Ibid.

86 U.S. Department of Justice. (2005, June 30). *U.S. Trustee Program – Bankruptcy Abuse Prevention and Consumer Protection Act of 2005 (BAPCPA) – Debtor Education.* Retrieved July 1, 2005, from www.usdoj.gov/ust/bacpa/debtor_education.htm.

Chapter 12

87 S.M. Brooks (personal communication, October 4, 2005)

88 Sachs, Jeffrey D., (2005, March 14). "How To End Poverty" (adapted from *The End of Poverty by Jeffrey D. Sachs*). *Time,* p. 47.

Chapter 14

89 "All the features of a luxury car for less." (2005, July). *Good Housekeeping,* p. 79.

90 Hope Wade (personal communication, December 4, 2005)

91 Hope Wade (personal communication, January 10, 2006)

Chapter 16

92 Kiyosaki, Robert T. (with Lechter, Sharon L.). (1999). *Rich Dad's Cashflow Quadrant.* New York, NY: Warner Books.

93 Pollan, Stephen M. and Levine, Mark. (1998). *Live Rich: Everything You Need To Know To Be Your Own Boss, Whoever You Work For.* New York, NY: HarperBusiness. pp. 83-90.

94 Kiyosaki, Robert T., (with Lechter, Sharon L.). (1998). *Rich Dad, Poor Dad.* New York, NY: TechPress, Inc.

95 G. Childs (personal communication, June 26, 2005)
B.J. Brooks (personal communication, January 31, 2006)

96 Stanley, T.J. and Danko, W.D. (1996). p. 8.

97 Ibid, p. 9.

98 Ibid, p. 10.

99 Dan Poynter's Para Publishing website. (1996-2004). Retrieved October 15, 2005, from http://www.ParaPublishing.com.

Chapter 17

100 Penn State Small Business Development Center (with SCORE). (n.d.). *Sample Business Plan Outline: Pre-Business Workshop.* University Park, PA.

101 Amy Feldman. (2005, December). "The cash-flow crunch." *Inc. Magazine.* p. 52.

APPENDIX A

PERSONALIZED BUDGET SHEET

For Pay Period Date: ________ / Next Pay date: ________

Breadwinner #1's net pay: $ _______._____

+ Breadwinner #2's net pay: $ _______._____

= Subtotal: $ ________.___

+ Carryover Balance: $ __________

= Total: $ ___________

Payment Methods:

$Cash **Check or M/O by Mail** **Debit** **Credit Card**

Pay-by-Phone **Pay-in-Person** **Online**

BUDGET ITEM	AMOUNT TO BE PAID	METHOD OF PAYMENT	PAYMENT DATE*
Place of Worship &/or Charity			
Mortgage or Rent			
Co-Op or Condo Maintenance			
Personal Allowance: Breadwinner #1 Breadwinner #2			
*Date you are actually paying the bill, regardless of due date			

BUDGET ITEM	AMOUNT TO BE PAID	METHOD OF PAYMENT	PAYMENT DATE*
Utilities: Electricity Gas/Heat Water Sanitation Telephone Cell Phone Internet Cable TV			
Student Loan(s)			
Credit Cards: AmEx MasterCard Visa Discover Dept. Store Other Credit Card(s)			
Children's Needs: Day Care Lunch Money Tuition & Fees School Supplies Uniform/Clothing Transportation Extracurricular activities Allowance			
Auto: Car Note Gas Insurance Repairs & Maintenance License & Registration			
Transportation: Subway Train Bus Ferry TaxiCab/Car Svc. Parking/Meter Tolls/E-ZPass			
*Date you are actually paying the bill, regardless of due date			

BUDGET ITEM	AMOUNT TO BE PAID	METHOD OF PAYMENT	PAYMENT DATE*
Groceries &/or Dining Out			
Dry Cleaning &/or Laundry			
Clothing			
Hair, Nails, & Personal Maintenance			
Doctor & Specialist visits Pharmaceutical			
Health Club Membership			
Recreation & Entertainment			
Savings/ Contingency fund			
Insurance premium account			
Investments			
Vacation club account			
Retirement			
Gift-giving account			
Other/Miscellaneous			
TOTAL EXPENSES:			
*Date you are actually paying the bill, regardless of due date			

Total Net Income: $_________._____

MINUS

Total Expenses this pay period: $_________._____

= Balance leftover in checking account to add to the next payday:

$_________._____

APPENDIX B

GROCERY LIST

ITEM	SUPER-MARKET?	99-CENT/ DOLLAR STORE?	WHOLE-SALE CLUB?	DO I HAVE A COUPON?
Rice			✓	Y
Light Bulbs	✓			N
Dish cloths		✓		N
Laundry Detergent		✓		N
Bread	✓			Y
Tea			✓	N

Post this list to your refrigerator, keep a list of what you need, and check off where you are going to purchase the item.

APPENDIX C

SAMPLE ORDER TRACKING FORM

CO. TELEPHONE #: ______________________

ITEM(S): ______________________________

ORDERED ON: ________ / ________ / ________

CUSTOMER SVC. REP. OR I.D.#: ________________

METHOD OF DELIVERY: ________________

TRACKING#: ________________

ETA: ________ // WHICH IS BETWEEN: ________ & ________ A.M./P.M.

COST: ________ // BREAKDOWN OF COST: ________

CREDIT CARD USED ________________ (use Land Line)

ORDER I.D./CONFIRMATION #: ________

DID YOU COPY OR
SCAN IN THE ITEM
BEFORE MAILING IT
FOR YOUR RECORDS?

YES NO N/A

MARK YOUR
CALENDAR
FOR DELIVERY
TIMEFRAME!

APPENDIX D

E-ZPASS TRAVEL LOG

DATE	DESTINATION	ROUTE	P=PERSONAL TRIP B=BUSINESS TRIP
08/16/05	BROOKLYN – CANARSIE	HOLLAND TUNNEL	P – CAROLYN'S BABY SHOWER
01/23/06	HARLEM – ACP STATE OFC BLDG	GWB	B – BUSINESS NETWORKING MEETING

APPENDIX E

MONEY SAVED IN MY/OUR HOUSEHOLD

MERCHANT	ITEM	REG. AMT. (BASE PRICE)	ACTUAL COST	SAVINGS	REASON FOR SAVINGS*
Home-Bed-Bath-Kitchen store	Roaster	$50	$25	$25	50% off sale
Office Supply store	Ink Cartridge	$46.99	$35.99	$11	frequency rewards coupon
Supermarket	sour crème French onion dip	$2.39	$2.19	20 cents	comparison shopping bet. brands
Electronics store	PCI card	$14.99	$4.99	$10	mail-in rebate
Drug store	box/cereal	$2.99	0	$2.99	buy 1, get 1 free
Association	Conference	$285	$260	$15	Early Bird Registration

*Reasons may include paying attention to merchant pricing mistakes or erroneous billing, comparison shopping, taking advantage of sales, use of coupons or discounts, reward checks, reimbursements, rebates, etc.

Total estimated savings based on the above examples: $64.19

Question: *If someone walked up to you right now and handed you $65, would you take it? Would you be able to use $65 elsewhere?*

CONTACT & ORDER INFORMATION

To order additional copies of:
How to Save Money and Organize Your Finances: Tales of an Urban Consumer

Call Toll-Free
1 (888) 280-7715
(credit card orders)

~ OR ~

Call Toll-Free
1 (888) 304-BOOK / 1 (888) 304-2665
(check or money orders)

~ OR ~

Download your Order Form from
www.RollingEnterprises.com
& Fax Toll-Free to 1 (866) 304-2299

~ OR ~

To order **online,** visit:
www.AuthorHouse.com

~ ~ ~

Bulk orders by corporations, churches, book clubs, libraries, organizations, etc. may be placed by calling
Toll-Free 1 (888) 280-7715

Other products offered by ROLLING ENTERPRISES LLC:

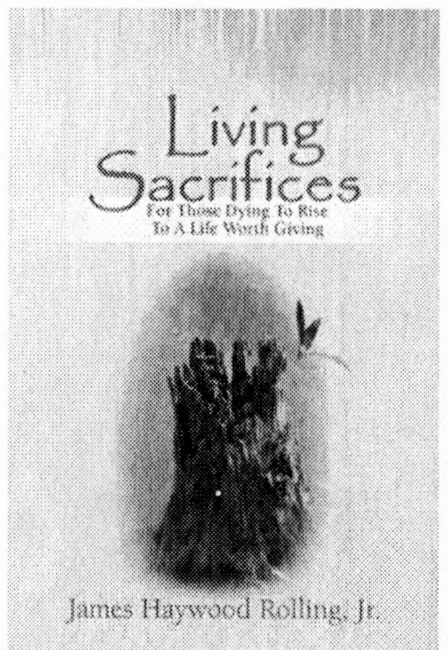

▸▸ *Living Sacrifices: For Those Dying To Rise To A Life Worth Giving*
(Pleasant Word)
by Dr. James Haywood Rolling, Jr.
(© 2003 James Haywood Rolling, Jr.)
Paperback • 208 pages • $15.99
ISBN 1-57921-522-X

Based on the 12th chapter of Romans in the New Testament Bible. Weaves together common sense prose, solid scriptural exposition, and candid personal testimony with unique parables and anecdotes to tell the good news of God's love, freely offered to both the loved and the unloved.

Come Look With Me: Discovering African American Art For Children

by Dr. James Haywood Rolling, Jr.
(© 2005 Lickle Publishing Inc.)
Hardcover • 32 pages • $15.95
ISBN: 1-890674-07-9

Profiles 12 prominent African-American Artists including Romare Beardon, Jacob Lawrence and Clementine Hunter; includes artists' biographies and encourages interactive learning with children.

The *Come Look With Me* series is endorsed by:

- American Educator
- Booklist, *American Library Association*
- Horn Book Magazine
- The School Library Journal

Fine art prints by James Haywwod Rolling, Jr., M.F.A.

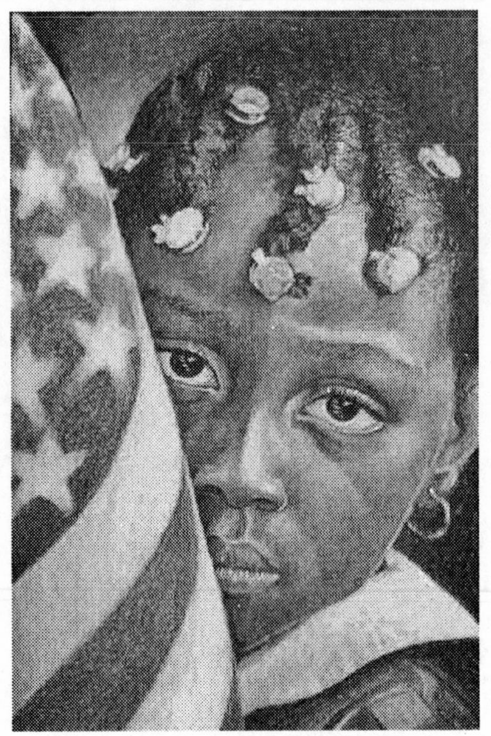

"emerging" © 1997

Yes! I/we would like to request more information:

____ I'd like to order additional copies of *How To Save Money and Organize Your Finances: Tales of an Urban Consumer*

____ To request a Financial Literacy Seminar by Me'Shae Brooks-Rolling, CSEP

____ To order *Living Sacrifices: For Those Dying To Rise To A Life Worth Giving* by James H. Rolling, Jr., Ed.D.

____ To order *Come Look With Me: Discovering African American Art For Children* by James H. Rolling, Jr., Ed.D.

____ To order art prints by James H. Rolling, Jr., Fine Artist

____ To request an all-day, joint seminar &/or book signing by James and Me'Shae Rolling

Contact Name: ____________________________________

Title: ____________________________________

Organization: ____________________________________

Address 1: ____________________________________

Address 2: ____________________________________

City, State, Zip Code: ____________________________________

Telephone #(s): ____________________________________

E-Mail Address(es): ____________________________________

To download and e-mail this form, visit:

www.RollingEnterprises.com

info@RollingEnterprises.com

~ or ~

Fax this form to:
Toll-Free 1 (866) 304-2299

~ or ~

Mail to this form to:
ROLLING ENTERPRISES LLC
210 W. Hamilton Avenue, #150
State College, PA 16801

~ ~ ~

ABOUT THE AUTHOR

Me'Shae Brooks-Rolling was born and raised in a small factory town in Indiana. She migrated to the East Coast via Syracuse University, where she met and married a New Yorker. Having resided in New York City for over a decade, she and her husband, James, have lived in the neighborhoods of Park Slope, Crown Heights and Spanish Harlem.

As a Special Events Planner & Professional Organizer, Me'Shae has worked in the corridors of City Hall, in the echelons of the federal government, on the Upper East Side of Manhattan, downtown on Wall Street, and on New York's most famous parades.

In the interim, Me'Shae has endured the hardship of unemployment, experienced the chokehold of debt, enjoyed the blessing of a handsome salary, and has achieved the peace of freedom from financial bondage.

She is a member of the National Association of Professional Organizers and the National Association of Female Executives.

Printed in the United States
48147LVS00003B/52-66

9 781425 916183